D1296868

Religious Drama 1

A LIVING AGE BOOK

RELIGIOUS DRAMA 1

Five Plays

FOR THE TIME BEING

THE FIRSTBORN

DAVID

THE ZEAL OF THY HOUSE

THE BLOODY TENET

Selected and Introduced
by MARVIN HALVERSON

Meridian Books

THE WORLD PUBLISHING COMPANY

CLEVELAND AND NEW YORK

All rights to these plays, including performance rights, are protected by their individual copyright. On the title page of each play, it is indicated from whom permissions have been—and in the future should be—obtained. Producers, amateur and professional, are expressly warned that performance rights cover not only production but readings; that it is not permissible to mimeograph and, in mimeograph form, to distribute any of this material; that permission is required to perform even part of any of these plays; and that owners of copyright, not producers, must decide when a "classroom" or "studio" performance or reading is actually "private." Lacking any better address, applicants for permission may address copyright holders or their agents c/o Meridian Books, The World Publishing Company, 119 West 57th Street, New York 19, New York.

An Original Living Age Book (Meridian)

Published by The World Publishing Company
2231 West 110th Street, Cleveland 2, Ohio

First printing March 1957
Seventh printing February 1964

Introduction by MARVIN HALVERSON

After centuries of alienation, we are witnessing in our day the return of drama to the churches and the recognition by churchmen of the religious dimensions of theater. Although it is now common knowledge that our drama has its roots in the liturgy of the Church, it is only in comparatively recent times that this historic relationship has taken on new life. One of the sources of renewal undoubtedly has been the growing awareness of the dramatic nature of the liturgy itself. While the historic shape of the liturgy, centering in Sermon and Supper with its attendant ritual acts, can never be regarded as tableaux or drama in itself, the liturgy nonetheless points to the divine drama of redemption. Christian faith sees life as a cosmic drama. The Biblical understanding of history as possessing a beginning, a middle, and an end, the creedal symbols of the Creation, the Crucifixion, and the Last Judgment, and the related acts of worship are the means by which man sees his participation in the cosmic drama of God's action and man's response.

Both the mood of our age and the religious climate in our churches have been such as either to misunderstand or reject this Biblical view of man and history. Thus we were not prepared either to accept a dramatic inheritance of religious meaning or to encourage contemporary drama of religious significance. However, the events of recent time and the renewal of theology today are sources of the striking resurgence of that religious drama which these plays represent. Although interest in religious drama is now widespread throughout this country, the renascence of such drama first began in Europe, where the moralism of a diffused Christianity was purged by the shock of wars and persecutions and renewed in the fire of the Gospel. In our own country churchmen are not as much at ease in bourgeois *Zions* and are becoming aware of the disquiets of our time. Thus one observes among churchmen a receptiveness to drama of depth and attentiveness to what the best voices in our theater disclose of the human situation today.

The probing character of our best theater, both in America and Europe, and its mode of asking questions that demand an existential reply, suggest that much modern drama is fundamentally religious. For religious drama appropriate to our day is more often that drama which poses questions rather than that which attempts to give answers. Thus the religious mind discerns the religious questions in the works of playwrights such as Williams, Miller, O'Neill, Camus, Sartre, and Beckett. However, the plays included in this anthology are representative not of this theater but rather of that drama which is more explicitly religious in theme and awareness. Dilemmas confronting men during episodes in the history of the church and the events of the Bible provide the subject matter. Yet while their stage is the past, these plays are contemporaneous in feeling. This is particularly true of Auden's *For the Time Being*, where the Eternal Act is inextricably related to the transient and fragmented now. However, beyond the return to Biblical themes and insights through contemporary vision these plays also represent the return of poetry to the theater. For the renewal of religious drama has been assisted by this restoration of poetry because the poetic approach is closer to the religious than the prevalent naturalism of nineteenth- and twentieth-century theater.

Thirty years ago Dr. Bell, then Dean of Canterbury and later Bishop of Chichester, wanted to stage a play in the chapterhouse of the cathedral church. A poet himself, Dr. Bell asked John Masefield to write a nativity play, which he promptly agreed to do. Masefield's *The Coming of Christ* was presented at Whitsuntide, 1928, with music by Gustav Holst. Subsequently T. S. Eliot, Dorothy Sayers, and Charles Williams, among others, responded to invitations to write plays. Through these efforts T. S. Eliot was introduced as a dramatist to the theater. There had been intimations of Eliot's interest in the renewal of drama through poetry, for as early as 1924 in treating "Four Elizabethan Dramatists" he had said: "I believe that the theatre has reached a point at which a revolution in principles should take place." The dramatic inadequacy of the theater, in Elizabethan as well as modern times, said Eliot, lay in the lack of a convention. Although that necessary convention might be in technique, in subject matter, in form, the surest convention was to be found in the liturgy. "Drama," said Eliot, "springs from religious liturgy, and it cannot afford to depart too far from religious liturgy." Also, he felt that verse was a necessary element in the recovery of drama. Mr. Eliot, however, did not make a direct contribution to the theater until 1933, when *The Rock* was written and produced in connection with a fund-raising effort for the rebuilding of London churches.

Although not a completed work, Eliot's *Sweeney Agonistes*, published in *The Criterion* in 1926-7, had pointed to his awareness of the role of myth in illumining man's situation. The emergence of myth as a decisive element in our literature since that time suggests Eliot, if not initiating a new factor in drama, was at least anticipating development of enormous significance for religious drama. John Lehmann pointed out that contemporary art and literature disclose an intense search for the myth and heritage of the past in awareness of the present. "The reason for this return to the kind of art that conceals a metaphysical meaning behind and above what it states is surely not far to seek." Although many are still sustained by the Christian religion and its symbols, the hold has been weakened. But their replacement by other ideologies has not satisfied the artist, for "life," says Lehmann, "is more complex and more mysterious than the textbooks of progress ever told us. And we look around for symbols that shall recreate faith within the enlarged circumference of this new awareness . . . even if those symbols should lead us back to a rediscovery of the central meaning of Christianity, restored through the discarding of outworn and corrupted images." This need to discover adequate symbols, the return to the hero-paradigms of Judaeo-Christian culture, to the Bible, and to history is demonstrated in each of the plays included in this anthology.

D. H. Lawrence's *David* is such an example of this return, although as a writer he stands outside the modern movement of religious drama. Lawrence, whose last completed book was a treatment of the Apocalypse, is now being widely recognized as a writer of deep religious sensitivity. His work is a prophetic protest against the despoliations of life by industrialism, narrow rationalism, and sterile religion. Throughout his life he was seeking the vital center through which the organic wholeness of existence might be perceived and fulfilled. Lawrence decried the blunted lives and blighted spirituality which derive from that peculiarly English form of social organization we have come to term "the Establishment." He was concerned with the health of society and wholeness of being out of a rare religious sensitivity. While he did not conform to ecclesiastical views of religion he was immersed in the Bible. His writing testifies that the Scriptural influence of his English Congregational background was indelible. For not only does he make use of the Biblical story, as in *David,* but his employment of Biblical imagery penetrates to the heart of meaning. While one might credit this freshness of insight to Lawrence's powerful imagination, it is also testimony to the renewing power of the Biblical image itself. *David* is a play that deals inevitably with the love of Jonathan and David, but its focus is even more on the tension between David and Saul. For Lawrence sees in David a fox-faced wisdom that gets him the kingdom over against the vitalities and subconscious forces that dominate Saul.* And in the prayer of Samuel the poetic and reli-

---

* Thus to Lawrence, Saul's brokenness is more human than David's calculation.

giously ecstatic quality of the play is seen in a way that makes most Biblical plays seem prosaic and devoid of life.

In Christopher Fry's work, drama and verse have achieved a union that has influenced commercial theater as well as religious drama. In *The Firstborn* as well as *A Sleep of Prisoners* one finds evidence of the myth's power to renew its life in the contemporary mind. Based on the figure of Moses, Fry's *The Firstborn* is a play of subtle understanding and effective dramatic device. The conflict between Moses and Pharaoh counterpoised by the inner conflict of Moses set the issues of power and its use and pose the question of ends and means. Drawing upon the powerful symbol of the Exodus and the surrounding action of that story, Fry establishes a dramatic dialogue between narrative and poetic commentary which concludes with the awareness that we are all bound together in a living tether. The curtain falls on Moses looking beyond the moment to

> "The morning, which still comes
> To Egypt as to Israel, the round of light
> Which will not wheel in vain.
> We must find our separate meaning
> In the persuasion of our days
> Until we meet in the meaning of the world.
> Until that time."

For W. H. Auden the place we meet is where the meaning of the world is fulfilled, the Event in which all events find their significance—the Christ through whose incarnation the *now* is seen through the *eternal* and the *now* invested with eternal meaning. *For the Time Being*, which Mr. Auden calls a Christmas Oratorio, is a remarkable fusion of poetry and religious insight. While technically not a play and not intended for performance in theater, *For the Time Being* is a brilliant work in verse which has been performed often as drama. Auden, like Eliot, turned to the theater as an important form of communication. However, this verse oratorio, rather than the plays, is his major contribution to the literature of religious drama. For in addition to his competence as a poet, Auden brings a personal awareness of the dislocations of our time into tension with a profound grasp of the Christian message. *For the Time Being* abounds in the paradoxes of life and the paradox of faith. Thus the work is confusing to the mind that sees Christianity as summed up in moralism and life fulfilled through legalism. It is religious drama arising out of our time which yet speaks to our time.

In all the plays one finds the perennial themes of power and pride with the possibility of redemption. Pride, the chief sin and the sin common to all men, is the "fatal flaw" in the Christian understanding of dramatic tragedy. Pride is the basis of dramatic development and particularly in *The Zeal of Thy House,* which was written by Dorothy Sayers for the Canterbury Festival in 1937. Although she was best known as a writer of detective stories, Dorothy Sayers was a theologian and a playwright. Her twelve radio plays on the Christ, *The Man Born to Be King,* and many other works intended for stage production, have established her in the company of dramatists who seek to serve the churches directly. It is not inappropriate, therefore, to include *The Zeal of Thy House,* which deals with the rivalries and pride involved in the building of the cathedral church at Canterbury.

The Bloody Tenet by James Schevill, an American poet, is also rooted in an episode of the life of the churches. Commissioned by Central Congregational Church in Providence, Rhode Island, and the Department of Worship and the Arts of the National Council of Churches, this play represents the intention of calling upon the poets and playwrights of our own country to contribute to this growing body of religious drama. Schevill's play, *The Bloody Tenet,* deals with Roger Williams, one of the intriguing figures in American history, who has become a symbol for freedom and religious liberty in this country. But Schevill has gone beyond the conflict between Roger Williams's conscience and the established authorities to the inner conflict between Williams's pride and God's will, out of which issued a train of events in American life which belie the privacy of man's lonely debate. The play has been cast in poetic form, at the same time incorporating much of the language of Williams himself.

The plays in this collection demonstrate the power of symbols and myths out of our past to illumine the present and define the issues of life in our time. But since religious drama embraces a range of expression even wider than that which is represented by this collection, subsequent volumes of *Religious Drama* have been published. The influence of medieval plays on modern theater is seen in *Religious Drama 2*, a collection of representative mystery and morality plays from the Middle Ages. *Religious Drama 3* returns to our own day with a selection of contemporary works representing a modern morality play form. Subsequent volumes will continue to make available in this format the best examples of extant dramatic literature as well as present new works of religious significance and dramatic merit.

December 9, 1959

ADVENT

I

> Darkness and snow descend;
> The clock on the mantelpiece
> Has nothing to recommend,
> Nor does the face in the glass
> Appear nobler than our own
> As darkness and snow descend
> On all personality.
> Huge crowds mumble—"Alas,
> Our angers do not increase,
> Love is not what she used to be";
> Portly Caesar yawns—"I know";
> He falls asleep on his throne,
> They shuffle off through the snow
> Darkness and snow descend.

SEMI-CHORUS:

> Can great Hercules keep his
> Extraordinary promise
> To reinvigorate the Empire?
> Utterly lost, he cannot
> Even locate his task but
> Stands in some decaying orchard
> Or the irregular shadow
> Of a ruined temple, aware of
> Being watched from the horrid mountains
> By fanatical eyes yet
> Seeing no one at all, only hearing
> The silence softly broken
> By the poisonous rustle
> Of famishing Arachne.

CHORUS:

> Winter completes an age
> With its thorough levelling;
> Heaven's tourbillions of rage
> Abolish the watchman's tower
> And delete the cedar grove.
> As winter completes an age,
> The eyes huddle like cattle, doubt
> Seeps into the pores and power
> Ebbs from the heavy signet ring;
> The prophet's lantern is out
> And gone the boundary stone,
> Cold the heart and cold the stove,
> Ice condenses on the bone:
> Winter completes an age.

SEMI-CHORUS:

> Outside the civil garden
> Of every day of love there
> Crouches a wild passion
> > To destroy and be destroyed.
> O who to boast their power
> Have challenged it to charge? Like
> Wheat our souls are sifted
> > And cast into the void.

CHORUS:

> The evil and armed draw near;
> The weather smells of their hate
> And the houses smell of our fear;
> Death has opened his white eye
> And the black hole calls the thief
> As the evil and armed draw near.
> Ravens alight on the wall,
> Our plans have all gone awry,
> The rains will arrive too late,
> Our resourceful general
> Fell down dead as he drank

And his horses died of grief,
Our navy sailed away and sank;
The evil and armed draw near.

II

NARRATOR:

If, on account of the political situation,
There are quite a number of homes without roofs, and men
Lying about in the countryside neither drunk nor asleep,
If all sailings have been cancelled till further notice,
If it's unwise now to say much in letters, and if,
Under the subnormal temperatures prevailing,
The two sexes are at present the weak and the strong,
That is not at all unusual for this time of year.
If that were all we should know how to manage. Flood, fire,
The desiccation of grasslands, restraint of princes,
Piracy on the high seas, physical pain and fiscal grief,
These after all are our familiar tribulations,
And we have been through them all before, many, many
        times.
As events which belong to the natural world where
The occupation of space is the real and final fact
And time turns round itself in an obedient circle,
They occur again and again but only to pass
Again and again into their formal opposites,
From sword to ploughshare, coffin to cradle, war to work,
So that, taking the bad with the good, the pattern composed
By the ten thousand odd things that can possibly happen
Is permanent in a general average way.

Till lately we knew of no other, and between us we
        seemed
To have what it took—the adrenal courage of the tiger,
The chameleon's discretion, the modesty of the doe,
Or the fern's devotion to spatial necessity:
To practise one's peculiar civic virtue was not
So impossible after all; to cut our losses

And bury our dead was really quite easy: That was why
We were always able to say: "We are children of God,
And our Father has never forsaken His people."

But then we were children: That was a moment ago,
Before an outrageous novelty had been introduced
Into our lives. Why were we never warned? Perhaps we
    were.
Perhaps that mysterious noise at the back of the brain
We noticed on certain occasions—sitting alone
In the waiting room of the country junction, looking
Up at the toilet window—was not indigestion
But this Horror starting already to scratch Its way in?
Just how, just when It succeeded we shall never know:
We can only say that now It is there and that nothing
We learnt before It was there is now of the slightest use,
For nothing like It has happened before. It's as if
We had left our house for five minutes to mail a letter,
And during that time the living room had changed places
With the room behind the mirror over the fireplace;
It's as if, waking up with a start, we discovered
Ourselves stretched out flat on the floor, watching our
    shadow
Sleepily stretching itself at the window. I mean
That the world of space where events re-occur is still there,
Only now it's no longer real; the real one is nowhere
Where time never moves and nothing can ever happen:
I mean that although there's a person we know all about
Still bearing our name and loving himself as before,
That person has become a fiction; our true existence
Is decided by no one and has no importance to love.
That is why we despair; that is why we would welcome
The nursery bogey or the winecellar ghost, why even
The violent howling of winter and war has become
Like a juke-box tune that we dare not stop. We are afraid
Of pain but more afraid of silence; for no nightmare
Of hostile objects could be as terrible as this Void.
This is the Abomination. This is the wrath of God.

III

CHORUS:

Alone, alone, about a dreadful wood
Of conscious evil runs a lost mankind,
Dreading to find its Father lest it find
The Goodness it has dreaded is not good:
Alone, alone, about our dreadful wood.

Where is that Law for which we broke our own,
Where now that Justice for which Flesh resigned
Her hereditary right to passion, Mind
His will to absolute power? Gone. Gone.
Where is that Law for which we broke our own?

The Pilgrim Way has led to the Abyss.
Was it to meet such grinning evidence
We left our richly odoured ignorance?
Was the triumphant answer to be this?
The Pilgrim Way has led to the Abyss.

We who must die demand a miracle.
How could the Eternal do a temporal act,
The Infinite become a finite fact?
Nothing can save us that is possible:
We who must die demand a miracle.

IV

RECITATIVE:

If the muscle can feel repugnance, there is still a false move
    to be made;
If the mind can imagine tomorrow, there is still a defeat
    to remember;
As long as the self can say "I," it is impossible not to rebel;
As long as there is an accidental virtue, there is a necessary
    vice:
And the garden cannot exist, the miracle cannot occur.

For the garden is the only place there is, but you will not
      find it
Until you have looked for it everywhere and found nowhere
      that is not a desert;
The miracle is the only thing that happens, but to you it will
      not be apparent,
Until all events have been studied and nothing happens
      that you cannot explain;
And life is the destiny you are bound to refuse until you
      have consented to die.

Therefore, see without looking, hear without listening,
      breathe without asking:
The Inevitable is what will seem to happen to you purely
      by chance;
The Real is what will strike you as really absurd;
Unless you are certain you are dreaming, it is certainly a
      dream of your own;
Unless you exclaim—"There must be some mistake"—you
      must be mistaken.

V

CHORUS:

O where is that immortal and nameless Centre from which
      our points of
   Definition and death are all equi-distant? Where
The well of our wish to wander, the everlasting fountain
   Of the waters of joy that our sorrow uses for tears?
O where is the garden of Being that is only known in Exist-
      ence
   As the command to be never there, the sentence by
      which
Alephs of throbbing fact have been banished into position,
   The clock that dismisses the moment into the turbine of
      time?
O would I could mourn over Fate like the others, the reso-
      lute creatures,

By seizing my chance to regret. The stone is content
With a formal anger and falls and falls; the plants are in-
   dignant
   With one dimension only and can only doubt
Whether light or darkness lies in the worse direction; and
   the subtler
   Exiles who try every path are satisfied
With proving that none have a goal: why must Man also
   acknowledge
   It is not enough to bear witness, for even protest is
   wrong?

Earth is cooled and fire is quenched by his unique excite-
   ment,
   All answers expire in the clench of his questioning hand,
His singular emphasis frustrates all possible order:
   Alas, his genius is wholly for envy; alas,
The vegetative sadness of lakes, the locomotive beauty
   Of choleric beasts of prey, are nearer than he
To the dreams that deprive him of sleep, the powers that
   compel him to idle,
   To his amorous nymphs and his sanguine athletic gods.

How can his knowledge protect his desire for truth from
   illusion?
   How can he wait without idols to worship, without
Their overwhelming persuasion that somewhere, over the
   high hill,
   Under the roots of the oak, in the depths of the sea,
Is a womb or a tomb wherein he may halt to express some
   attainment?
   How can he hope and not dream that his solitude
Shall disclose a vibrating flame at last and entrust him
   forever
   With its magic secret of how to extemporise life?

THE ANNUNCIATION

I

THE FOUR FACULTIES:

Over the life of Man
We watch and wait,
The Four who manage
His fallen estate:
We who are four were
Once but one,
Before his act of
Rebellion;
We were himself when
His will was free,
His error became our
Chance to be.
Powers of air and fire,
Water and earth,
Into our hands is given
Man from his birth:

INTUITION:

As a dwarf in the dark of
His belly I rest;

FEELING:

A nymph, I inhabit
The heart in his breast;

SENSATION:

A giant, at the gates of
His body I stand;

THOUGHT:

His dreaming brain is
My fairyland.

TUTTI:

Invisible phantoms,
The forms we assume are
Adapted to each
Individual humour,
Beautiful facts or true
Generalisations,
Test cases in Law or
Market quotations:
As figures and formulae
Chemists have seen us,
Who to true lovers were
Putti of Venus.

Ambiguous causes
Of all temptation,
We lure men either
To death or salvation:
We alone may look over
The wall of that hidden
Garden whose entrance
To him is forbidden;
Must truthfully tell him
What happens inside,
But what it may mean he
Alone must decide.

II

THOUGHT:

The garden is unchanged, the silence is unbroken.
Truth has not yet intruded to possess
Its empty morning nor the promised hour
Shaken its lasting May.

INTUITION:

The human night,
Whose messengers we are, cannot dispel
Its wanton dreams, and they are all we know.

SENSATION:

My senses are still coarse
From late engrossment in a fair. Old tunes
Reiterated, lights with repeated winks,
Were fascinating like a tic and brought
Whole populations running to a plain,
Making its lush alluvial meadows
One boisterous preposter. By the river
A whistling crowd had waited many hours
To see a naked woman swim upstream;
Honours and reckless medicines were served
In booths where interest was lost
As easily as money; at the back,
In a wet vacancy among the ash cans,
A waiter coupled sadly with a crow.

FEELING:

I have but now escaped a raging landscape:
There woods were in a tremor from the shouts
Of hunchbacks hunting a hermaphrodite;
A burning village scampered down a lane;
Insects with ladders stormed a virgin's house;
On a green knoll littered with picnics
A mob of horses kicked a gull to death.

INTUITION:

Remembrance of the moment before last
Is like a yawning drug. I have observed
The sombre valley of an industry
In dereliction. Conduits, ponds, canals,
Distressed with weeds; engines and furnaces
At rust in rotting sheds; and their strong users
Transformed to spongy heaps of drunken flesh.
Deep among dock and dusty nettle lay
Each ruin of a will; manors of mould
Grew into empires as a westering sun
Left the air chilly; not a sound disturbed
The autumn dusk except a stertorous snore

That over their drowned condition like a sea
Wept without grief.

THOUGHT:
                              My recent company
Was worse than your three visions. Where I was,
The haunting ghosts were figures with no ground,
Areas of wide omission and vast regions
Of passive colours; higher than any squeak,
One note went on for ever; an embarrassed sum
Stuck on the stutter of a decimal,
And points almost coincident already
Approached so slowly they could never meet.
There nothing could be stated or constructed:
To Be was an archaic nuisance.

INTUITION:
Look. There is someone in the garden.

FEELING:
The garden is unchanged, the silence is unbroken
For she is still walking in her sleep of childhood:
Many before
Have wandered in, like her, then wandered out
Unconscious of their visit and unaltered,
The garden unchanged, the silence unbroken:
None may wake there but One who shall be woken.

THE ANGEL GABRIEL:
Wake.

III

GABRIEL:
Mary, in a dream of love
Playing as all children play,
For unsuspecting children may

Express in comic make-believe
The wish that later they will know
Is tragic and impossible;
Hear, child, what I am sent to tell:
Love wills your dream to happen, so
Love's will on earth may be, through you,
No longer a pretend but true.

MARY:

What dancing joy would whirl
My ignorance away?
Light blazes out of the stone,
The taciturn water
Burst into music,
And warm wings throb within
The motionless rose:
What sudden rush of Power
Commands me to command?

GABRIEL:

When Eve, in love with her own will,
Denied the will of Love and fell,
She turned the flesh Love knew so well
To knowledge of her love until
Both love and knowledge were of sin:
What her negation wounded, may
Your affirmation heal today;
Love's will requires your own, that in
The flesh whose love you do not know,
Love's knowledge into flesh may grow.

MARY:

My flesh in terror and fire
Rejoices that the Word
Who utters the world out of nothing,
As a pledge of His word to love her
Against her will, and to turn
Her desperate longing to love,

Should ask to wear me,
From now to their wedding day,
For an engagement ring.

GABRIEL:

Since Adam, being free to choose,
Chose to imagine he was free
To choose his own necessity,
Lost in his freedom, Man pursues
The shadow of his images:
Today the Unknown seeks the known;
What I am willed to ask, your own
Will has to answer; child, it lies
Within your power of choosing to
Conceive the Child who chooses you.

IV

SOLO AND CHORUS:

Let number and weight rejoice
In this hour of their translation
Into conscious happiness:
For the whole in every part,
The truth at the proper centre
(*There's a Way. There's a Voice.*)
Of language and distress
Is recognised in her heart
Singing and dancing.

Let even the great rejoice.
Though buffeted by admirers
And arrogant as noon,
The rich and the lovely have seen
For an infinitesimal moment
(*There's a Way. There's a Voice.*)
In another's eye till their own
Reflection came between,
Singing and dancing.

Let even the small rejoice
Though threatened from purple rostra
And dazed by the soldier's drum
Proclaiming total defeat,
The general loquacious Public
(*There's a Way. There's a Voice.*)
Have been puzzled and struck dumb,
Hearing in every street
Singing and dancing.

Let even the young rejoice
Lovers at their betrayal
Weeping alone in the night,
Have fallen asleep as they heard,
Though too far off to be certain
(*There's a Way. There's a Voice.*)
They had not imagined it,
Sounds that made grief absurd,
Singing and dancing.

Let even the old rejoice
The Bleak and the Dim, abandoned
By impulse and regret,
Are startled out of their lives;
For to footsteps long expected
(*There's a Way. There's a Voice.*)
Their ruins echo, yet
The Demolisher arrives
Singing and dancing.

THE TEMPTATION OF ST. JOSEPH

I

JOSEPH:

My shoes were shined, my pants were
                    cleaned and pressed,

And I was hurrying to meet
   My own true Love:
But a great crowd grew and grew
Till I could not push my way through,
   Because
A star had fallen down the street;
   When they saw who I was,
The police tried to do their best.

CHORUS (*off*):

> *Joseph, you have heard*
> *What Mary says occurred;*
> *Yes, it may be so.*
> *Is it likely? No.*

JOSEPH:

> The bar was gay, the lighting well-designed,
> And I was sitting down to wait
>   My own true Love:
> A voice I'd heard before, I think,
> Cried: "This is on the House. I drink
>   To him
> Who does not know it is too late";
>   When I asked for the time,
> Everyone was very kind.

CHORUS (*off*):

> *Mary may be pure,*
> *But, Joseph, are you sure?*
> *How is one to tell?*
> *Suppose, for instance . . . Well . . .*

JOSEPH:

> Through cracks, up ladders, into waters deep,
> I squeezed, I climbed, I swam to save
>   My own true Love:
> Under a dead apple tree
> I saw an ass; when it saw me

It brayed;
A hermit sat in the mouth of a cave;
When I asked him the way,
He pretended to be asleep.

CHORUS (*off*):

Maybe, maybe not.
But, Joseph, you know what
Your world, of course, will say
About you anyway.

JOSEPH:

Where are you, Father, where?
Caught in the jealous trap
Of an empty house I hear
As I sit alone in the dark
Everything, everything,
The drip of the bathroom tap,
The creak of the sofa spring,
The wind in the air-shaft, all
Making the same remark
Stupidly, stupidly,
Over and over again.
Father, what have I done?
Answer me, Father, how
Can I answer the tactless wall
Or the pompous furniture now?
Answer them . . .

GABRIEL:

No, you must.

JOSEPH:

How then am I to know,
Father, that you are just?
Give me one reason.

GABRIEL:

No.

JOSEPH:

> All I ask is one
> Important and elegant proof
> That what my Love had done
> Was really at your will
> And that your will is Love.

GABRIEL:

> No, you must believe;
> Be silent, and sit still.

II

NARRATOR:

For the perpetual excuse
Of Adam for his fall—"My little Eve,
God bless her, did beguile me and I ate,"
    For his insistance on a nurse,
All service, breast, and lap, for giving Fate
Feminine gender to make girls believe
That they can save him, you must now atone,
    Joseph, in silence and alone;
While she who loves you makes you shake with fright,
Your love for her must tuck you up and kiss good night.

For likening Love to war, for all
The pay-off lines of limericks in which
The weak resentful bar-fly shows his sting,
    For talking of their spiritual
Beauty to chorus-girls, for flattering
The features of old gorgons who are rich,
For the impudent grin and Irish charm
    That hides a cold will to do harm,
Today the roles are altered; you must be
The Weaker Sex whose passion is passivity.

For those delicious memories
Cigars and sips of brandy can restore

To old dried boys, for gallantry that scrawls
　　In idolatrous detail and size
A symbol of aggression on toilet walls,
For having reasoned—"Woman is naturally pure
Since she has no moustache," for having said,
　　"No woman has a business head,"
You must learn now that masculinity,
To Nature, is a non-essential luxury.

　　Lest, finding it impossible
To judge its object now or throatily
Forgive it as eternal God forgives,
　　Lust, tempted by this miracle
To more ingenious evil, should contrive
A heathen fetish from Virginity
To soothe the spiritual petulance
　　Of worn-out rakes and maiden aunts,
Forgetting nothing and believing all,
You must behave as if this were not strange at all.

　　Without a change in look or word,
You both must act exactly as before;
Joseph and Mary shall be man and wife
　　Just as if nothing had occurred.
There is one World of Nature and one Life;
Sin fractures the Vision, not the Fact; for
The Exceptional is always usual
　　And the Usual exceptional.
To choose what is difficult all one's days
As if it were easy, that is faith. Joseph, praise.

III

SEMI-CHORUS:

　　　　Joseph, Mary, pray for those
　　　　Misled by moonlight and the rose,
　　　　For all in our perplexity.
　　　　Lovers who hear a distant bell

That tolls from somewhere in their head
Across the valley of their dream—
"All those who love excessively
Foot or thigh or arm or face
Pursue a louche and fatuous fire
And stumble into Hell"—
Yet what can such foreboding seem
But intellectual talk
So long as bodies walk
An earth where Time and Space
Turn Heaven to a finite bed
And Love into desire?
Pray for us, enchanted with
The green Bohemia of that myth
Where knowledge of the flesh can take
The guilt of being born away,
Simultaneous passions make
One eternal chastity:
Pray for us romantics, pray.

BOYS' SEMI-CHORUS:

> Joseph, Mary, pray for us,
> Independent embryos who,
> Unconscious in another, do
> Evil as each creature does
> In every definite decision
> To improve; for even in
> The germ-cell's primary division
> Innocence is lost and sin,
> Already given as a fact,
> Once more issues as an act.

SEMI-CHORUS:

> Joseph, Mary, pray for all
> The proper and conventional
> Of whom this world approves.
> Pray for us whose married loves
> Acquire so readily

The indolent fidelity
Of unaired beds, for us to whom
Domestic hatred can become
A habit-forming drug, whose will
To civil anarchy,
Uses disease to disobey
And makes our private bodies ill.
O pray for our salvation
Who take the prudent way,
Believing we shall be exempted
From the general condemnation
Because our self-respect is tempted
To incest not adultery:
O pray for us, the bourgeoisie.

BOYS' SEMI-CHORUS:

Joseph, Mary, pray
For us children as in play
Upon the nursery floor
We gradually explore
Our members till our jealous lives
Have worked through to a clear
But trivial idea
Of that whence each derives
A vague but massive feel
Of being individual.
O pray for our redemption; for
The will that occupies
Our sensual infancy
Already is mature
And could immediately
Beget upon our flesh far more
Expressions of its disbelief
Than we shall manage to conceive
In a long life of lies.

CHORUS:

Blessed Woman,
Excellent Man,

Redeem for the dull the
Average Way,
That common ungifted
Natures may
Believe that their normal
Vision can
Walk to perfection.

THE SUMMONS

I

STAR OF THE NATIVITY:
I am that star most dreaded by the wise,
For they are drawn against their will to me,
Yet read in my procession through the skies
The doom of orthodox sophrosyne:
I shall discard their major preservation,
All that they know so long as no one asks;
I shall deprive them of their minor tasks
In free and legal households of sensation,
Of money, picnics, beer, and sanitation.

Beware. All those who follow me are led
Onto that Glassy Mountain where are no
Footholds for logic, to that Bridge of Dread
Where knowledge but increases vertigo:
Those who pursue me take a twisting lane
To find themselves immediately alone
With savage water or unfeeling stone,
In labyrinths where they must entertain
Confusion, cripples, tigers, thunder, pain.

THE FIRST WISE MAN:
    To break down Her defences
        And profit from the vision

That plain men can predict through an
    Ascesis of their senses,
With rack and screw I put Nature through
    A thorough inquisition:
But She was so afraid that if I were disappointed
I should hurt Her more that Her answers were disjointed—
    I did. I didn't. I will. I won't.
She is just as big a liar, in fact, as we are.
    To discover how to be truthful now
    Is the reason I follow this star.

THE SECOND WISE MAN:

    My faith that in Time's constant
        Flow lay real assurance
    Broke down on this analysis—
        At any given instant
    All solids dissolve, no wheels revolve,
        And facts have no endurance—
And who knows if it is by design or pure inadvertence
That the Present destroys its inherited self-importance?
    With envy, terror, rage, regret,
We anticipate or remember but never are.
    To discover how to be living now
    Is the reason I follow this star.

THE THIRD WISE MAN:

    Observing how myopic
        Is the Venus of the Soma,
    The concept Ought would make, I thought,
        Our passions philanthropic,
    And rectify in the sensual eye
        Both lens-flare and lens-coma:
But arriving at the Greatest Good by introspection
And counting the Greater Number, left no time for affection,
    Laughter, kisses, squeezing, smiles:
And I learned why the learned are as despised as they are.
    To discover how to be loving now
    Is the reason I follow this star.

THE THREE WISE MEN:

    The weather has been awful,
        The countryside is dreary,
    Marsh, jungle, rock; and echoes mock,
        Calling our hope unlawful;
    But a silly song can help along
        Yours ever and sincerely:
At least we know for certain that we are three old sinners,
That this journey is much too long, that we want our dinners,
    And miss our wives, our books, our dogs,
But have only the vaguest idea why we are what we are.
    To discover how to be human now
    Is the reason we follow this star.

STAR OF THE NATIVITY:

Descend into the fosse of Tribulation,
Take the cold hand of Terror for a guide;
Below you in its swirling desolation
Hear tortured Horror roaring for a bride:
O do not falter at the last request
But, as the huge deformed head rears to kill,
Answer its craving with a clear I Will;
Then wake, a child in the rose-garden, pressed
Happy and sobbing to your lover's breast.

II

NARRATOR:

Now let the wife look up from her stove, the husband
Interrupt his work, the child put down its toy,
That His voice may be heard in our Just Society
    Who under the sunlight
Of His calm, possessing the good earth, do well. Pray
Silence for Caesar: stand motionless and hear
In a concourse of body and concord of soul
    His proclamation.

RECITATIVE:

CITIZENS OF THE EMPIRE, GREETING. ALL MALE PERSONS
WHO SHALL HAVE ATTAINED THE AGE OF TWENTY-ONE YEARS
OR OVER MUST PROCEED IMMEDIATELY TO THE VILLAGE,
TOWNSHIP, CITY, PRECINCT OR OTHER LOCAL ADMINISTRA-
TIVE AREA IN WHICH THEY WERE BORN AND THERE REGISTER
THEMSELVES AND THEIR DEPENDENTS IF ANY WITH THE PO-
LICE. WILFUL FAILURE TO COMPLY WITH THIS ORDER IS
PUNISHABLE BY CONFISCATION OF GOODS AND LOSS OF CIVIL
RIGHTS.

NARRATOR:

You have been listening to the voice of Caesar
Who overcame implacable Necessity
By His endurance and by His skill has subdued the
 Welter of Fortune.
It is meet, therefore, that, before dispersing
In pious equanimity to obey His orders,
With well-tuned instruments and grateful voices
 We should praise Caesar.

III

FUGAL-CHORUS:

Great is Caesar: He has conquered Seven Kingdoms.
The First was the Kingdom of Abstract Idea:
Last night it was Tom, Dick and Harry; tonight it is S's
 with P's;
Instead of inflexions and accents
There are prepositions and word-order;
Instead of aboriginal objects excluding each other
There are specimens reiterating a type;
Instead of wood-nymphs and river-demons,
There is one unconditioned ground of Being.
Great is Caesar: God must be with Him.

Great is Caesar: He has conquered Seven Kingdoms.
The Second was the Kingdom of Natural Cause:

Last night it was Sixes and Sevens; tonight it is One and
    Two;
Instead of saying, "Strange are the whims of the Strong,"
We say, "Harsh is the Law but it is certain";
Instead of building temples, we build laboratories;
Instead of offering sacrifices, we perform experiments;
Instead of reciting prayers, we note pointer-readings;
Our lives are no longer erratic but efficient.
Great is Caesar: God must be with Him.

Great is Caesar; He has conquered Seven Kingdoms.
The Third was the Kingdom of Infinite Number:
Last night it was Rule-of-Thumb, tonight it is To-a-T;
Instead of Quite-a-lot, there is Exactly-so-many;
Instead of Only-a-few, there is Just-these;
Instead of saying, "You must wait until I have counted,"
We say, "Here you are. You will find this answer correct";
Instead of a nodding acquaintance with a few integers
The Transcendentals are our personal friends.
Great is Caesar: God must be with Him.

Great is Caesar: He has conquered Seven Kingdoms.
The Fourth was the Kingdom of Credit Exchange:
Last night it was Tit-for-Tat, tonight it is C.O.D.;
When we have a surplus, we need not meet someone with
    a deficit;
When we have a deficit, we need not meet someone with
    a surplus;
Instead of heavy treasures, there are paper symbols of
    value;
Instead of Pay at Once, there is Pay when you can;
Instead of My Neighbour, there is Our Customers;
Instead of Country Fair, there is World Market.
Great is Caesar: God must be with Him.

Great is Caesar; He has conquered Seven Kingdoms.
The Fifth was the Kingdom of Inorganic Giants:
Last night it was Heave-Ho, tonight it is Whee-Spree;

When we want anything, They make it;
When we dislike anything, They change it;
When we want to go anywhere, They carry us;
When the Barbarian invades us, They raise immovable
    shields;
When we invade the Barbarian, They brandish irresistible
    swords;
Fate is no longer a fiat of Matter, but a freedom of Mind.
Great is Caesar: God must be with Him.

Great is Caesar: He has conquered Seven Kingdoms.
The Sixth was the Kingdom of Organic Dwarfs:
Last night it was Ouch-Ouch, tonight it is Yum-Yum;
When diseases waylay us, They strike them dead;
When worries intrude on us, They throw them out;
When pain accosts us, They save us from embarrassment;
When we feel like sheep, They make us lions;
When we feel like geldings, They make us stallions;
Spirit is no longer under Flesh, but on top.
Great is Caesar: God must be with Him.

Great is Caesar: He has conquered Seven Kingdoms.
The Seventh was the Kingdom of Popular Soul:
Last night it was Order-Order, tonight it is Hear-Hear;
When he says, You are happy, we laugh;
When he says, You are wretched, we cry;
When he says, It is true, everyone believes it;
When he says, It is false, no one believes it;
When he says, This is good, this is loved;
When he says, That is bad, that is hated.
Great is Caesar: God must be with Him.

IV

NARRATOR:
These are stirring times for the editors of newspapers:
History is in the making; Mankind is on the march.

The longest aqueduct in the world is already
Under construction; the Committees on Fen-Drainage
And Soil-Conservation will issue very shortly
Their Joint Report; even the problems of Trade Cycles
And Spiralling Prices are regarded by the experts
As practically solved; and the recent restrictions
Upon aliens and free-thinking Jews are beginning
To have a salutary effect upon public morale.
True, the Western seas are still infested with pirates,
And the rising power of the Barbarian in the North
Is giving some cause for uneasiness; but we are fully
Alive to these dangers; we are rapidly arming; and both
Will be taken care of in due course: then, united
In a sense of common advantage and common right,
Our great Empire shall be secure for a thousand years.
    If we were never alone or always too busy,
Perhaps we might even believe what we know is not true:
But no one is taken in, at least not all of the time;
In our bath, or the subway, or the middle of the night,
We know very well we are not unlucky but evil,
That the dream of a Perfect State or No State at all,
To which we fly for refuge, is a part of our punishment.
    Let us therefore be contrite but without anxiety,
For Powers and Times are not gods but mortal gifts from
        God;
Let us acknowledge our defeats but without despair,
For all societies and epochs are transient details,
Transmitting an everlasting opportunity
That the Kingdom of Heaven may come, not in our present
And not in our future, but in the Fullness of Time.
Let us pray.

V

CHORALE:

> Our Father, whose creative Will
> Asked Being for us all,

Confirm it that Thy Primal Love
May weave in us the freedom of
The actually deficient on
    The justly actual.

Though written by Thy children with
    A smudged and crooked line,
The Word is ever legible,
Thy Meaning unequivocal,
And for Thy Goodness even sin
    Is valid as a sign.

Inflict Thy promises with each
    Occasion of distress,
That from our incoherence we
May learn to put our trust in Thee,
And brutal fact persuade us to
    Adventure, Art, and Peace.

THE VISION OF THE SHEPHERDS

I

THE FIRST SHEPHERD:

The winter night requires our constant attention,
    Watching that water and good-will,
Warmth and well-being, may still be there in the morning.

THE SECOND SHEPHERD:

    For behind the spontaneous joy of life
There is always a mechanism to keep going,

THE THIRD SHEPHERD:

    And someone like us is always there.

THE FIRST SHEPHERD:

We observe that those who assure us their education
    And money would do us such harm,
How real we are just as we are, and how they envy us,
    For it is the centreless tree
And the uncivilised robin who are the truly happy,
    Have done pretty well for themselves:

THE SECOND SHEPHERD:

Nor can we help noticing how those who insist that
    We ought to stand up for our rights,
And how important we are, keep insisting also
    That it doesn't matter a bit
If one of us gets arrested or injured, for
    It is only our numbers that count.

THE THIRD SHEPHERD:

In a way they are right,

THE FIRST SHEPHERD:

                    But to behave like a cogwheel
    When one knows one is no such thing,

THE SECOND SHEPHERD:

Merely to add to a crowd with one's passionate body,
    Is not a virtue.

THE THIRD SHEPHERD:

              What is real
About us all is that each of us is waiting.

THE FIRST SHEPHERD:

    That is why we are able to bear
Ready-made clothes, second-hand art and opinions
    And being washed and ordered about;

THE SECOND SHEPHERD:

That is why you should not take our conversation

Too seriously, nor read too much
Into our songs;

THE THIRD SHEPHERD:

        Their purpose is mainly to keep us
From watching the clock all the time.

THE FIRST SHEPHERD:

For, though we cannot say why, we know that something
   Will happen:

THE SECOND SHEPHERD:

        What we cannot say,

THE THIRD SHEPHERD:

Except that it will not be a reporter's item
   Of unusual human interest;

THE FIRST SHEPHERD:

That always means something unpleasant.

THE SECOND SHEPHERD:

                    But one day or
The next we shall hear the Good News.

II

THE THREE SHEPHERDS:

       Levers nudge the aching wrist;
          "You are free
          Not to be,
          Why exist?"
      Wheels a thousand times a minute
          Mutter, stutter,
      "End the self you cannot mend,
     Did you, friend, begin it?"
         And the streets

Sniff at our defeats.
Then who is the Unknown
Who answers for our fear
As if it were His own,
So that we reply
Till the day we die;
"No, I don't know why,
But I'm glad I'm here"?

III

CHORUS OF ANGELS:

Unto you a Child,
A Son is given.
Praising, proclaiming
The ingression of Love,
Earth's darkness invents
The blaze of Heaven,
And frigid silence
Meditates a song;
For great joy has filled
The narrow and the sad,
While the emphasis
Of the rough and big,
The abiding crag
And wandering wave,
Is on forgiveness:
Sing Glory to God
And good-will to men,
All, all, all of them.
Run to Bethlehem.

SHEPHERDS:

Let us run to learn
How to love and run;
Let us run to Love.

CHORUS:

Now all things living,
Domestic or wild,
With whom you must share
Light, water, and air,
And suffer and shake
In physical need,
The sullen limpet,
The exuberant weed,
The mischievous cat,
And the timid bird,
Are glad for your sake
As the new-born Word
Declares that the old
Authoritarian
Constraint is replaced
By His Covenant,
And a city based
On love and consent
Suggested to men,
All, all, all of them.
Run to Bethlehem.

SHEPHERDS:

Let us run to learn
How to love and run;
Let us run to Love.

CHORUS:

The primitive dead
Progress in your blood,
And generations
Of the unborn, all
Are leaping for joy
In your veins today
When the Many shall,
Once in your common
Certainty of this

Child's lovableness,
Resemble the One,
That after today
The children of men
May be certain that
The Father Abyss
Is affectionate
To all Its creatures,
All, all, all of them.
Run to Bethlehem.

AT THE MANGER

I

MARY:
O shut your bright eyes that mine must endanger
With their watchfulness; protected by its shade
Escape from my care: what can you discover
From my tender look but how to be afraid?
Love can but confirm the more it would deny.
    Close your bright eye.

Sleep. What have you learned from the womb that bore you
But an anxiety your Father cannot feel?
Sleep. What will the flesh that I gave do for you,
Or my mother love, but tempt you from His will?
Why was I chosen to teach His Son to weep?
    Little One, sleep.

Dream. In human dreams earth ascends to Heaven
Where no one need pray nor ever feel alone.
In your first few hours of life here, O have you
Chosen already what death must be your own?

How soon will you start on the Sorrowful Way?
　　Dream while you may.

II

FIRST WISE MAN:
Led by the light of an unusual star,
We hunted high and low.

SECOND WISE MAN:
　　　　　　　　Have travelled far,
For many days, a little group alone
With doubts, reproaches, boredom, the unknown.

THIRD WISE MAN:
Through stifling gorges.

FIRST WISE MAN:
　　　　　　　Over level lakes,

SECOND WISE MAN:
Tundras intense and irresponsive seas.

THIRD WISE MAN:
In vacant crowds and humming silences,

FIRST WISE MAN:
By ruined arches and past modern shops,

SECOND WISE MAN:
Counting the miles,

THIRD WISE MAN:
　　　　　　　And the absurd mistakes.

THE THREE WISE MEN:
O here and now our endless journey stops.

FIRST SHEPHERD:
We never left the place where we were born,

SECOND SHEPHERD:
Have only lived one day, but every day,

THIRD SHEPHERD:
Have walked a thousand miles yet only worn
The grass between our work and home away.

FIRST SHEPHERD:
Lonely we were though never left alone.

SECOND SHEPHERD:
The solitude familiar to the poor
Is feeling that the family next door,
The way it talks, eats, dresses, loves, and hates,
Is indistinguishable from one's own.

THIRD SHEPHERD:
Tonight for the first time the prison gates
Have opened.

FIRST SHEPHERD:
                        Music and sudden light

SECOND SHEPHERD:
Have interrupted our routine tonight,

THIRD SHEPHERD:
And swept the filth of habit from our hearts.

THE THREE SHEPHERDS:
O here and now our endless journey starts.

WISE MEN:
Our arrogant longing to attain the tomb,

SHEPHERDS:
Our sullen wish to go back to the womb,

WISE MEN:
To have no past.

SHEPHERDS:
        No future,

TUTTI:
              Is refused.
And yet, without our knowledge, Love has used
Our weakness as a guard and guide.
              We bless

WISE MEN:
Our lives' impatience.

SHEPHERDS:
        Our lives' laziness,

TUTTI:
And bless each other's sin, exchanging here

WISE MEN:
Exceptional conceit

SHEPHERDS:
        With average fear.

TUTTI:
Released by Love from isolating wrong,
Let us for Love unite our various song,
Each with his gift according to his kind
Bringing this child his body and his mind.

III

WISE MEN:

Child, at whose birth we would do obsequy
For our tall errors of imagination,
Redeem our talents with your little cry.

SHEPHERDS:

Clinging like sheep to the earth for protection,
We have not ventured far in any direction:
Wean, Child, our ageing flesh away
From its childish way.

WISE MEN:

Love is more serious than Philosophy
Who sees no humour in her observation
That Truth is knowing that we know we lie.

SHEPHERDS:

When, to escape what our memories are thinking,
We go out at nights and stay up drinking,
Stay then with our sick pride and mind
The forgetful mind.

WISE MEN:

Love does not will enraptured apathy;
Fate plays the passive role of dumb temptation
To wills where Love can doubt, affirm, deny.

SHEPHERDS:

When, chafing at the rule of old offences,
We run away to the sea of the senses,
On strange beds then O welcome home
Our horror of home.

WISE MEN:

Love knows of no somatic tyranny;

For homes are built for Love's accommodation
By bodies from the void they occupy.

SHEPHERDS:

When, exhausting our wills with our evil courses,
We demand the good-will of cards and horses,
    Be then our lucky certainty
    Of uncertainty.

WISE MEN:

Love does not fear substantial anarchy,
But vividly expresses obligation
With movement and in spontaneity.

SHEPHERDS:

When, feeling the great boots of the rich on our faces,
We live in the hope of one day changing places,
    Be then the truth of our abuse
    That we abuse.

WISE MEN:

The singular is not Love's enemy;
Love's possibilities of realisation
Require an Otherness that can say *I*

SHEPHERDS:

When in dreams the beasts and cripples of resentment
Rampage and revel to our hearts' contentment,
    Be then the poetry of hate
    That replaces hate.

WISE MEN:

Not In but With our time Love's energy
Exhibits Love's immediate operation;
The choice to love is open till we die.

SHEPHERDS:

O Living Love, by your birth we are able
Not only, like the ox and ass of the stable,

To love with our live wills, but love,
Knowing we love.

TUTTI:
O Living Love replacing phantasy,
O Joy of life revealed in Love's creation;
Our mood of longing turns to indication:
Space is the Whom our loves are needed by,
Time is our choice of How to love and Why.

THE MEDITATION OF SIMEON

SIMEON: As long as the apple had not been entirely digested, as long as there remained the least understanding between Adam and the stars, rivers and horses with whom he had once known complete intimacy, as long as Eve could share in any way with the moods of the rose or the ambitions of the swallow, there was still a hope that the effects of the poison would wear off, that the exile from Paradise was only a bad dream, that the Fall had not occurred in fact.

CHORUS: *When we woke, it was day; we went on weeping.*

SIMEON: As long as there were any roads to amnesia and anaesthesia still to be explored, any rare wine or curiosity of cuisine as yet untested, any erotic variation as yet unimagined or unrealised, any method of torture as yet undevised, any style of conspicuous waste as yet unindulged, any eccentricity of mania or disease as yet unrepresented, there was still a hope that man had not been poisoned but transformed, that Paradise was not an eternal state from which he had been forever expelled, but a childish state which he had permanently outgrown, that the Fall had occurred by necessity.

CHORUS: *We danced in the dark, but were not deceived.*

SIMEON: As long as there were any experiments still to be undertaken in restoring that order in which desire had once rejoiced to be reflected, any code of equity and obligation upon which some society had not yet been founded, any species of property of which the value had not yet been appreciated, any talent that had not yet won private devotion and public honour, any rational concept of the Good or intuitive feeling for the Holy that had not yet found its precise and beautiful expression, any technique of contemplation or ritual of sacrifice and praise that had not yet been properly conducted, any faculty of mind or body that had not yet been thoroughly disciplined, there was still a hope that some antidote might be found, that the gates of Paradise had indeed slammed to, but with the exercise of a little patience and ingenuity would be unlocked, that the Fall had occurred by accident.

CHORUS: *Lions came loping into the lighted city.*

SIMEON: Before the Positive could manifest Itself specifically, it was necessary that nothing should be left that negation could remove; the emancipation of Time from Space had first to be complete, the Revolution of the Images, in which the memories rose up and cast into subjection the senses by Whom hitherto they had been enslaved, successful beyond their wildest dreams, the mirror in which the Soul expected to admire herself so perfectly polished that her natural consolation of vagueness should be utterly withdrawn.

CHORUS: *We looked at our Shadow, and, Lo, it was lame.*

SIMEON: Before the Infinite could manifest Itself in the finite, it was necessary that man should first have reached that point along his road to Knowledge where, just as it rises from the swamps of Confusion onto the sunny slopes of Objectivity, it forks in opposite directions towards the One and the Many; where, therefore, in order to proceed at all, he must decide which is Real and which only Appearance, yet at the same time cannot escape the knowledge that his choice is arbitrary and subjective.

CHORUS: *Promising to meet, we parted forever.*

SIMEON: Before the Unconditional could manifest Itself under the conditions of existence, it was necessary that man should first have reached the ultimate frontier of consciousness, the secular limit of memory beyond which there remained but one thing for him to know, his Original Sin, but of this it is impossible for him to become conscious because it is itself what conditions his will to knowledge. For as long as he was in Paradise he could not sin by any conscious intention or act: his as yet unfallen will could only rebel against the truth by taking flight into an unconscious lie; he could only eat of the Tree of the Knowledge of Good and Evil by forgetting that its existence was a fiction of the Evil One, that there is only the Tree of Life.

CHORUS: *The bravest drew back on the brink of the Abyss.*

SIMEON: From the beginning until now God spoke through His prophets. The Word aroused the uncomprehending depths of their flesh to a witnessing fury, and their witness was this: that the Word should be made Flesh. Yet their witness could only be received as long as it was vaguely misunderstood, as long as it seemed either to be neither impossible nor necessary, or necessary but not impossible, or impossible but not necessary; and the prophecy could not therefore be fulfilled. For it could only be fulfilled when it was no longer possible to receive, because it was clearly understood as absurd. The Word could not be made Flesh until men had reached a state of absolute contradiction between clarity and despair in which they would have no choice but either to accept absolutely or to reject absolutely, yet in their choice there should be no element of luck, for they would be fully conscious of what they were accepting or rejecting.

CHORUS: *The eternal spaces were congested and depraved.*

SIMEON: But here and now the Word which is implicit in the Beginning and in the End is become immediately explicit, and that which hitherto we could only passively fear as the incomprehensible I AM, henceforth we may actively love with comprehension that THOU ART. Wherefore, having seen Him, not in some prophetic vision of what might be, but with the eyes of our own weakness as to what actually is, we are bold to say that we have seen our salvation.

CHORUS: *Now and forever, we are not alone.*

SIMEON: By the event of this birth the true significance of all other events is defined, for of every other occasion it can be said that it could have been different, but of this birth it is the case that it could in no way be other than it is. And by the existence of this Child, the proper value of all other existences is given, for of every other creature it can be said that it has extrinsic importance but of this Child it is the case that He is in no sense a symbol.

CHORUS: *We have right to believe that we really exist.*

SIMEON: By Him is dispelled the darkness wherein the fallen will cannot distinguish between temptation and sin, for in Him we become fully conscious of Necessity as our freedom to be tempted, and of Freedom as our necessity to have faith. And by Him is illuminated the time in which we execute those choices through which our freedom is realised or prevented, for the course of History is predictable in the degree to which all men love themselves, and spontaneous in the degree to which each man loves God and through Him his neighbour.

CHORUS: *The distresses of choice are our chance to be blessed.*

SIMEON: Because in Him the Flesh is united to the Word without magical transformation, Imagination is redeemed from promiscuous fornication with her own images. The tragic conflict of Virtue with Necessity is no longer confined to the Exceptional Hero; for disaster is not the impact of a curse upon a few great families, but issues continually from the hubris of every tainted will. Every invalid is Roland defending the narrow pass against hopeless odds, every stenographer Brunnhilde refusing to renounce her lover's ring which came into existence through the renunciation of love.

Nor is the Ridiculous a species any longer of the Ugly; for since of themselves all men are without merit, all are ironically assisted to their comic bewilderment by the Grace of God. Every Cabinet Minister is the wood-cutter's simple-minded son to whom the fishes and the crows are always whispering the whereabouts of the Dancing Water or the Singing Branch, every heiress the washerwoman's butter-fingered daughter on whose pillow the fairy keeps laying the herb that could cure the Prince's mysterious illness.

Nor is there any situation which is essentially more or less interesting than another. Every tea-table is a battle-field littered with old catastrophes and haunted by the vague ghosts of vast issues, every martyrdom an occasion for flip cracks and sententious oratory.

Because in Him all passions find a logical In-Order-That, by Him is the perpetual recurrence of Art assured.

CHORUS: *Safe in His silence, our songs are at play.*

SIMEON: Because in Him the Word is united to the Flesh without loss of perfection, Reason is redeemed from incestuous fixation on her own Logic, for the One and the Many are simultaneously revealed as real. So that we may no longer, with the Barbarians, deny the Unity, asserting that there are as many gods as there are crea-tures, nor, with the philosophers, deny the Multiplicity, asserting that God is One who has no need of friends and is indifferent to a World of Time and Quantity and Horror which He did not create, nor, with Israel, may we limit the co-inherence of the One and the Many to a special case, asserting that God is only concerned with and of concern to that People whom out of all that He created He has chosen for His own.

For the Truth is indeed One, without which is no salvation, but the possibilities of real knowledge are as many as are the creatures in the very real and most ex-citing universe that God creates with and for His love, and it is not Nature which is one public illusion, but we who have each our many private illusions about Nature.

Because in Him abstraction finds a passionate For-The-Sake-Of, by Him is the continuous development of Science assured.

CHORUS: *Our lost Appearances are saved by His love.*

SIMEON: And because of His visitation, we may no longer desire God as if He were lacking: our redemption is no longer a question of pursuit but of surrender to Him who is always and everywhere present. Therefore at every moment we pray that, following Him, we may depart from our anxiety into His peace.

CHORUS: *Its errors forgiven, may our Vision come home.*

THE MASSACRE OF THE INNOCENTS

I

HEROD: Because I am bewildered, because I must decide, because my decision must be in conformity with Nature and Necessity, let me honour those through whom my nature is by necessity what it is.

To Fortune—that I have become Tetrarch, that I have escaped assassination, that at sixty my head is clear and my digestion sound.

To my Father—for the means to gratify my love of travel and study.

To my Mother—for a straight nose.

To Eva, my coloured nurse—for regular habits.

To my brother, Sandy, who married a trapeze-artist and died of drink—for so refuting the position of the Hedonists.

To Mr. Stewart, nicknamed The Carp, who instructed

me in the elements of geometry through which I
came to perceive the errors of the tragic poets.

To Professor Lighthouse—for his lectures on The
Peloponnesian War.

To the stranger on the boat to Sicily—for recommending to me Brown on Resolution.

To my secretary, Miss Button—for admitting that my
speeches were inaudible.

There is no visible disorder. No crime—what could
be more innocent than the birth of an artisan's child? To-
day has been one of those perfect winter days, cold,
brilliant, and utterly still, when the bark of a shepherd's
dog carries for miles, and the great wild mountains come
up quite close to the city walls, and the mind feels in-
tensely awake, and this evening as I stand at this window high up in the citadel there is nothing in the whole
magnificent panorama of plain and mountains to indicate that the Empire is threatened by a danger more
dreadful than any invasion of Tartars on racing camels
or conspiracy of the Praetorian Guard.

Barges are unloading soil fertiliser at the river wharves.
Soft drinks and sandwiches may be had in the inns at
reasonable prices. Allotment gardening has become popular. The highway to the coast goes straight up over the
mountains and the truck-drivers no longer carry guns.
Things are beginning to take shape. It is a long time
since anyone stole the park benches or murdered the
swans. There are children in this province who have
never seen a louse, shopkeepers who have never handled
a counterfeit coin, women of forty who have never hidden in a ditch except for fun. Yes, in twenty years I
have managed to do a little. Not enough, of course.
There are villages only a few miles from here where
they still believe in witches. There isn't a single town
where a good bookshop would pay. One could count on
the fingers of one hand the people capable of solving the

problem of Achilles and the Tortoise. Still it is a beginning. In twenty years the darkness has been pushed back a few inches. And what, after all, is the whole Empire, with its few thousand square miles on which it is possible to lead the Rational Life, but a tiny patch of light compared with those immense areas of barbaric night that surround it on all sides, that incoherent wilderness of rage and terror, where Mongolian idiots are regarded as sacred and mothers who give birth to twins are instantly put to death, where malaria is treated by yelling, where warriors of superb courage obey the commands of hysterical female impersonators, where the best cuts of meat are reserved for the dead, where, if a white blackbird has been seen, no more work may be done that day, where it is firmly believed that the world was created by a giant with three heads or that the motions of the stars are controlled from the liver of a rogue elephant?

Yet even inside this little civilised patch itself, where, at the cost of heaven knows how much grief and bloodshed, it has been made unnecessary for anyone over the age of twelve to believe in fairies or that First Causes reside in mortal and finite objects, so many are still homesick for that disorder wherein every passion formerly enjoyed a frantic licence. Caesar flies to his hunting lodge pursued by ennui; in the faubourgs of the Capital, Society grows savage, corrupted by silks and scents, softened by sugar and hot water, made insolent by theatres and attractive slaves; and everywhere, including this province, new prophets spring up every day to sound the old barbaric note.

I have tried everything. I have prohibited the sale of crystals and ouija-boards; I have slapped a heavy tax on playing cards; the courts are empowered to sentence alchemists to hard labour in the mines; it is a statutory offence to turn tables or feel bumps. But nothing is really effective. How can I expect the masses to be sensible when, for instance, to my certain knowledge, the captain of my own guard wears an amulet against the Evil

Eye, and the richest merchant in the city consults a medium over every important transaction?

Legislation is helpless against the wild prayer of longing that rises, day in, day out, from all these households under my protection: "O God, put away justice and truth for we cannot understand them and do not want them. Eternity would bore us dreadfully. Leave Thy heavens and come down to our earth of waterclocks and hedges. Become our uncle. Look after Baby, amuse Grandfather, escort Madam to the Opera, help Willy with his home-work, introduce Muriel to a handsome naval officer. Be interesting and weak like us, and we will love you as we love ourselves."

Reason is helpless, and now even the Poetic Compromise no longer works, all those lovely fairy tales in which Zeus, disguising himself as a swan or a bull or a shower of rain or what-have-you, lay with some beautiful woman and begot a hero. For the Public has grown too sophisticated. Under all the charming metaphors and symbols, it detects the stern command, "Be and act heroically"; behind the myth of divine origin, it senses the real human excellence that is a reproach to its own baseness. So, with a bellow of rage, it kicks Poetry downstairs and sends for Prophecy. "Your sister has just insulted me. I asked for a God who should be as like me as possible. What use to me is a God whose divinity consists in doing difficult things that I cannot do or saying clever things that I cannot understand? The God I want and intend to get must be someone I can recognise immediately without having to wait and see what he says or does. There must be nothing in the least extraordinary about him. Produce him at once, please. I'm sick of waiting."

Today, apparently, judging by the trio who came to see me this morning with an ecstatic grin on their scholarly faces, the job has been done. "God has been born," they cried, "we have seen him ourselves. The World is saved. Nothing else matters."

One needn't be much of a psychologist to realise that if this rumour is not stamped out now, in a few years it is capable of diseasing the whole Empire, and one doesn't have to be a prophet to predict the consequences if it should.

Reason will be replaced by Revelation. Instead of Rational Law, objective truths preceptible to any who will undergo the necessary intellectual discipline, and the same for all, Knowledge will degenerate into a riot of subjective visions—feelings in the solar plexus induced by undernourishment, angelic images generated by fevers or drugs, dream warnings inspired by the sound of falling water. Whole cosmogonies will be created out of some forgotten personal resentment, complete epics written in private languages, the daubs of school children ranked above the greatest masterpieces.

Idealism will be replaced by Materialism. Priapus will only have to move to a good address and call himself Eros to become the darling of middle-aged women. Life after death will be an eternal dinner party where all the guests are twenty years old. Diverted from its normal and wholesome outlet in patriotism and civic or family pride, the need of the materialistic Masses for some visible Idol to worship will be driven into totally unsocial channels where no education can reach it. Divine honours will be paid to silver teapots, shallow depressions in the earth, names on maps, domestic pets, ruined windmills, even in extreme cases, which will become increasingly common, to headaches, or malignant tumours, or four o'clock in the afternoon.

Justice will be replaced by Pity as the cardinal human virtue, and all fear of retribution will vanish. Every corner-boy will congratulate himself: "I'm such a sinner that God had to come down in person to save me. I must be a devil of a fellow." Every crook will argue: "I like committing crimes. God likes forgiving them. Really the world is admirably arranged." And the ambition of every young cop will be to secure a death-bed repentance. The New Aristocracy will consist exclusively of hermits, bums, and permanent invalids. The Rough Diamond, the Consumptive Whore, the bandit who is good to his mother, the epileptic girl who has a way with animals will be the heroes and heroines of the New Tragedy when the general, the statesman, and the philosopher have become the butt of every farce and satire.

Naturally this cannot be allowed to happen. Civilisation must be saved even if this means sending for the military, as I suppose it does. How dreary. Why is it that in the end civilisation always has to call in these professional tidiers to whom it is all one whether it be Pythagoras or a homicidal lunatic that they are instructed to exterminate. O dear, Why couldn't this wretched infant be born somewhere else? Why can't people be sensible? I don't want to be horrid. Why can't they see that the notion of a finite God is absurd? Because it is. And suppose, just for the sake of argument, that it isn't, that this story is true, that this child is in some inexplicable manner both God and Man, that he grows up, lives, and dies, without committing a single sin? Would that make life any better? On the contrary it would make it far, far worse. For it could only mean this; that once having shown them how, God would expect every man, whatever his fortune, to lead a sinless life in the flesh and on earth. Then indeed would the human race be plunged into madness and despair. And for me personally at this moment it would mean that God had given me the power to destroy Himself. I refuse to be taken in. He could not play such a horrible practical joke. Why should He dislike me so? I've worked like a slave. Ask anyone you like. I read all official dispatches without skipping. I've taken elocution lessons. I've hardly ever taken bribes. How dare He allow me to decide? I've tried to be good. I brush my teeth every night. I haven't had sex for a month. I object. I'm a liberal. I want everyone to be happy. I wish I had never been born.

II

SOLDIERS:

When the Sex War ended with the slaughter of the Grand-
mothers,
They found a bachelor's baby suffocating under them;
Somebody called him George and that was the end of it:
　　They hitched him up to the Army.
　　George, you old debutante,
　　How did you get in the Army?

In the Retreat from Reason he deserted on his rocking-
horse
And lived on a fairy's kindness till he tired of kicking her;
He smashed her spectacles and stole her check-book and
mackintosh
　　Then cruised his way back to the Army.
　　George, you old numero,
　　How did you get in the Army?

Before the Diet of Sugar he was using razor-blades
And exited soon after with an allergy to maidenheads;
He discovered a cure of his own, but no one would patent
it,
　　So he showed up again in the Army.
　　George, you old flybynight,
　　How did you get in the Army?

When the Vice Crusades were over he was hired by some
Muscovites
Prospecting for deodorants among the Eskimos;
He was caught by a common cold and condemned to the
whiskey mines,
　　But schemozzled back to the Army.
　　George, you old Emperor,
　　How did you get in the Army?

Since Peace was signed with Honour he's been minding his
  business;
But, whoops, here comes His Idleness, buttoning his uni-
  form;
Just in tidy time to massacre the Innocents;
  He's come home to roost in the Army.
  George, you old matador,
  Welcome back to the Army.

III

RACHEL:

On the Left are grinning dogs, peering down into a solitude
  too deep to fill with roses.
On the Right are sensible sheep, gazing up at a pride
  where no dream can grow.
Somewhere in these unending wastes of delirium is a lost
  child, speaking of Long Ago in the language of
  wounds.
Tomorrow, perhaps, he will come to himself in Heaven.
But here Grief turns her silence, neither in this direction,
  nor in that, nor for any reason.
And her coldness now is on the earth forever.

THE FLIGHT INTO EGYPT

I

JOSEPH:
Mirror, let us through the glass
No authority can pass.

MARY:
Echo, if the strong should come,
Tell a white lie or be dumb.

VOICES OF THE DESERT:
It was visitors' day at the vinegar works
In Tenderloin Town when I tore my time;
A sorrowful snapshot was my sinful wage:
Was that why you left me, elusive bones?
Come to our bracing desert
Where eternity is eventful,
For the weather-glass
Is set at Alas,
The thermometer at Resentful.

MARY:
The Kingdom of the Robbers lies
Between Time and our memories;

JOSEPH:
Fugitives from Space must cross
The waste of the Anonymous.

VOICES OF THE DESERT:
How should he figure my fear of the dark?
The moment he can he'll remember me,
The silly, he locked in the cellar for fun,
And his dear little doggie shall die in his arms.
Come to our old-world desert
Where everyone goes to pieces;
You can pick up tears
For souvenirs
Or genuine diseases.

JOSEPH:
Geysers and volcanoes give
Sudden comical relief;

MARY:
And the vulture is a boon
On a dull hot afternoon.

VOICES OF THE DESERT:
All Father's nightingales knew their place,
The gardens were loyal: look at them now.
The roads are so careless, the rivers so rude,
My studs have been stolen; I must speak to the sea.
  Come to our well-run desert
  Where anguish arrives by cable,
    And the deadly sins
    May be bought in tins
  With instructions on the label.

MARY:
Skulls recurring every mile
Direct the thirsty to the Nile;

JOSEPH:
And the jackal's eye at night
Forces Error to keep right.

VOICES OF THE DESERT:
In a land of lilies I lost my wits,
Nude as a number all night I ran
With a ghost for a guest along green canals;
By the waters of waking I wept for the weeds.
  Come to our jolly desert
  Where even the dolls go whoring;
    Where cigarette-ends
    Become intimate friends,
  And it's always three in the morning.

JOSEPH AND MARY:
Safe in Egypt we shall sigh
For lost insecurity;
Only when her terrors come
Does our flesh feel quite at home.

II

RECITATIVE:

Fly, Holy Family, from our immediate rage,
That our future may be freed from our past; retrace
    The footsteps of law-giving
  Moses, back through the sterile waste,

Down to the rotten kingdom of Egypt, the damp
Tired delta where in her season of glory our
    Forefathers sighed in bondage;
  Abscond with the Child to the place

That their children dare not revisit, to the time
They do not care to remember; hide from our pride
    In our humiliation;
  Fly from our death with our new life.

III

NARRATOR:

Well, so that is that. Now we must dismantle the tree,
Putting the decorations back into their cardboard boxes—
Some have got broken—and carrying them up to the attic.
The holly and the mistletoe must be taken down and burnt,
And the children got ready for school. There are enough
Left-overs to do, warmed-up, for the rest of the week—
Not that we have much appetite, having drunk such a lot,
Stayed up so late, attempted—quite unsuccessfully—
To love all of our relatives, and in general
Grossly overestimated our powers. Once again
As in previous years we have seen the actual Vision and
    failed
To do more than entertain it as an agreeable
Possibility, once again we have sent Him away,
Begging though to remain His disobedient servant,

The promising child who cannot keep His word for long.
The Christmas Feast is already a fading memory,
And already the mind begins to be vaguely aware
Of an unpleasant whiff of apprehension at the thought
Of Lent and Good Friday which cannot, after all, now
Be very far off. But, for the time being, here we all are,
Back in the moderate Aristotelian city
Of darning and the Eight-Fifteen, where Euclid's geometry
And Newton's mechanics would account for our experience,
And the kitchen table exists because I scrub it.
It seems to have shrunk during the holidays. The streets
Are much narrower than we remembered; we had forgotten
The office was as depressing as this. To those who have
    seen
The Child, however dimly, however incredulously,
The Time Being is, in a sense, the most trying time of all.
For the innocent children who whispered so excitedly
Outside the locked door where they knew the presents to be
Grew up when it opened. Now, recollecting that moment
We can repress the joy, but the guilt remains conscious;
Remembering the stable where for once in our lives
Everything became a You and nothing was an It.
And craving the sensation but ignoring the cause,
We look round for something, no matter what, to inhibit
Our self-reflection, and the obvious thing for that purpose
Would be some great suffering. So, once we have met the
    Son,
We are tempted ever after to pray to the Father;
"Lead us into temptation and evil for our sake."
They will come, all right, don't worry; probably in a form
That we do not expect, and certainly with a force
More dreadful than we can imagine. In the meantime
There are bills to be paid, machines to keep in repair,
Irregular verbs to learn, the Time Being to redeem
From insignificance. The happy morning is over,
The night of agony still to come; the time is noon:
When the Spirit must practise his scales of rejoicing
Without even a hostile audience, and the Soul endure

A silence that is neither for nor against her faith
That God's Will will be done, that, in spite of her prayers,
God will cheat no one, not even the world of its triumph.

IV

CHORUS:
He is the Way.
Follow Him through the Land of Unlikeness;
You will see rare beasts, and have unique adventures.

He is the Truth.
Seek Him in the Kingdom of Anxiety;
You will come to a great city that has expected your return
    for years.

He is the Life.
Love Him in the World of the Flesh;
And at your marriage all its occasions shall dance for joy.

THE FIRSTBORN

A Play in Three Acts

CHRISTOPHER FRY

TO MY MOTHER AND MY BROTHER

CHARACTERS

IN THE ORDER OF THEIR APPEARANCE

ANATH BITHIAH, *Pharaoh's sister*

TEUSRET, *Pharaoh's daughter*

SETI THE SECOND, *the Pharaoh*

RAMASES, *his son*

MOSES

AARON, *his brother*

MIRIAM, *his sister*

SHENDI, *Miriam's son*

Two overseers, a Minister (KEF)

A guard and a servant

The action of the play takes place in the summer of 1200 B.C., alternating between Pharaoh's palace and Miriam's tent.

ACT ONE

SCENE ONE: *The terrace of the palace of Seti the Second, at Tanis. A morning in the summer of 1200 B.C. A flight of steps (unseen) leads down through a gate to open ground. The terrace looks out upon an incompleted pyramid.*

A scream.

Enter from the palace ANATH BITHIAH, *a woman of fifty, sister to the Pharaoh, and* TEUSRET, *a girl of fifteen, the Pharaoh's daughter.*

ANATH: What was it, Teusret?

TEUSRET: Did you hear it too?

ANATH: Some man is dead. That scream was password to a
    grave.

  Look there: up go the birds!

TEUSRET: The heat on this terrace!

  You could bake on these stones, Aunt Anath.

ANATH: Ask who it was.

TEUSRET: They're working steadily at father's tomb.

  There's no sign of trouble.

ANATH: We're too far off to see.

  We should know more if we could see their faces.

TEUSRET (*calling down the steps*): Guard! Come up here.

ANATH: I should like to be certain.

  Oh, that pyramid! Everyday, watching it build,

  Will make an old woman of me early.

  It will cast a pretty shadow when it's done.

  Two hundred more men were taken on to-day,

  Did you know that, Teusret? Your father's in a hurry.

  Their sweat would be invaluable to the farmers in this
    drought.

  What pains they take to house a family of dust.

TEUSRET: It's a lovely tomb.

ANATH: Yes, so it may be.
But what shall we do with all that air to breathe
And no more breath? I could as happily lie
And wait for eternal life in something smaller.

Enter A GUARD.

TEUSRET: What was that scream we heard?

GUARD: It's nothing, madam.

ANATH: You are right. Nothing. It was something once
But now it is only a scare of birds in the air
And a pair of women with their nerves uncovered;
Nothing.

TEUSRET: Who was it screamed?

GUARD: One of the builders
Missed his footing, madam; merely an Israelite.
They're digging him into the sand. No, over to the left.

TEUSRET: Oh yes, I see them now.—That was all I wanted.

Exit THE GUARD.

So that's all right.

ANATH: Can you remember your cousin?

TEUSRET: Why, which cousin?

ANATH: My foster son. You knew him
When you were little. He lived with us in the palace.

TEUSRET: The birds are back on the roof now.

ANATH: Moses, Teusret.

TEUSRET: What, Aunt? Yes, I think I remember. I remember
A tall uncle. Was he only a cousin?
He used to drum his helmet with a dagger
While he sang us regimental marches to get us to sleep.
It never did. Why?

ANATH: No reason. I thought of him.
Well, they've buried the man in the sand. We'd better
Find our morning again and use what's left.

TEUSRET: Why did you think of him? Why *then* particularly?

ANATH: Why not then? Sometimes he blows about my brain

Like litter at the end of a public holiday.
I have obstinate affections. Ask your father.
He would tell you, if it wasn't impolitic
To mention Moses, what a girl of fire
I was, before I made these embers.
He could tell you how I crossed your grandfather,
And your grandfather was a dynasty in himself.
Oh Teusret, what a day of legend that was!
I held forbidden Israel in my arms
And growled on my stubborn doorstep, till I had my
    way.

TEUSRET: What do you mean?

ANATH: Well, never mind.

TEUSRET: I do.
You've told me so far.

ANATH: Keep it to yourself then.
The summer of '24 had brilliant days
And unprecedented storms. The striped linen
You once cut up for a doll's dress was the dress
Made for me that summer. It was the summer
When my father, your grandfather, published the pro-
nouncement.

TEUSRET: What pronouncement?

ANATH: That all the boys of Jewdom
Should be killed. Not out of spite, Teusret; necessity.
Your grandfather ordered that Defence of the Realm be
    painted
At the head of the document, in azure and silver.
It made it easier for him.

TEUSRET: Were they killed?

ANATH: Yes, they all died of a signature. Or we thought
    so,
Until the thirtieth of August. I went bathing on that
    day.
I was a girl then, Teusret, and played with the Nile
As though with a sister. And afterwards as I waded
To land again, pushing the river with my knees,
The wash rocked a little ark out

Into the daylight: and in the ark I found
A tiny weeping Israel who had failed
To be exterminated. When I stooped
With my hair dripping on to his face
He stopped in a screwed-up wail and looked.
And when I found my hands and crowded him
Into my breast, he buried like a burr.
And when I spoke I laughed, and when I laughed
I cried, he was so enchanting. I was ready
To raise a hornet's nest to keep him; in fact
I raised one. All the court flew up and buzzed.
But what could they do? Not even my Pharaoh-father
Could sting him out of my arms. So he grew up
Into your tall cousin, Egyptian
From beard to boots and, what was almost better,
A soldier of genius. You don't remember
How I held you on this terrace, to see him come home
    from war?
It was ten years ago. Do you remember
The shrieking music, and half Egypt shouting
Conqueror! Peacemaker!

TEUSRET: No.

ANATH: They have all tried to forget.
They have blotted him out of the records, but not out
Of my memory.

TEUSRET: Why did they blot him out?
I can never get at the truth of what came next.
I sometimes overhear his name muttered
In the corridors, between servants or the soldiers.
But when they see me they stop their conversation.
I have seen my father fidget at the name of a battle
And change the subject. What is it all about?
Moses was a prince of this house, my cousin.
Now he is someone not to be spoken of.
"The murder" I've heard them say, and "Since the mur-
    der"
What did he do? Did he go mad or something?

ANATH: I might have known that I should say too much.

TEUSRET: Aunt, you must tell me.

ANATH: Well, no doubt I meant to.
The day I held you here, he came as the conqueror
Of Abyssinia. In all the windows and doors
Women elbowed and cracked their voices; and men
Hung on the gates and the trees; and children sang
The usual songs, conducted by their teachers.
As for me, nothing would stop me shaking.
As for him, as for Moses, he was as tired
As a dog, and stumbled when he climbed the steps to
    the palace.
There was a brilliant reception. He was decorated
By your grandfather.

TEUSRET: Yes, but what happened to make him—

ANATH: All right, I'm coming to it, Teusret. The day
    after,
For the country-side also to be able to see the hero,
He went to inspect the city being built at Pithom.—
My book was closed from that day forward.
He went round with an officer who unfortunately
Was zealous but unintelligent. Silly man:
Silly, silly man. He found a labourer
Idling or resting, and he thought, I suppose,
"I'll show this prince that I'm worth my position"
And beat the workman. A Jewish bricklayer.
He beat him senseless.

TEUSRET: And then?

ANATH: What happened then
I only know out of the sleepless nights
Which I endured afterwards. In those nights
I made myself a knowledge, and believe it.
Moses turned—turned to what was going on—
Turned himself and his world turtle. It was
As though an inward knife scraped his eyes clean.
The General of Egypt, the Lion and the Prince
Recognized his mother's face in the battered body
Of a bricklayer; saw it was not the face above
His nursery, not my face after all.

He knew his seed. And where my voice had hung till
   then
Now voices descending from ancestral Abraham
Congregated on him. And he killed
His Egyptian self in the self of that Egyptian
And buried that self in the sand.

TEUSRET: Aunt—
    Enter A GUARD.

GUARD: The Pharaoh.
  Madam, the Pharaoh is here.

ANATH: Can we look innocent?
    Enter SETI. *Exit* THE GUARD.

TEUSRET: Good morning, father.

SETI: Go indoors, my Teusret.
    Exit TEUSRET.

ANATH: Is the day such vexation? Did you listen to me
  And sleep apart from your empire for one night?
  You didn't. Egypt has argued in the dark again
  While the night struck bitter bells on every clock.
  Look at you! Your eyes are deaf with listening
  To your wretched pillows, Seti.

SETI: Where is Moses?

ANATH: Seti!

SETI: Where is Moses? You will know.
  In what country? Doing what?

ANATH: Why Moses?

SETI: I need him.

ANATH: I've no reason to remember.
  I'm without him.

SETI: But you know.

ANATH: Why should I know?
  Why should I? When the sun goes down do I have to
    know
  Where and how it grovels under the world?
  I thought he was a dust-storm we had shut outside.
  Even now I sometimes bite on the grit.

SETI: Time has made it easier. The men are dead
  Who wanted his death-sentence. I must have him home.

ANATH: Indeed you've not slept!

SETI: I have found him necessary.
  Libya is armed along the length of her frontier,
  And the South's like sand, shifting and uncertain.
  I need Moses.—We have discarded in him
  A general of excellent perception.

ANATH: He's discarded, rightly or wrongly. We've let him
  go.

SETI: Deeds lie down at last, and so did his.
  Out in the wilderness, after two days' flight,
  His deed lay down, knowing what it had lost him.
  Under the boredom of thorn-trees his deed cried out
  For Egypt and died. Ten years long he has lugged
  This dead thing after him. His loyalty needn't be questioned.

ANATH: We're coming to something strange when a normal day
  Opens and lets in the past. He may remember
  Egypt. He's in Midian.

SETI: In what part of Midian?

ANATH: Wherever buckets are fetched up out of wells
  Or in his grave.

SETI: We'll find him. If we have to comb
  Midian to its shadows we'll find him.

ANATH: He's better where he is.

SETI: He is essential to my plans.

ANATH: I tell you
  He is better where he is. For you or me
  He's better where he is.
  We have seen different days without him
  And I have done my hair a different way.
  Leave him alone to bite his lips.

SETI: He and I
  Were boys who went well together, in spite of a difference
  In age. He was old for his years. We were excellent
  friends.

ANATH: Boys go home from school. After a time
  All boys become initials cut in wood.
SETI: Prepare yourself to see him back.

    His eye is caught by something below and beyond the terrace.

                          What's this,
  What is this crowd?
ANATH: It's Ramases! No qualms
  For the dynasty, with a son as popular as he is.
SETI: There's half the city round him. Where are his
    guards?
ANATH: There: a little behind.
SETI: The boy's too careless
  Of himself. This mobbing is a fever and out of propor-
    tion.
  You would think he had brought them a conquest; he
    might be a hero
  The way they cheer him. They're even climbing the
    gates
  To see him come through. What is the matter with
    you?
ANATH: What do you mean?
SETI: You're shaking.
ANATH: Nonsense, Seti.
SETI: I'm not altogether at rest in the way he's growing,
  Not altogether pleased with his free-and-easy good hu-
    mor,
  His good graces for no-matter-whom.
  The young have keys that we have lost. They enter
  Life by doors which were better never unlocked.
  This easily-come-by popularity, for instance,
  Is a danger above all dangerous to princes.
  I don't like his drift or trust his politics.
ANATH: What are his politics?
SETI: Exactly so;
  What are they? There are no politics more dangerous
  Than politics that don't seem to exist.
  I can trust my enemy, trust him to be my enemy,

But Ramases follows unpredictable instincts.
They'll turn on him one of these days, like lion-cubs
Who play so innocently and later on
Find a mouth for blood. He must learn to abdicate
His heart and let the needs of Egypt rule there.

ANATH: He will learn. He is learning.

SETI: Egypt should pray so.

ANATH: I would hazard a guess that Egypt's women
Have prayed for him often enough. Ra, raising
An eyebrow stiff with the concentration of creation
Probably says: That boy again? We'd better
Make something of him early and have them satisfied.
O, Ramases will be all right.

SETI: I hope,
I hope.

Enter RAMASES, *a boy of eighteen.*

RAMASES: Did you see the excitement? I think it's the drought.
Like the air, we're all quivering with heat.
Do you find that, Aunt? Either you must sleep like the dead
Or something violent must happen.

ANATH: Look: your father.

RAMASES: I didn't see you, father. I'm sorry, sir.
Did I interrupt state matters?

SETI: If they had been,
We should have fetched you here. What morning have
you had?

RAMASES: Holiday—books rolled up, military exercises
Over, and no social engagements. I've been fowling
Down at the marshes.

ANATH: Any luck?

RAMASES: Not much flesh
But a paradise of feathers. I was out before daybreak.

ANATH: It's a good marksman who hunts by batlight.

RAMASES: But I
Waited for daylight. Until then the marsh was a torpor.
I clucked and clapped as the sun rose

And up shot so much whistle and whirr
I could only hold my spear and laugh.
All the indignant wings of the marshes
Flocking to the banner of Tuesday
To avoid the Prince of Egypt!
Off they flapped into the mist
Looking about for Monday
The day they had lived in peace: and finding nothing
Back they wheeled to Tuesday.
I had recovered myself by then and killed
One that had the breast of a chestnut.
At last he could feel the uninterrupted darkness
Of an addled egg. I watched his nerves flinching
As they felt how dark that darkness was.
I found myself trying to peer into his death.
It seemed a long way down. The morning and it
Were oddly separate,
Though the bird lay in the sun: separate somehow
Even from contemplation.

ANATH: Excellent spirits
To make a success of a holiday.

RAMASES: Only for a moment.

SETI: This afternoon I have business for you. (*He turns to
go in.*)

RAMASES: Very well.

SETI: Was that thunder?

ANATH: They're dumping new stone for the pyramid.

RAMASES: Two men came through the marshes before I
left;
Jews, but not our Jews: or one of them
Was not; he seemed a man of prosperity
Although some miles of sun and dust were on him.

SETI: Aliens?

RAMASES: Yes; but one of them I felt
I should have known. I stared but couldn't place him.
He stood so strongly up out of some recollection
And yet what was it? How could I have known him?
I passed then again as I came home. They stood

To watch the crowd. I looked across and smiled
But got no smiles from them. They looked, and yet
They seemed to look back in their minds
Rather than out at me. And one, the tall one—
ANATH: Very tall?
RAMASES: Yes, he was tall. It was he
Who is somehow in my memory.
ANATH: Seti—
SETI: Well?
ANATH: Is it possible that someone hasn't waited to be recalled?
Is it possible?
SETI: It is not possible.
ANATH: Your thoughts are leaning that way too.
Sometimes the unaccountable stalks in.
SETI: Which way were they travelling, Ramases?
RAMASES: This way. If I had only thought of them sooner
We could have seen them go by.—Sir!
They are standing here at the foot of the stairway. How long
Can they have been there? They're standing without moving,
Gazing up: not conversing, but looking up:
Who let them through? Shall I speak to them?
ANATH: He has stood all day under my brain's stairway.
Seti, who is there? Which foremost, Ramases?
The tall one?
RAMASES: Yes. Who's in your mind?
ANATH: The tall one.
The tall one.
RAMASES *goes down the steps.*
So he is back; and small-talk
Has to block a draught up ten years old.
God help me.
SETI: Why has he come?
ANATH: You said he longed
For Egypt.

SETI: I think so.

ANATH: But what am I in Egypt?
A dead king's daughter.

Re-enter RAMASES, *followed by* MOSES *and* AARON.

SETI: I am tempted to call this a visitation and not
A visit. What words can I find to fit
So ghostly a homecoming?

RAMASES (*to* ANATH).

Who is this man?

SETI: Understand you are welcome. Whatever uncertainty
You have can go. We welcome you. Look who is here.

ANATH: He has seen me. We have looked at one another.

SETI: We'll absolve ourselves of the ten years. Who is
this?

MOSES: My brother.

SETI: I had not heard you had a brother.

ANATH: A brother, a sister—and a mother. All the three.

SETI: Our lives at their most coincidental bring the gods
Very near. I told my sister we must have you back.
And so we must, and so Egypt must; and it seems
That we have. You are come promptly at the word,
Moses.

MOSES: This is not why I came.

SETI: You would scarcely foresee it.

MOSES: I am not who you think. I am a stranger.

SETI: Not by a vein or a hair. The past is forgotten.
You are a prince of Egypt.

MOSES: The prince of Egypt
Died the day he fled.

SETI: What do you mean?

MOSES: That prince of Egypt died. I am the Hebrew
Smitten out of the shadow of that prince,
Vomited out of his dry lips, the cry
Whipped off the sanded tongue of that prince of Egypt.

SETI: What has this long discomfort done for you,
My friend? It has made you bitter.

MOSES: Make no mistake;
I have done very well for myself. I haven't come to
beg.
Why was it you decided to ask me to come back?
SETI: Isn't it time we laid the crippling ghost
That haunts us? You evidently thought so too
To come so far.
MOSES: You've a better reason than that.
SETI: Why should you want reasons when you have come
On your own initiative? Why are you here?
I am asking you candidly. Why did you come?
MOSES: My blood heard my blood weeping
Far off like the swimming of fear under the sea,
The sobbing at night below the garden. I heard
My blood weeping. It is here it wept and weeps.
It was from here I heard coming this drum of despair,
The hidden bullfrog of my brothers' grief:
Under your shoes, under your smile, and under
The foundations of your tomb. From Egypt.
ANATH: What was it, Seti, that lay down and died?
SETI: Why are you here?
MOSES: To be close to this
That up to now has only made me uneasy,
As though a threat of evil whispered beyond
Control under the wind. I could be
Uneasy and still eat in Midian.
I could be Pharaoh in Midian, but in Egypt
I knew I should be Moses.
SETI: Still you haven't
Answered my question. Come, what do you want?
MOSES: First, that you should know what you are doing.
SETI: Take care, Moses.
ANATH: And secondly?
MOSES: What can I hope
From that until he has understood the first?
SETI: What is this mood you have come in which is so
ready

To abuse a decent welcome? There is something ship-
wreck
About you that will not do for peaceful places.
Steady yourself if we're to understand one another.
I am the Pharaoh, Moses, not the young uncle
Of the Heliopolis classroom, nor your messroom
brother.
Well, go on.

MOSES: A man has more to be
Than a Pharaoh. He must dare to outgrow the security
Of partial blindness. I'm not speaking now
To your crown; I'm speaking to your merciless mischief.

SETI: You have coarsened during your exile. What you say
Hasn't even the virtue of clarity. If you wish
To consider my offer of reinstatement, go
And consider. I can be patient. Egypt can do
Her work on you like a generous woman, given
Her time. (*He glances at* ANATH.)
          Midian will wash off in the Nile.
Go on, go on, I shall not remember this morning.

MOSES: I think you will. My brother has lived these days
In amongst Israel, while I was sleeping.
He knows both the truth and the injury better than I
can.
He has had refuge, this last year, close to your border.
He was hunted out for his friendship to flesh and blood,
And so he has lain with his ear against the door
Hearing pain but unable to come to it.
He stands here with me now so that what shall be said
Shall be truthfully said and what you shall hear
Will have earned hearing because the teller lived it.

AARON: Twelve hundred thousand Israelites are under
Your dominion. Of these two hundred and twenty thou-
sand
Only, are men. The rest are in the proportion
Of four hundred and fifty thousand women
And five hundred and thirty thousand children.

SETI: I have my census-takers.

AARON: So perhaps
Has Death got his; but I think he has not referred
His undertakings to your dynastic understanding.
Here I have his estimate: between April and July
Sixty-one deaths suffered in old age
But an old age of forced labour, their backs bent twice,
Under the weight of years and under the mule-whip.
Also thirty-eight deaths of healthy men
Who made some show of reluctance or momentary
Impatience.

MOSES: That was a good cure. They are now
Patient for all eternity.

AARON: Also the deaths
Of seven pregnant women, forced to dig
Until they had become their own gravediggers.
Also the deaths of nineteen children, twelve
Unofficial crucifixions . . .

SETI: This is intolerable
Singsong! Am I to compose the epitaphs
For every individual grave of this trying summer?
I have my figures. I do not need yours.

MOSES: Twelve hundred thousand. These are the men
I have come to find. They are the wound in my mind.
They show me myself covered in blood: and you
Are there, staring back at yourself from that mortal
Mirror, twelve hundred thousand times yourself,
Which, like a dog with its own reflection,
You don't recognize. No recollection?
Not of this child, elect in its private maze?
Not of this boy rashly making manhood
Out of a clumsy alteration? Is this some other
Form of life than yours? What; is nothing like?
The girls dandling to-morrow, the young men
Trying to justify to-day, old men
Sitting by monuments of memory—
All these licking their fingers of experience

To turn the page.—No! I am mistaken.
They are only pestilence-carriers and tomb makers.
But the worst pestilence they carry is the cruelty
Of Pharaoh. That is what I have come to show you.

SETI: Very well; you have introduced yourself;
I have understood you. Is it not a pity
That you had taken up this attitude
Before you were aware of mine? I can see
How, knowing, as you must, your own capabilities,
You would fill those listless hours of your exile
With dreams of action. Action is what I have for you.
But there's a whiff of anarchy about you.
You cannot hope that I should like it. A generalship—
The confidence of Egypt—these do not look well
On an agitator. Something has to go.—
I have put men to a purpose who otherwise
Would have had not the least meaning.

MOSES: Aaron,
What am I doing fitting one word against another
To see them melt as soon as they touch this man?
Not the least meaning, except the meaning
Of the breath in your lungs, the mystery of existing
At all. What have we approached or conceived
When we have conquered and built a world? Even
Though civilisation became perfect? What then?
We have only put a crown on the skeleton.
It is the individual man
In his individual freedom who can mature
With his warm spirit the unripe world.
What would you make of man? If you diminish him
To a count of labouring limbs, you also will dwindle
And be an unmeaning body, decomposing
Imperceptibly under heavy ornaments.
They are your likeness, these men, even to nightmares.
I have business with Egypt, one more victory for her,
A better one than Ethiopia:
That she should come to see her own shame
And discover justice for my people.

SETI: You have fermented in your Midian bottle.
   But lately I have learnt an obstinate patience.
   We should have done better to have met
   Out of the sun. We can do better than this
   And so we shall yet, later, at a cooler time.
   Where will you sleep? We will see you have food.
   Do you remember, I wonder, the palace nectarine?

   MOSES *and* AARON *go towards the steps.*

   I said, where will you lodge?

MOSES: With my sister, Miriam.

SETI (*to* ANATH): Do you know where that is?

ANATH: Perfectly.

SETI (*going in*):   Very well.

ANATH: Now he will not sleep again tonight.

MOSES: I hope that none of us will sleep again
   Until we all can sleep.

ANATH: And so once more
   We see each other. You have chosen a fine day.

   MOSES *waits.* ANATH *says no more. He goes with*
   AARON.

ANATH: I taught him to walk, Ramases. I also taught him
   To speak and say his alphabet. I taught you your
   Alphabet also; and also Teusret hers.
   I have been a really useful woman.

RAMASES: Where
   Does his sister live?

ANATH: Why do you want to know?

RAMASES: I wondered where it might be.

ANATH: She has a tent
   By the brick-kiln.

RAMASES: We used to ride that way
   And leave presents on a woman there. Was that
   The sister?

ANATH: Yes; Miriam. His sister Miriam.
   Ramases, let what has happened work itself out.
   Don't finger it. Do you hear me?

RAMASES: I liked that man.

ANATH: So have others before you. Do not finger it.
  Your father is not always quite at his best.
RAMASES: I know my father.
ANATH: Maybe.
RAMASES: I seem to love him.
ANATH: You should.
RAMASES: And yet I could like that man.
ANATH: Well, like that man; but do not raise a hand
  To help that man; do not sing with that man
  Or let him make his nest in your brain. Like him,
  Ramases, forget him, and let us live in peace.
RAMASES: I shall go and find him.
ANATH: Ramases, come here.
  Do you want to make yourself look like a laughable
    puppy
  Bounding after his heels? Stay where you are.
  I ask it of you. I ask you to put him from your mind.
  Do you hear? I ask you to forget him.
RAMASES: How?
ANATH: What would make it difficult?
RAMASES: Can you forget him?
ANATH: He has gone.
RAMASES: And something of us, I think, went with him.
ANATH: Well, you will let him go. I have asked you.
RAMASES: No.
  I love you, you know that. But trust me a little.
  I shall be discreet.
        Exit RAMASES.
ANATH: Ramases!—No,
  What should I be doing, turning his feet
  Towards my fears? (*She goes to the parapet.*)
                      I guess at a reticent power
  Above the days of our life.
  Our most convinced actions are only questions,
  And the power will answer as it wishes.
  If I do not act, it will still answer.
  But it will not have been my question.
        Enter TEUSRET.

TEUSRET: Aunt Anath—

ANATH: Do you remember, Teusret?
A man fell from the pyramid—only this morning.

Curtain

SCENE TWO: MIRIAM'S *tent.* MOSES *(in the entrance)*.
MIRIAM.

MOSES: Miriam! Miriam!

MIRIAM: Is it my brother? Yes;
You have his immovable look. Aaron told me
To expect you.

MOSES: Can you be Miriam?

MIRIAM: A kind
Of residue. Sit down, if you don't mind.
I dislike answering questions. Ask me nothing.
I am very well; I have nothing to offer you
To drink.

MOSES: I'm glad to be with you after so long.

MIRIAM: You will find it very tiresome after five or six
minutes.
I repeat myself unendurably, like the Creation.
Your only hope is to deaden yourself to me
And it.

AARON *(in the entrance)*: Your name runs like fire, like
an ostrich!
You didn't wait to hear, but the sergeant at the gate
Is full of it. They've started campaigns of gossip
And altercation in the assembly-gardens—
As soon as this; before you've even been seen!

MOSES: And what will this do for us?

AARON: Surely it suggests
They're taking sides? It was noticed a minister's wife

Was wearing an M in small lilies; her daughter snatched
   them off
And threw them among the pigeons. How can Seti
Assure himself what size your faction is?
Egypt loves and hates you inextricably.

MOSES: Egypt is afraid. Love me? No;
   They're afraid to be without me.

AARON: That will pass for love.

MOSES: They love me from the bottom of their greed.
   Give me the bad news. What men have we lost?

MIRIAM: So you're not only here on a visit to your sister.

AARON: Here is a list. It's not complete.

MIRIAM: I've had
   Enough of trouble.

MOSES: Rahnor, Janeth, Pathrusim—
   Is he lost? Pathrusim? The sand of Egypt
   Is abominably the richer.—Hadoram, Seth,
   Havilah, Dodanim . . .

MIRIAM: Why do you read
   Dead men's names? There are some of us still breath-
     ing.
   Your sister, for example, is still alive,
   Figuratively speaking. I imagined
   You would have plenty to tell me. Have you not?
   Am I always to know nothing of you?

MOSES: These names are what I am.

MIRIAM: They are yesterday's life. I liked many of them
   very well;
   But we no longer have anything in common.

AARON: Are we to forget them because we have lost
   them?

MIRIAM: To wish
   To be with them comes too easily.

MOSES: This tent
   Is stifling.

MIRIAM: I keep it closed. I have no liking
   For what goes on outside.

MOSES: When do they say
  The mountains last had rain?

MIRIAM: Nine months ago.

MOSES: It's time for parturition.
  Look: what you shut out is a withering city.
  City of Egypt. This land once I worshipped,
  And now I cannot be sure what I bring against her
  In my heart. This noon, like every other noon,
  Still groans with the laborious wheels which drew
  The Nile water. There is little difference
  Between ourselves and those blindfolded oxen.
  We also do the thing we cannot see,
  Hearing the creaking pivot and only knowing
  That we labour.

MIRIAM: Why did you bring him? Take yourselves off!
  This is my tent, and it's not for restless hands.
  He's a dangermaker still. Only watch his hands!

AARON: What has he said, Miriam?

MIRIAM: I have a son
  And that is all I rest on. There's a man
  Who should have been my brother. A king's daughter
  Swallowed him and spat out this outlaw. I'll
  Not have any more in the family.

AARON: What should make them?

MIRIAM: You and he. I know. Two years ago
  I had it all: the surly men coming in here,
  One at a time by signal, hardly nodding
  Towards me, covering the table with their knife-cuts
  To show how revolution must come, and freedom,
  And idiocy; till a beetle striking the lamp
  Or the coal settling, would shiver through us all
  As though a dagger had sung into the pole.
  And Espah and Zoad are dead from it. And you
  In a night of loud hyenas went over the border.
  Not again. I'll keep my nights of sleep, and I'll keep
  My son.

AARON: In this country of murder?

MIRIAM: I'll keep my son
In whatever country.

MOSES: Happily?

MIRIAM: We have
A way of living. We have the habit. Well?
It becomes a kind of pleasantness.

MOSES: You have gone
With the dead after all, but you pretend not to see them.
Miriam, we have to speak to them with our lives.
Death was their question to us, and our lives
Become their understanding or perplexity.
And by living to answer them, we also answer
Our own impermanence. But this rule of Egypt
Denies us life, Miriam, and gives us nothing
With which we can outspeak our graves.

MIRIAM: I am angry;
The pity is I am angry. I must pretend
You have said nothing.

AARON: But do you understand him?
In fact, do I understand him?

MIRIAM: In fact, do we need to?
I've no doubt he is kind, but not our kind. Very well,
I will say something. I'll say he's a sightseer;
And we keep our experience.

MOSES: When I was a child,
Miriam, and you came like comfort to the huge
Nursery of the Pharaohs, we'd go hand
In hand along your stories, Hebrew stories
Which like contraband you put quietly in
To become my nature. What have you for me now?

MIRIAM: How she disliked me then! But what a talent
For condescension she had. I never saw you
After you were a child except by waiting
Among the crowd in the streets. There was no need
To come from Midian to tell me what my life is;
I have a bowing acquaintance with it. I knew it
When I hid you to save you from the knives.

Before I could talk it talked to me
In most difficult words.

MOSES: What words, Miriam?

MIRIAM: Pogrom, for one. And the curses of children
When I ran towards them expecting to play.
We have a wildfowl quality of blood,
Moses, temptation for sportsmen.

MOSES: Go on.

MIRIAM: With what
If you please? Do you know the secret which will
    change
Our spoor? Our grandfather was stoned. I imagine
Creation tried our blood, and brought it in guilty.

MOSES: It was the verdict of Chaos.

MIRIAM: The thick of Chaos
Can still be smelt in the air, then. It was never
Properly resolved.

MOSES: And I believed
I had strength!

MIRIAM: Your quarrel is with what things are.

MOSES: Above all, with what I am, the inconsiderable
Life, born of such distances of suffering
And experiences, such an orgasm of mankind,
Such hewing of a foothold in the rockface
Of darkness, such aeons of cause and purport,
Jets and flares of a vision and the blaze
Of undecipherable fury, ages
Of moons rising into airs of sleep,
Of suns relenting down into the hills
Away from triumph, beyond defeat—and yet
My spirit, fruit of these life-throes of time,
Paces the condemned cell, the human body,
Incapable, weaponless, fettered with flesh, drinking
The moisture of the walls. Is the spirit
So masterly, that nature must obstruct it
Or be consumed? I feel it. Oh, it points!
I am there, beyond myself, if I could reach
To where I am. Miriam, you have shown me too much.

MIRIAM: One grows accustomed.

AARON: You will find the approach
And the means you want, I'm confident. Something
Will soon open a way to action.

RAMASES (*in the tent-opening*): Uncle.
I knew you as that. When I have thought of you
It has been as my uncle. You may not like it.
You may not want to see me, even.

MIRIAM: The palace!

AARON: Well, why not? Another man has been royal
And is here.

MIRIAM: Has been, has been.

RAMASES: Moses.

MOSES: Welcome and unwelcome.

RAMASES: I haven't come
From my father. I used schoolboy's worship, like myrrh
And cassia, with gums of memory,
To perpetuate you: the immense and affable
God in general's uniform, who came
And went between wars, who filled the schoolroom; and I
Could call him uncle. So when the memory
Broke its wrappings, and stood speaking like a man
On a noonday terrace, I decided to come nearer.

MOSES: Come on, then, and send the god to vanish finally
Into the lie that he always was.

RAMASES: You spoke
To my father too suddenly.

MOSES: Yes, we're precipitous,
We gods. We threw off the world, vegetable
And animal too, on the impulse of an imaginative
Moment. But we lost interest.

RAMASES: You mean
I'm a boy to you still.

MOSES: You came by your boyhood honestly.
Mine I stole. I had no right to it.

AARON: Why
Do you turn him away, Moses? Why not talk to him?

MOSES: What would we talk of, Aaron? What quiet sub-
     ject?
   They tell me centuries of horror brood
   In this vivid kindgom of fertile mud. Do you think
   If we swung the rattle of conversation
   Those centuries would fly off like so many crows?
   They would wheel above us and come to feed again.

AARON: But what do you think of? I sometimes call you,
     to myself,
   A gate without a key. You'll open when you will.
   Such a gate must lead somewhere, so I believe,
   Though perhaps that sounds fanciful. Where shall we
     find a better
   Opportunity?

RAMASES: I have my father mapped
   So that I know which way to travel. Listen,
   Uncle—he says he would have recalled you, which
     means
   He needs you here. He'll be friendly if you let him.
   I kept a buckle of your uniform—this one, the lion-
     head.
   Take it again, take our army and be our general.
   You'll become inseparable from Egypt's safety;
   Then he will listen. Then you can direct
   His goodwill past yourself to these Israelites.

AARON: It's true. You have the buckle, and we're agreed,
     then.
   My dreams were less; not a third as felicitous.

MOSES: Egypt and Israel both in me together!
   How would that be managed? I should wolf
   Myself to keep myself nourished. I could play
   With wars, oh God, very pleasantly. You know
   I prosper in a cloud of dust—you're wise
   To offer me that. And Egypt would still be,
   In spite of my fathers, a sufficient cause.

AARON: Yes, it would be sufficient.

MOSES: Splendid, then.
   What armour shall I wear? What ancestral metal

Above my heart? Rib, thighbone and skull:
Bones from the mines of Egypt. I will clank
To Egypt's victory in Israel's bones.
Does this please you? Does it not? Admire
How when preparing a campaign I become
Oblivious to day and night, and in
The action, obsessed. How will that do? I make
My future, put glory into Egypt, enjoy myself
Into your father's confidence—yes, that,
I know; and being there, perhaps I coax
Little concessions for the Hebrew cause
To justify me.—Idiot, idiot!
I should have lost them, Aaron, and be lost,
More than when in Midian I sat
Over my food and let them trudge in my bowels.

AARON: I have faith in your judgment. Nevertheless, **this**
is

Something to be thought of, a reality of a kind.

MOSES: Like adultery.

MIRIAM: Offer of a generalship?
Of course I don't understand. But like adultery?
To be a general? Do you mean us to think
You would refuse—

MOSES: You both would like to see
Your brother fat, but your brother has a fancy
To be as lean as Israel.

MIRIAM: Where do you see
Israel now?

MOSES: Where do I see God?
Be certain, Israel is. I am here to be a stone
In her sling, out of her gall.

RAMASES: Will you promise to be patient?
There will be difficulties to be got over;
I have a father. But at some future time
When I am Pharaoh—

MOSES: By then I may be free
To let my bones talk of their disinterest

In the world's affairs: and whether it is Hebrew
Or Egyptian, man will cry for me no longer.

MIRIAM: Listen!

AARON: What is it?

MIRIAM: Nothing, nothing—I imagined—
Why should he be back at this time? What
Could bring him now? Listen!

MOSES: What do you hear?

MIRIAM: It's the whistle he gives when he's reaching
    home.

AARON: Her son.
It's Shendi.

MIRIAM: Something has happened. The negro lynx
Was in my sleep last night praying to become
A man, but only dead birds came out of its mouth.
Why is the palace here? What are you doing here
In my home? He cannot even come home.

RAMASES: Is this
Egypt?

MIRIAM: Do you hear him again? No nearer, no nearer.
He is being prevented. Can I get to him
Without being seen? Stay where you are. No one
Must see me, no one.

       She goes out. In a moment AARON *follows her.*

RAMASES: You all think of me
As an enemy.

MOSES: We're not enemies so much
As creatures of division. You and I,
Ramases, like money in a purse,
Ring together only to be spent
For different reasons.

RAMASES: Different? How am I
To be spent, then?

MOSES: How? Why, upon solids,
On heritage, the one thing positive.
Our roots are the element which gives us purpose
And life. There will be summers to come which need
The lotus. That will be for you.

RAMASES: So let
　The lotus stink. Am I never to see you?
MOSES: No,
　It would be better, never. Forget me, Ramases.
RAMASES: That anyway is impossible. I know
　I bear your mark, and how will you obliterate
　That? Do you forget the feel of the year
　When you were as I am? They count me as a man,
　Just. But the boy is still in my head and mouth.
　I feel him there. I speak him. I should burn
　Throne and lotus gladly if I could break
　Myself of boyhood, if burning would do it. But you
　Are clear and risen roundly over the hazes.
　You have the formula. I need it.
MOSES: Clear?
　Evidence of that! Where in this drouthy
　Overwatered world can you find me clarity?
　What spirit made the hawk? a bird obedient
　To grace, a bright lash on the cheek of the wind
　And drawn and ringed with feathered earth and sun,
　An achievement of eternity's birdsmith. But did he
　Also bleak the glittering charcoal of the eyes
　And sharpen beak and claws on his hone of lust?
　What language is life? Not one I know.
　A quarrel in God's nature. But you, at least,
　Are pronounceable: heir of Egypt, heir of Egypt.
　That is yourself.
RAMASES: You mean I'm of no value
　Except to be Egypt's ornament.
MOSES: Of much
　Value, infinite.
RAMASES: But we stay unfriendly?
MOSES: Because I taste your boyhood and remember mine
　And like them both.
RAMASES: But even so—
MOSES: You shall stay as you are.
RAMASES: Exactly as I am, a friend of Moses.

MOSES: They're coming with Shendi. Keep with me in
the shadow.

  Enter MIRIAM *and* AARON, *supporting* SHENDI.

MIRIAM: He has been so strong. Are you ill? How are you
ill?

You can speak, surely you can speak? We don't know
them;

That's what is worst—our own—even in childhood

They say so little.

AARON: Lie here, Shendi.

MIRIAM: Still

And quiet. What shall I do for him? They're ourselves

But quite dark to us. Things happen without warning.

AARON: Give him this water.

MIRIAM: A sip, and then you shall have more.

My fingers are hot. I must drench my hands. Aaron,

We have been unhappy. What can we do with water?

A sip again. I feel your heart in your forehead.

SHENDI: They'll come.

MIRIAM: Keep yourself quiet.

SHENDI: Yes, they will come,

They'll come for me, they'll find me!

AARON: What have you done?

MIRIAM: Done?

SHENDI: What are you holding me for? Must I always

Be held? It was the sun! Don't you know that?

They make madmen in the sun. Thousands of madmen

Have been made in the sun. They say nothing, nothing at
all,

But suddenly they're running—no, not they,

It's only their bodies that are running: the madmen

Are still standing in the sun, watching their bodies

Run away. Can they kill me for that? Or what, or what?

It was the strike that made it happen!

AARON: What have you said?

What strike?

MIRIAM: He's ill!

SHENDI: No, it was the sun; not the strike,
   The sun. The noise of the strike, the whips.
AARON: The strike?
   What was it? What has happened?
SHENDI: The spermy bastards!
   They make us hit the earth like spit.
MIRIAM: What are you saying?
   Don't ask him any more!
AARON: I'll make him tell me. What strike?
   What has happened?
SHENDI: I don't know what has happened.
   The brickmakers began it. A youngster was with me,
   Twelve years old, and he left me to watch the trouble.
   I saw them take him away, they dragged him off
   To the captain at the gate, because he was watching.
   It has nothing to do with it. It's the sun. Have you
     heard
   The order? They'll not give us straw to make the
     bricks;
   We must gather the straw ourselves; but the tale of
     bricks
   Must be more, more! What does it matter? Who says
   It matters? They're coming for me.
MIRIAM: It cannot happen,
   Shendi, it cannot.
MOSES: Cannot happen, cannot be.
   Cannot. Earth, life, ourselves are impossibility;
   Impossible even as lie or legend. What is this Pharaoh
   Who answers me with this? Does he hope
   To make himself exist? Tell him it isn't possible.
   Existence is beyond conception.
SHENDI: Who's that?
   My uncle, is it? The great fellow that was.
   The man who thought he was Egypt. Have you come
   To try again, murderer? Look at your crop of relations
   And how they do in the land you dunged for us.
   Never mind. You did very well.—Oh, what will happen?

Do you hear that? They're whipping the side of the
    tent.

You know I can't stand up, they've come for me,

You know it was the sun—uncle, uncle!

MIRIAM: It was neighbours talking, it was only the neigh-
    bours.

      —Aaron,

It was neighbours talking. Wasn't it, wasn't it?

    Enter TWO OVERSEERS.

                          No, no!

1ST OVERSEER: Nice family. Here's the man we want.

2ND OVERSEER: Get up,

Little rat. So you'd strike? We'll teach you striking.

  Striking's our specialty. Eh? Not bad! We'll strike him!

MIRIAM: He's sick—can't you see?

1ST OVERSEER: That's enough of that.

RAMASES: What is this?

Weren't you told I had sent for him?

2ND OVERSEER: My crimes!

RAMASES: Well, weren't you told?

1ST OVERSEER: No, sir; no, your holiness; not told.

  I beg pardon, sir. I didn't see you, my lord, didn't see
    you.

RAMASES: I tell you now. I sent for him. Go away.

1ST OVERSEER: Yes, lord.

2ND OVERSEER: Yes, almighty.

    They back away out of sight.

MIRIAM: You're here, Shendi, you're here. The prince has
    kept you.

He spoke for you. Forgive me, I'm more afraid than
    ever.

Forgive me. Relief is very like an illness.

SHENDI: No one warned—What are you doing with me?

Is it a trick? What did I say before they came?

My lord, I was ill. I don't know what is happening.

RAMASES: Nothing is happening. You can rest.

AARON: For us

Much is happening. I begin to have hope.

Eh, Moses? This is the boy who will be our man,
The palace key. In the belly of our misfortune
We find our hope.

MOSES: We're not ready to hope
Or to despair; not ready to doubt or to believe.
We're equipped to do no more than confront ourselves.
And if we were equipped for more, hoping
Or despairing, I wouldn't use him. My need is something
Different: I need to know how good
Can be strong enough to break out of the possessing
Arms of evil: good, rectitude,
The popular song, whistled by the world in the streets;
And evil whistles the same air back again.
Gigantic, mastering evil! And what we accept
As good, breaks it less than the incision of wheat
Breaks the ground. Where shall I look for triumph?
Somewhere, not beyond our scope, is a power
Participating, but unharnessed, waiting
To be led towards us. Good has a singular strength
Not known to evil; and I, an ambitious heart
Needing interpretation. But not through this boy,
Never through this boy. I will not use him!

Curtain

SCENE THREE: *A room in the Palace, giving on to the terrace of Scene One.* ANATH *is standing on the terrace.* TEUSRET's *voice is heard calling "Ramases! Ramases!" It draws nearer.* ANATH *comes into the room and listens for* TEUSRET's *voice which now comes from farther away. She turns to go back to the terrace. Enter* RAMASES.

ANATH: Have you seen him?
RAMASES: Moses?

ANATH: Have you seen your father?

RAMASES: He made me a present of my future, with the
    royal seal
  Attached. Did you know?

ANATH: I have to wish you happiness.
  Dear, be happy. There's nothing better to be looked for.
  Happiness is sometimes hard to recognize.
  It seems so to keep company with the unlikely.
  Teusret is looking for you.

RAMASES: Where is she?

ANATH: Everywhere.
  Put your hand in one place, she is already
  Beating her wings in another.

RAMASES: Listen—look—
  What is it, this that has captured me? This "now,"
  This exact truth of time—certainly truth—
  The moment we're now crossing. Can this truth
  Vanish? Look, your shadow thrown over the chair,
  That dog's jerking bark, the distance of whistling,
  A gate clanging-to, the water thrown into the yard,
  Your fingers travelling your bracelet, my voice—listen,
  My voice—your breathing—
      TEUSRET *is heard calling* RAMASES.
  And Teusret running through the empty rooms.
  It is true for us now, but not till now, and never
  To be again. I want it for myself.
  This is my life.
      Enter TEUSRET.
      It has gone.

TEUSRET: I've found you at last.
  Where have you been hidden? Where were you?

RAMASES: With father.

TEUSRET: For an hour!
  No one could tell me. The rooms were all deserted.
  Just as it happens in my sleep sometimes; but then
  The door on the other side of the room is always
  Closing behind you, and the room is empty—I never
  Come to you.

RAMASES: But, awake, it's different. You find me.

TEUSRET: Why did he talk for so long?

RAMASES: I'm to be married
He says.

TEUSRET: I had a riddle to ask you. Fareti
Taught it to me.

RAMASES: What is it?

TEUSRET: Ramases,
When will you be married?

RAMASES: Soon, he says.

TEUSRET: Why? Why? You can't! What does he mean?
Then—if you did—Why have you said so? Oh,
Why did you say it?

RAMASES: Teusret—

TEUSRET: Who is it?

RAMASES: The Syrian.
Her name is Phipa.

TEUSRET: Do you think that's pretty?
Phipa, Phipa, Phipa! The noise a flute makes
When the mouth's too full of saliva. You won't do it.

RAMASES: What can I say?

ANATH: Teusret, we all, you will find,
Belong to Egypt: our lives go on the loom
And our land weaves. And the gods know we need
Some such alliance. If the dynasty is safe
We can at least be partly ourselves. He will need
Both of us still.

TEUSRET: He won't. He will be changed.
The days will be different and I shall be the same.
How shall I be happy then?

Enter SETI.

Will *you* be?
Are you glad?

SETI: Can you imagine, Teusret,
The frantic compulsion which first fetched man forming
And breathing out of the earth's dust? Such
A compulsion of beauty has this Phipa of Syria,
With the addition of wit and a good head for business.

She's immensely rich. Homegoing sailors,
When there are no stars, steer perfectly for Syria
Merely by thinking of her. So they say.
A figure of her, hung under the bows
And kissing the wake, ensures a harvest of fish.

TEUSRET: What a tale!

SETI: Well, yes, but she has beauty.

TEUSRET: Flowers for Ramases
Then! We must make it an occasion. I'll fetch my lute
And celebrate. Garlands! I'll make you into
A nice little afternoon god. Don't go away.

RAMASES: Here, Teusret—

TEUSRET: You have earned a ceremony.
Would you rather have me in tears? This isn't silliness
But a proper formality. I need to do it.
Wait here, all of you.
        Exit TEUSRET.

ANATH: Let her do what she must.

RAMASES (*sings*): "If under my window
The dark will not lose me
No one will see me a maiden again." Father,
I have something to ask you. It has to do with Moses.

SETI: He needn't trouble you.

RAMASES: Nor any of us. But haven't you
Overlooked his nephew?

SETI: This is nothing to you.
Nothing to you at all.

RAMASES: Nothing at all.
Moses has a sister and a nephew.
The nephew's a labourer. Might there not here be a
    way
By which you could come at Moses?

SETI: Statesmanship,
My son, is the gods' gift to restrain their own
Infidelities to man. As for Moses,
I'll comprehend him when he's comprehensible.

RAMASES: Such as a commission for this nephew; or a
    place in the palace.

Or whatever you consider is best. What would you
   wish?
What do you say? Can you talk of honours
To a man whose family is unhonoured? I don't know,
But you will know.

SETI: Who told you to speak of him?
What do you know of this name that you're bandying?
   Anath?
You have stared enough at that pyramid. Is this
Your influence?

ANATH: Am I a planet, to be
So influential? No, Seti; it is not.
I would rather infect him with something less dubious
Than the blood of Moses.

                Enter TEUSRET *with a lute and flowers.*

TEUSRET: Look, I have them. I got them
Out of my room. They were round my bronze Isis.
Shall I have offended her?

SETI: Do you know this nephew?

ANATH: I've seen him.

SETI: How did he promise?

ANATH: He promised to be male,
As though he might have the ability for a beard
I thought.

TEUSRET: Are you all ready for the ceremony?
Ramases, you must be in a chair; this chair.

RAMASES: Can it be tried?

SETI: What is it now?

RAMASES: To mark
My coming of age. May I commission the nephew?

SETI: That is still to be known. I must have precise
Information of him. Now forget the question.
The window on the east side of your room
Is the window that looks toward Syria.

TEUSRET: Why must you go
Before you see Ramases in flowers? And when
Have you ever heard me play on my lute?

        Exit SETI

Has no one

Told him he has a daughter?

ANATH: The flowers were schooled

With salamanders, to be so enduring

In this furnace.

RAMASES: Will he really do it?

ANATH: The land

Is rocking, remember. He'll take hold even of grass.

TEUSRET: Let me begin. Neither of you has any sense

Of occasion. These on your shoulders. What *are* flowers?

What is the bridge to be crossed, I wonder,

From a petal to being a wing or a hand? These

For your brows. Does the scent of them sicken you?

My pollen fingers.

RAMASES: They're shattering already.

TEUSRET: Some of them are too full.

RAMASES: You've brought me the garden.

Here's an earwig on my hand.

TEUSRET: Tread on it. Now

You're ripe to receive a god. Isn't he, Aunt?

Does he look noble? My brother in bloom.

RAMASES (*treading on the earwig*): Out goes he. Let's get

your singing over.

TEUSRET (*staring*): I have to remember you. Sing with me.

ANATH: I?

Sing? With the crack in my voice? Not songs for

bridegrooms.

Only songs in the minor, where a false note

Can be taken to be excessive sensibility.

TEUSRET: Nothing, nothing will go on in the old way.

I wonder, can I remember which is the key? (*She

touches the lute*)

RAMASES: Did you know my father had ordered the Isra-

elites

To gather their own straw?

ANATH: Yes, I knew.

RAMASES: Why did he?

ANATH: A little show of invulnerability.

RAMASES: Is Moses safe here?

TEUSRET: I wish there were echoes in this room,
A choir of them, to be company for my voice.
You will have to help me when I lose myself.

(*Sings*)   Why should there be two
          Where one will do,
      Step over this shadow and tell me
         And my heart will make a ring
           Sighing in a circle
         And my hands will beckon and bring
       The maiden fortune who befell me
          O fortune, fortune.

    Enter SETI.

You see, father,—doesn't he look married already?

(*Sings*)   Why do we breath and wait
          So separate?
      The whirl in the shell and the sand
         Is time going home to time
           Kissing to a darkness.
      So shall we go, so shall we seem
        In the gardens, hand in hand.
          O fortune, fortune.

     So changed against the sun—

    She is interrupted by MOSES, *who enters bearing in
    his arms a dead Israelite boy.*

ANATH: What are we to have now?

RAMASES: The wrong of a right.

SETI: What is this? Isn't it enough that you broke
Into Egypt unasked but you must—

MOSES: This is your property.
Of little value. Shall I bury it in your garden?
You need have no anxiety. It will not grow.

ANATH: Oh, in the name of the gods—

SETI: Is your reason gone?

MOSES (*laying the body at* SETI's *feet*): Look: worthless,
worthless.

The music needn't stop.

You killed him.

SETI: As I thought; you've let your brain
Suffer in this heat. I saw, in the first few words
You spoke this morning, it would end in this.

TEUSRET: Ramases!

SETI: You frighten children, you see.
It's too ambitious.

TEUSRET: That boy!

RAMASES: That isn't death
Lying on the ground.

TEUSRET: It is! It is! It is!

SETI: Well? Tell me: is it an act of sanity
To carry this child here? I'm sorry to see it.
Take him and have him buried. You know it wasn't
Done by me.

MOSES: It was done of you. You'll not
Escape from yourself through the narrows between By
    and Of.
Your captain killed him on the metal of your gates, as
    with
A score of others. If it wasn't done of you
Fetch the captain, condemn him to death, and watch
How he'll stare.

SETI: I'll see the man. It's understood.

MOSES: Who understands? And what is understood?
If you move your foot only a little forward
Your toe will be against your power. Is this
How you imagined your strength to be—ungrowing,
Unbreathing, a child, and dead? Out of him
Comes your army, your fleet, the cliff of gold
You move on, pride, place, adulation
And name—out of this contemptible chrysalis—
Not this, not even this, but this destroyed,
This refused to itself. Fetch in your captain,
Fetch in your thousand captains, and condemn them
For the murder of your power.

SETI: What would I give
  To see you for a moment with your old grasp
  And intelligence. Nature, you may remember,
  Is lavish, and in return for being understood,
  Not hoarded, gives us civilisation.
  Would you have the earth never see purple
  Because the murex dies? Blame, dear Moses,
  The gods for their creative plan which is
  Not to count the cost but enormously
  To bring about.

MOSES: And so they bring about
  The enormity of Egypt. Is that the full
  Ambition of your gods? Egypt is only
  One golden eruption of time, one flying spark
  Attempting the ultimate fire. But who can say
  What secrets my race has, what unworked seams
  Of consciousness in mind and soul? Deny
  Life to itself and life will harness and ride you
  To its purpose. My people shall become themselves,
  By reason of their own god who speaks within them.
  What I ask is that I may lead them peaceably
  Into the wilderness for a space, to find
  Their god and so become living men at last.

SETI: More favours, something new. What god is this?

MOSES: The inimitable patience who doesn't yet
  Strike you down.

SETI: He and I have something in common
  If he has patience. Shall I plough your madness
  And sow what I can of perception, or is the ground
  Too arid with your envy? My trust is Egypt
  And the maturity of the world. Where should I look
  For my worth, if I plunged my hand into the body
  Of the kingdom, and with a pale flower smell of hu-
      manity
  Released each bone and blessed each nerve and drop
  Of blood and left them to the elements?
  Or, gathering them in again when each by the wonder
  Of its individual god had learnt a new

Desire of life, put them with their untutored
Ambitions back to the corporate achievement,
To watch their incoherence? Where then
Is the painfully acquired stature and beauty
Of mankind?

MOSES: Where is it now? Your stature and beauty
Is an untarred fleet which the waves rot while it rides
them.
You know well enough the dark places of the fish
Under your palace floor: invasion is probable,
Unrest is in and out of doors, your southern half
Splits from the north, the lords at your table
Are looking down at their hands. And flowing through
all
Is the misery of my blood. Let that be clean
First, and then the flesh may heal.

SETI: Your god
Has already taken your senses into his bosom;
No doubt he'll fetch your race to join them. But I
Can't laugh. The public ear goes too easily
To bed with lies. I have nursed you enough.
Now dungeons can nurse you. Your god can find you
Behind the walls and return your reason when he will.

ANATH: Seti! Are you sure? Will the surly half
Of Egypt believe he was mad?

SETI: Do you still play
At being his mother?

ANATH: Do you think I do?
If you could see what my heart does, you could watch
me
Destroying him.

MOSES: If you destroy me, Seti,
Destruction will end with you.

RAMASES: There could have been
Some other way than this. Is only Israel
Present to you, as once it was only Egypt?
Are you still Moses? Or who? Who are you?

ANATH: Does he know?

SETI: A man without laws.

MOSES: What are the laws,
Other than those laws, stupendous and balancing,
Which made the hurl of smiting, infamous fires
Wheel in perfection, perpetually,
In great unaltering constellations:
The devotion in time and place and appearance,
Memory of the first unrolling of light:
At the centre of which are we, uncentred man,
Pointing in distraction at nothing but our existence.
What are the laws? Tell me, you taker of lives!
I am here by fury and the heart. Is that not
A law? I am here to appease the unconsummated
Resourceless dead, to join life to the living.
Is that not underwritten by nature? Is that
Not a law? Do not ask me why I do it!
I live. I do this thing. I was born this action.
Who can say for whom, for what ultimate region
Of life? A deed is what it becomes. And yet
What are the laws? Despite you, through you, upon
    you,
I am compelled.

        A distant long cracking sound of thunder. MOSES
        jerks back his head to listen.

                        Are we overheard? Behind
The door that shuts us into life, there is
An ear.

ANATH: The mountains are breaking the drought at last!

MOSES: It is not as we suppose! We are the fools
Of sense and sight. What shall I believe?
What league have we, the human, with the greater
Than human? Nothing is as we suppose!
The stream of Israel's cause has surely turned
The wheel that contains us. Now, if only to make
Death excel, life shall live. Am I given the power
To do what I am?

ANATH: Do what you are! Be unborn,
Or a name spoken savagely before I lived.

The power to do what you are is self-destruction.
Ask it, ask it then, demand it! Crave it!
Dispossess time of your white face. Be unborn,
Unexisting, even though in going
You take the world with you!
MOSES: Am I given the power?
    What says the infinite eavesdropper?

> *From horizon to horizon the sky is beaten into*
> *thunder.*

Curtain to Act One

ACT TWO

SCENE ONE: MIRIAM'S *tent, the evening of the same day.*
MOSES, AARON.

MOSES: Has something come between us, or into what
    Back room of your mind have you gone? You watch
        each word
    As it comes out of my mouth, but I cannot see
    What you do with it after you have watched.
    You've something to say.
AARON: I have nothing.
MOSES: Must we bring
    Lights to each other?
AARON: Why do you have to say this?
MOSES: The present is always falling behind me. I seem
    To do what was done long ago, and yet I still
    Must grope and pummel to bring it into being.
    It's the switch of time on our flanks, to make us
    Pull the heavy moment.—Look: I shall divide them
    Into groups a hundred or a hundred and fifty strong,

Each with a man to lead them, one they can trust,
Such as this man you mention, Morshad—
And the man I spoke with this evening. Put them down.

AARON: Morshad and Zedeth. Yes, I have them.

MOSES: And then
This morning's rioting, the man who started that,
Whatever his name is. Will they listen to him again?

     AARON goes to the tent-opening and looks out.
He made his move too early, some few days
Too soon.

AARON: I thought I felt the earth quiver.

MOSES: What is he called?

AARON: The earth has moved. It stirred
Like an animal. Moses!

MOSES: The man has a name. Put him down.

AARON: Something unnatural has come awake
Which should have slept until time was finished.
I haven't made this out of fear. Or what
Is fear? Is it this—uncoiling, unexampled!
Listen! Did you hear a roar? A building
Has collapsed. The dust is like a cloud, higher
Than the city. Will you see?

MOSES: We have something more to do
Than to listen to falling cities. The dust will settle
While we Hebrews die. Come on; give me the names.

AARON: It's you, yourself! You see, it's yourself! I knew
It wasn't I! And this is why I couldn't
Answer you. You have gone under yourself,
Under yourself or wherever it is—as though
Your reasonable plans and normal behaviour
Were a deception covering something
Utterly different. Were you waiting for this—
This, outside—this obsessed appalling sunset?
You see, I'm to pieces. Why does this mean nothing to
you?
Why won't you come and see it?

MOSES: The names, the names.

    MIRIAM stands in the opening, with a pitcher.

MIRIAM: All the water is blood.

AARON: Miriam! What is happening to the city?

MIRIAM: There's no water, no water. Nothing but blood.

AARON: Then my fear has foundation. The sun has set
On truth altogether. The evening's a perjury!
Let none of us be duped by it.

MIRIAM: Did you really
Believe the world? So did we all. The water
Is blood. The river floods it over the fields.
The wells stink of it.

AARON: What are you saying?

MIRIAM: Go out then
And see it yourself. The men who were thirsty
enough
To drink what came, are lying at the well-heads
Vomiting.

MOSES: What men? Ours?

MIRIAM: Egyptians.

MOSES: Miriam,
What have you there?

MIRIAM: I filled my pitcher. We all
Filled our pitchers, everyone, in spite of—
Do you think we believed it could happen to us? To
them
Perhaps, something might happen; to the others but not
To ourselves.

MOSES (*bringing his hand out of the pitcher*). Not to ourselves. To the others.

MIRIAM: Your hand
Has water on it! It is water!

MOSES: From which well
Was this drawn?

MIRIAM: Our own. Are we likely to use the Egyptians'?
But I saw it, we all saw it.

MOSES: The sun this last hour
Has been that colour. Doesn't it at evening
Fall directly on our well?

MIRIAM: The sun? Are we

Talking about the sun? Tell me I'm lying
And look at my feet. We slopped in blood flooding
From the Nile. I saw the Egyptians who drank it.

MOSES: The Nile.
The Egyptians! But this water came from our well
Not theirs.—Was I waiting, Aaron? I was waiting
Without expectation. But surely, I already knew?
And you—did you guess, as well, that we are such a
    part
Of the whole, more than time made clear to us?
Such projects of the unending, here projected
Into passing actions? We with our five bare fingers
Have caused the strings of God to sound.
Creation's mutehead is dissolving, Aaron.
Our lives are being lived into our lives.
We are known!

MIRIAM: Do you think it was you who made the Egyptians
Vomit? We may as well all be mad. The world
Has a disease. Let me away from it, and from you,
And away from myself. Where is Shendi?

AARON: What's this?
Isn't there confusion enough? Confusion I call it!
A contradiction of what we have always known
To be conclusive: an ugly and impossible
Mistake in nature. And you, you of all men
Accept it, identify yourself with it. It must be
Denied. What has become of you since yesterday?
Is it not possible still to be plain men
Dealing with a plain situation? Must we see
Visions? You were an unchallengeable leader once.
That is the man I follow. A plain soldier.

MIRIAM: Where can Shendi be?

MOSES: The plainest soldier is sworn to the service of rid-
    dles.
Our strategy is written on strange eternal paper.
We may decide to advance this way or that way
But we are lifted forward by a wind

And when it drops we see no more of the world.
Shall we live in mystery and yet
Conduct ourselves as though everything were known?
If, in battle upon the sea, we fought
As though on land, we should be more embroiled
With water than the enemy. Are we on sea
Or land, would you say?

AARON: Sea? Land? For pity's sake
Stay with reality.

MOSES: If I can penetrate
So far.

MIRIAM: What will you do for us? Not as much
As sleep will do, if there is any way
We can come at sleep. Do you think that we
Can sink fear in that water in the pitcher?
Why hasn't Shendi come home yet? It's past his time.
He should have stayed here the rest of the day.
Will you let me out of this intolerable night?
Are we going to stand here for ever?

SHENDI (*in the tent-opening*):   Mother!

MIRIAM: Shendi,
Has nothing happened to you? Let me see you and be
Reassured. Were you harmed by what I saw?

SHENDI: What have you seen? Nothing happened? Every-
    thing!
We've stepped across to a new life. Where were we liv-
    ing?
It was the appearance, of course, the appearance of hell.
Nothing like it at all, except in our minds, our poor
Minds. I was going to make you try to guess,
But such an idea could never come at a guess.
Never; it couldn't. They've made me an officer!

MIRIAM: I don't—understand what you mean.

SHENDI: Your son! You see?
They've made him an officer. Like an Egyptian officer.
Like? I am one. We didn't know, that was all,
The world is perfectly fair, something to laugh at.

The ridiculous difference between me this morning
And now! They found I was better with head than
   hands.

MIRIAM: Shendi, did you come by way of the wells? Did
   you see them?

SHENDI: I expect so. They say they're diseased. Can
   you imagine
How I felt when they took me by the arm and led me
Apart from the other men? I almost fought them.
I knew I was going to be beaten—

MIRIAM: Shendi, stop!
What are you saying?

SHENDI: Hell is done, done,
Done with, over!

MOSES: For you.

MIRIAM: They would never do it.
But then to-night everything is to be believed.
Nothing has any truth and everything is true.

AARON: I believe it. Perhaps you will think I'm gullible
But here is something recognizable and encouraging.
An evocation, if you like, of better things;
And, considering the Pharaoh, as a gesture a prodigy.
You've already achieved something, Moses,
And in a way—

SHENDI: *He* has achieved? Achieved what?
You didn't hear what they said to me. This has nothing
To do with my uncle. You have my uncle on the brain.

AARON: I can see what you mean.

SHENDI: I report at the officers' quarters
In half an hour. I'll take some of my things
Along with me now. Has the world always been known
To spring such wonders, do you think? You're to live
   with me,
Mother, do you understand? Follow on later
And ask for the new officer. At the officers' quarters.
Have you something you can give me to wrap this linen
   in?

The Libyans have broken across the border and massa-
cred
Two companies of the border regiment.

AARON: What?
A massacre? When was this?

SHENDI: I don't know when.
Where have you put my razor? Four hundred Egyptians
Killed, they say. They talked as though
I were already one of themselves. They say
There's also a rumour of revolution in the south

AARON: Moses, do you hear?

SHENDI: Where is my razor?

MIRIAM: There.
Did you see the wells? I don't know what life's doing.
I don't know how we're to think.

AARON: Ambitiously.
These incidents all march our way. The Libyans
Over the border—revolution—Time
Is preparing for us with a timely unrest.
We came to Egypt at the perfect hour as it happens.

SHENDI: That's enough of talk like that!

MIRIAM: As it happens;
If we knew what happens. Shendi an officer!
Will this be what we want, at last? As the Nile
Happens into blood. Shendi an officer.

SHENDI: And the officers' quarters, remember: comfort.

MIRIAM: As massacre
And revolution happens. As to-morrow
Happens, whatever happens to-morrow.

SHENDI: Come on,
I must go.

MOSES: Refuse this commission.

SHENDI: What did you say?

MOSES: Refuse this commission.

MIRIAM: Refuse it?

SHENDI: Listen to that!
As my uncle happens, this is no surprise.

Only one of the family must rise
And glow in Egypt. We see the Hebrew sky
Must only bear one star, and at that a meteor
Which has fizzled. The rest of us can keep
Against the ground, our light withering
Into painful roots, and lose the whole damned world
Because Moses prefers it. But in spite of that,
In spite of that, generous brother of my mother,
We hope to live a little.

AARON: As who does not?
The Pharaoh, I quite see, will have his motives.
But we can outmove motives to our advantage;
And here surely is a kind of proffered hand.

MIRIAM: Why should he refuse? How could he refuse? He
      couldn't.
But who except you would say he should?

SHENDI: It's clear
Why he says it. It was he who came back for recognition
And I have got it.

MOSES: Make yourself live, then, Shendi;
But be sure it is life. The golden bear Success
Hugs a man close to its heart; and breaks his bones.
We come upon ourselves, as though we were chance,
Often by the most unwilling decisions
Our maturities hide themselves from our wishes.
And where at last we touch our natures into life
Is at that drastic angle of experience
Where we divide from our natures. What have they
      said,
These Egyptians? Come with us and we'll treat you
      well.
Not, come with us and we will treat
You and your people well.

AARON: They will come in time
Even to say that.

SHENDI (to MOSES): This sounds well
Indeed, from you!

MIRIAM: Shendi is to be all
That he can become—all; and I say so,
I who made him. Am I to go on holding
The guilt for his unhappiness when opportunity
Offers to deliver me from it? Guilt it was,
And damnation, for giving him birth. This will let me
    loose!

SHENDI: Why do we listen to him? I know how to value
The first fairness I've known. If you think so little
Of being alive, uncle, you will find they're assembling
Spears to flash on Libya. Why not make something
Of that? The tradition is that, once upon a time,
You didn't know the meaning of apprehension
Or fear—back in those days when it was you
They treated well.

ANATH (*in the tent-opening*): Does he still not appre-
    hend
Or fear?

SHENDI: Madam, madam—

ANATH: What are you doing
To Egypt, Moses?

MOSES: What have you come for?

ANATH: You.
And have you really no fear? You are afraid
Of me, I think. Isn't it I who possess
That level of yourself which you are in torment
To see again? Can something you do not want
Be so great a relentless need? Not anything
Of me, but what I have of you. Your thoughts
Cannot accept me, but I am here. Oh,
Poor man, I am here!

MOSES: I'm stronger than memory.

ANATH: It sucks the blood.
What are you doing to Egypt, Moses?

MOSES: What
Is Egypt doing to Egypt?

ANATH: Or Egypt to you.
You shall try your strength against memory the insect.

Come with me. I came by the old walks.
What have I seen? You shall come with me
And see it and tell me, and see the men and women
Bewildered in the doorways, for the name of their world
Has changed from home to horror. And is this
What you have in your heart for Egypt? Then favour me
And also have it in your eyes.

MOSES: But why
Do you come to me? To whose blood has the Nile
Turned? It isn't mine. Can it be the spilt blood
Of Israelites that is flowing back on Egypt?
Why come to me?

ANATH: He wants reason! Rationalize
The full moon and the howling dog. I have less
Inclination to be here than the dog has to howl.
If you come with me to Seti, he's ready to talk to you.

MOSES: We've talked already.

ANATH: He'll let you take your Hebrews
To make their worship, or whatever you want of them,
On some conditions which he'll tell you.

AARON: Good.
Events are moving.

MOSES: If Seti is so ready,
Why did you make the walk through the ominous evening
To remind me that I'm in Egypt?

ANATH: Because he is sitting
Pressing his thumbs together, wedged inactive
In between his decision and pride. What it is
To have to do with men! They live too large.
Isn't it so, Miriam? I'm ready to take you.

MOSES: I'll come.

AARON: This will be a great day for Israel.

MIRIAM: My son has been made an officer.

ANATH: I shall be glad
Not to be alone this time, with the earth
Wavering to a hint of doom. I suppose

There have to be powers of darkness, but they should keep
    To the rules. The sky is lighter. The worst may be over.

MOSES: Aaron, you will come too.

AARON: It has been easier
    Than I should have thought possible this morning.
        Exeunt ANATH, MOSES *and* AARON.

SHENDI: What is this business the Pharaoh has with my uncle?

MIRIAM: I mustn't think of Moses. Many things
    I must be sure to keep my thoughts quite away from.
    What is it we have to do? A dark mind
    And he has followed that woman.

SHENDI: Will he try to stop my commission going through?

MIRIAM: No, no, he's forgotten it.

SHENDI: What does he matter, then?
    I'm an officer!

MIRIAM: How could the water be blood, Shendi?

SHENDI: What?

MIRIAM: I'll put your things together for you.
    How grand we shall be!

    Curtain

SCENE TWO: *A room in the Palace.* SETI. ANATH.

ANATH: Keep the window covered, Seti. The terrace
    Crackles with dying locusts. I looked out.
    I seemed to look within, on to myself,
    When I stood there and looked out over Egypt.
    The face of all this land is turned to the wall.
    I looked out, and when I looked to the north I saw

Instead of quiet cattle, glutted jackals,
Not trees and pasture but vulture-bearing boughs
And fields which had been sown with hail. And looking
To the south I saw, like falling ashes after fire,
Death after thirst, death after hunger, death
After disease. And when I looked to the east
I saw an old woman ridding herself of lice;
And to the west, a man who had no meaning
Pushing thigh-deep through drifts of locusts.

SETI: Well; these things are finished

ANATH: And what happens
Now? What will you do when the mourners have done
Wailing, and men look across the havoc of their fields
And the bones of their cattle and say: You did this,
What happens now?

SETI: Why am I to be blamed
For all the elemental poisons that come up fungoid
Out of the damps and shadows which our existence
Moves in? Can I put peace into the furious
God—epilepsy of earthquake and eruption?
What am I but one of those you pity?

ANATH: You tricked him, you tricked Moses, and not
   once
But seven times. First when I, against
All my self-warning, approached the unapproachable
And brought him to you. Didn't you make him promises
Then, and break them? And that night your promises
Plagued our ears with a croaking mockery,
With an unceasing frog-echo of those words
Which had meant nothing; with a plague of frogs!
A second time you made promises, and a third time
And a fourth: seven times you've broken them
While the stews of creation had their way with Egypt.

SETI: You say this, concoct this legend; you have become
Infected with the venom that's against me.

ANATH: No, I've no venom. I've no more efficacy
Than a fishwife who has been made to breed against
Her will; and so I'm shrill and desperate.

No power against misery! That's what our lives add up
    to.
Our spacious affability, our subtle intelligence,
Our delicate consciousness of worlds beyond the world,
Our persuasive dignity when sacrificing to the gods,
Our bodies and our brains can all become
Slutted with lice between afternoon and evening.
You tricked him a second time, and that is what
You saw: sweet made foul. And then the third time
And we became the dungheap, the lusted of flies,
The desirable excretion. Our pleasantness was flyblown
SETI: I've suffered this once with Egypt—
ANATH: You tricked Moses.
And what has come of it I would bring back to you
Until pity came out of you like blood to the knife,
Remembering how disease swept all the cattle,
How we could not sleep for intolerable lowing
Till daylight rounded up the herds of wolftorn
Death. You tricked him, and that feculent moment
Filthied our blood and made of us a nation
Loathsome with boils. You had stirred up the muck
Which the sweet gods thought fit to make us of
When they first formed man, the primal putrescence
We keep hidden under our thin dress of health.
What a pretty world, this world of filthmade kings!
When, after the sixth time, the hail came down,
I laughed. The hail was hard, metallic, cold
And clean, beating on us with the ferocity
Of brainbright anger. As cut diamonds, clean,
Clean, and fit to be beaten down by. When
It stamped out the gardens and cracked the skulls of
    birds
It bruised away the memory of vermin
And struck our faces fairly. If then, if only
Then our consciousness had gone clean out,
Or if then you had let these Israelites go with Moses,
We should not now so vainly
Shuffle our fingers in the dust to find

The name we once were known by. But you tricked
For the seventh time, and then the curse of the locusts
Strangled the whole air, the whole earth,
Devoured the last leaf of the old life
That we had sometime lived. The land is naked
To the bone, and men are naked beyond the bone,
Down to the barest nakedness which until now
Hope kept covered up. Now climb and sit
On the throne of this reality, and be
A king.

SETI:
        Anath! These plagues were not my doing
And you know they were not. No man would say I
caused them.
Only a woman with her mind hung
With a curtain of superstition would say so.

ANATH: I admit it.
I am superstitious. I have my terrors.
We are born too inexplicably out
Of one night's pleasure, and have too little security:
No more than a beating heart to keep us probable.
There must be other probabilities.
You tricked Moses after I had gone myself
To bring him to you, and what followed followed.

SETI: It is true I made certain concessions to Moses
And reconsidered them. I was prepared
To let him have his way, if in return
He would use his great abilities to our advantage.
But am I to have no kind of surety
That he'll return, after this godhunt of his?
I said to him Take the men but their wives and children
Must remain. And then I went further: I told him to
take
Both men and women, but the children must stay. And
at last
I only insisted on their cattle, since our cattle
Were dead. I'll not be panicked by this chain
Of black coincidence, which he with his genius
For generalship has taken advantage of.

He presumes upon the eternal because he has
No power to strike his bargain. I have not done
These things to Egypt. I'll not hear it be said.

ANATH: Well, they're done. Blame has no value anyway.
There's not one of us whose life doesn't make mischief
Somewhere. Now after all you've had to give way.
We must calculate again, calculate without Moses.
I picked unhappy days in those girlhood rushes.
But at least we can sweep away the locusts.

SETI: You understand
There will be no postponement of Ramases' marriage.
We can look forward to that, and the change of fortune
Which I shall force presently. I haven't by any means
Put my policy aside.

ANATH: What do you mean?
Moses by now has called the assembly of the Hebrews.
By now Egypt has heard the news. Moses
Has taken policy out of your hands.

SETI: I sent
Word after him.

ANATH: Seti! What word did you send?
What have you done now against our chance
Of rest? What word did you send? Answer me, Seti!
Your promise you said this time was final. There was
No need or possibility of another word.
What have you done?

SETI: I have only been careful
To protect your future. Even before Moses
Had gone three steps from the palace there came the
    news
Of another defeat. Fate has taken a hammer
To chip and chip and chip at our confidence.
But while I still have Moses to come at my call
I have not lost him. And while he needs my help
He will continue to come. And when he is tired—
We'll make a bargain.

ANATH: All this, then, over again.
You're mad. It isn't we who make the bargains

In this life, but chance and time. I tell you it's madness!
—Listen!

SETI: I heard nothing.

ANATH: It is Teusret.

She draws aside the curtain and goes on to the terrace.

TEUSRET (*unseen*): Ramases!

SETI: What's the matter? She sounds afraid.

ANATH: Teusret! Teusret! What has happened to you?

TEUSRET (*unseen*): Where is Ramases?
Where is he?

ANATH: Come here, my frightened darling.
I haven't seen Ramases. But we are here,
Your father and I.

SETI: Is she hurt?

ANATH: She is no longer
Yesterday's Teusret. I have been watching how
She cannot altogether recognize who she now is.
Yesterday's Teusret was for yesterday's world.

SETI: She shouldn't call and cry where everyone can watch
her.

TEUSRET *comes on to the terrace.* ANATH *takes
her in her arms.*

ANATH: What is it? Take your head out of my heart
And tell me what it is. Each of us just now
Is an odd number with himself, but between us
We should be able to add up to something even.
Put yourself with me and see what we come to.

TEUSRET: Oh, Aunt!

ANATH: Can it be said?

TEUSRET: Nothing can really be said,
Do you believe that? When I try for words
I disappear from myself.

SETI: Come to me a moment, Teusret.
Now, what has frightened you? Tell me; we can't have
you crying.

TEUSRET: My thoughts! They went—inside—the world. I
don't

Seem to be able to get out. I think it's impossible
To live any more. What can I do?

ANATH: Insist on living.
More curious things happen than happiness.

TEUSRET: No, happiness is the most curious of all.
While I was reading, the last weeks
Came again and put their hands across
The page and closed themselves over me
Until I was inside the world. And there,
Ruling everything, is a whirlpool, trying
To escape, disguising and disguising itself,
Spitting out intricate concoctions of itself,
Shrill birds, bearded animals, heartbreaking
And perfumed flowers, delirious design
And complexity, flesh, near-flesh, seeing, seeing
To escape, with claw, voice, wing, appetite,
Beauty, fang, colour and poison, all
Nothing but a maddened beating against the walls
Of space, all consuming themselves or consuming
Others or being consumed.—And that's the sun
Rising and setting and the smooth endless
Music of the Nile. Oh the pretence
Of good when everything is hateful!

ANATH: But you
Are not, and I hope I am not, so there
Are two things to put back into the world.

TEUSRET: Aunt—

SETI: I have something to show you, Teusret.
We're not altogether destitute, you will see,
Of what is fine.

TEUSRET: What can you show me?

SETI: A vein
Of the earth. How does this seem to you?

He has brought out from a casket a collar of precious stones.

TEUSRET: O father.
Let me see! Perfect, perfect thing.
I'm too warm. Being held will melt it.

SETI: Drops of cornelian.
  These are diamonds. Hebrew labourers dug them.
  Now, Anath, you see how ill we could afford
  To lose them.

ANATH: Our grandmother wore these.
  It is a pity that all the love-affairs
  Between women and their jewels are broken off.

TEUSRET: May I wear it?

SETI: You can try it on.
  It is for Phipa when she comes.

TEUSRET: The world
  Is spun for Phipa! Everything for that girl!
  Even these, though they seem to chatter so merrily
  With the light, even these are the enemy! They go
  To make Ramases welcome to her. There's beauty!

SETI: If that is how they affect you, give them back
  To me.

TEUSRET: Take them! They were merely cast up
  By the whirlpool anyway. If you can pretend
  That our lives are still going on and if you can plan
  Days and days of triumph because Ramases
  Is going to marry a girl he has never met,
  That's your own dream-story. You can't make me clap
    hands
  And say that it's true. But you're using him for Egypt's
  Purpose, and whether he's happy or unhappy
  To you it's equally good. Let us alone!
  You've got to let us alone!

     She is running towards the door. Enter RAMASES.
     She cries out his name. He puts her arms gently
     away from him, intent on his father. She runs past
     him and out.

RAMASES: Father,
  Is it true you've withdrawn your latest promise to
    Moses?

SETI: Whatever I have done or not done isn't to be said
  In a sentence.

RAMASES: They say it's true. Wherever I have gone
Dank rumour has been rising off the pavements, chilling
Into the heart of the people: "Pharaoh has refused
Moses again. What new disastrous day
Is coming?" I tell you I've been out walking
Under the burning windows of the people's eyes.
You've stood fast long enough. Let Moses take
The Hebrews.

SETI: So you also are afraid of magic
And believe that this tall Moses can make a business
Out of curses? Do you suppose if I surrendered to him
There would be any less roaring in the wind
Or less infection in disease? Why
Aren't you beside me like another man,
Instead of so fretting me with nursery behaviour
That I could strike you? I made life in your mother
To hand me strength when I should need it. That life
Was you. I made you exactly for this time
And I find you screeching to escape it.

RAMASES: I have been
Through streets that no men should have to walk in.
You must let the Hebrews go. Father, you must!

SETI: You know nothing, you little fool, nothing! Govern
By your idiocy when I am dead.

RAMASES: What
Will you leave for me to govern, or what by then
Shall I have become, what figure of faded purple
Who clears his throat on an unimportant throne?
I am to you only the boy who comes
To the door to say goodnight on his way to bed.
It's you who invite the future but it's I
Who have to entertain it, remember that.
What is expedience for you may become
Dark experience for me. And these last weeks
I've heard the future's loping footfall, as plague
Came after plague, and I knew the steps
Were not passing but approaching. You

Were persuading them. They came each time a little
Nearer, and each time closer to me.

Keep your word to Moses. Let him take them.

SETI: I tell you it isn't possible.

RAMASES: Then get
Yourself another heir, and make him eat
Your black bread of policy. Marry yourself
To this girl from Syria. My plans are different.

SETI: Your plans are different! You insolent cub, you
    spoiled
Insolent cub! And so your plans are different?
You've already made your plans!

RAMASES: Wait. What
Was that noise?

ANATH: The old familiar. A man crying out.
What difference is one man's groaning more or less?

RAMASES (*looking from the terrace*): Oh horrible! What
    is it that makes men
And makes them like this man? Abortions of nature.
It is true what they said.

ANATH: What is true?

RAMASES: What the other officers said, what I thought
    they spread
About out of malice: that Shendi outstruts them all,
Drives the Hebrews harder than any Egyptian
Drives them, hits them down with a readier fist,
And smiles and thrives under the admiration
Of the overseers. Go out on the terrace if you doubt me
And see him, Shendi, the son of Miriam, a Jew
Beating a Jew.

SETI: So perhaps at last,
So perhaps at last you will have seen
That what you thought was child's play, black and white,
Is a problem of many sides. And you will kindly
Wait and learn. This fellow does the work
Which you yourself suggested he should do
And does it conscientiously, without sentiment.

RAMASES: I suggested he should do it. Yes.

I put the whip in his hand. I raised that arm.
I struck that Jew. I did it. I did not know
How the things we do, take their own life after
They are done, how they can twist themselves
Into foul shapes. I can now see better
The deathly ground we live on. Yes, all right,
I have surrendered. Whatever happens will happen
Without me. I've finished meddling.

ANATH: Ramases!
Of all the Jews one Jew has done this.

RAMASES: It might be
A thousand instead of one.

ANATH: Ramases, only
One Jew!

SETI: Would you even encourage the traitor
In my son, because of your fear of this Moses?

ANATH: Yes,
I would make him rebellious, and if I could I would make
Every limb of your body rebellious;
I'd paralyse that pride which with such cunning
Packs us into a daily purgatory
Of apprehension.

SETI: The purgatory may save you
From damnation. But turn yourselves all against me.
I stand now living and breathing only to protect
This country from disintegration.

ANATH: Oh
The gods, how we fumble between right and wrong,
Between our salvation and our overthrow,
Like drunk men with a key in the dark who stand
At the right door but cannot get out of the cold.
May the moment of accident bless us.

RAMASES: I shall not
Rebel again. That will be one trouble less.

SETI: Stand beside me. We're almost of equal height
And may yet come to be of equal mind;
And if that is so, one of us will find

The way of escape out of this distress
Of ours, either you or I.
    Enter KEF, *a Minister to the Pharaoh.*

KEF: My lord Pharaoh.

SETI: News; come on.

KEF: Better to hear it alone.

SETI: Bad news. Well, let's have it. Catastrophe
Is no longer my secret. Let us have it all.

KEF: My lord—

SETI: Go on, go on,

KEF: A report that the Libyans
Have annihilated the reinforcing fifth
Division.

SETI: It is impossible.

KEF: They were surrounded
And surprised. Only six men got through.

SETI: Six men.

RAMASES: Six men.

SETI: They make me a pack-horse to carry despair.
They load me to the last inch.
    Enter TEUSRET.

TEUSRET: Moses has come
Again. I saw him walking like a lion
Behind bars, up and down in your battered garden,
Ramases. The sentries had tried to hold him
But he broke through their spears as though he didn't
    see them.
He looked at me, his eyes the colour of anger;
He looked at me and gripped a mulberry-bough
And broke it, and said Go to your father, fetch me
Your father.

SETI: He can walk longer and break more boughs.
He shall wait, and find that Egypt is hard ground
Under his lion's walk. (*To* KEF) Go out to the over-
    seers
And tell them to tighten discipline, to give
No rest to those Hebrews, not to let man, woman
Or child straighten their backs while they still stand.

I shall not see him until I choose; and, when
I choose, for his people's sake, he'll do what I need.
See this done.

    Exit KEF.

ANATH: Seti, take care; take care
What you do.

SETI: Let Moses think again what behaviour
Is best, best to save his people.

    Exit.

ANATH: And all
We can do is to wait, wait and wait in this
Uneasy entrance hall of doubtful omen,
Feeling like pale petitioners who have already
Waited beyond all bearing.

TEUSRET: Ramases,
What is it? Why are you so silent? Are you afraid
As well? Are you afraid? Are you, Ramases?

RAMASES: Why should I be? The sweet part of the
    world's
All over, but that's nothing. It had to go.
My mind had lutes and harps and nodding musicians
Who drowned my days with their casual tunes. They
    have been
Paid off by this honest hour. And now I hear
My voice raised in deathly quiet. It's insufferable
That my voice, without the accompaniment of good
    fortune,
Should be so out of key, so faltering,
So cracking with puberty.—Aunt Anath,
What's the meaning of my manhood, to be found
So helpless, to be so helpless: an arbitrary thing
Of nerves and brain which this ambitious mud
We loyally call World and Planet, has spawned
Upon itself to give itself passion,
Five senses and despair. What is there to do
Which I could do and haven't yet seen?

ANATH: We're no longer alone.

    MOSES *stands in the doorway.*

TEUSRET: Look, Ramases.

MOSES: Where is Seti?

ANATH: He will not see you.

MOSES: When will he learn? When,
When, when will he learn? We have agonized
This land with anger for too many days.

ANATH: You
And he together. No birth is worth this labour.

MOSES: For three hundred years the pangs of this coming
deliverance
Have been suffered by my people, while Egypt played.
But now Egypt suffers, and she says
This is a new hell. But hell is old;
And you yourself sitting in sunlight
Embroidered on it with your needle. Hell
Is old, but until now
It fed on other women, that is all.

ANATH: And all is the innocent as well as the guilty;
All is the small farmer and the singing fisherman
And the wife who sweeps; to-morrow's boy as well
As yesterday's. All these, while Seti twists
To have his way, must go to your fire like sticks.

RAMASES (*looking from the terrace*): The gods help them
now! The gods help those Hebrews!

MOSES: It must be one people or another, your people
Or mine. It is Seti who like a monstrous mole
Blindly throws up this mountain of pain. I
Am the conscript of an autocracy of grief.
Injuries, nursed in sullen obliterated graves,
Anguish that is lost in dust—sometime
That time-gone sea of troubled hands, my forefathers'
Martyrdom, signed me away, gave an oath for my heart
Long before I lived. And deflected purpose
Or altered ambition, or the stirred and terrible affections
Cannot discharge me. You appeal to Moses,
But Moses is now only a name and an obedience.
It is the God of the Hebrews, springing out
Of unknown ambush, a vigour moving

In a great shadow, who draws the supple bow
Of his mystery, to loose this punishing arrow
Feathered with my fate; he who in his hour
Broke the irreparable dam which kept his thought,
Released the spumy cataract birth and death
To storm across time and the world;
He who in his morning
Drew open the furious petals of the sun;
He who through his iron fingers
Lets all go, lets all waste and go,
Except, dearly retained in his palm, the soul:
He, the God of my living, the God of the Hebrews,
Has stooped beside Israel
And wept my life like a tear of passion
On the iniquity of Egypt.

ANATH: So the great general steps down to captaincy.
I wonder. Does this god use you
Or do you use this god? What is this divinity
Which with no more dexterity than a man
Rips up good things to make a different kind
Of good? For any god's sake, if you came here
To get justice, also give justice.
In this mood the lot goes headlong.

MOSES: Headlong!
And our memories too. And our hands which once
Knew how to come together, must now forever
Hide themselves in our dress. We are utterly separate.

RAMASES: Look at the sky! A sea of cloud, blind-black,
Is pouring on to the beaches of the sun!

TEUSRET: Oh, it will swamp the sailing of the air!
The sky will be gone from us, it's taking the sky!
What shall we do?

ANATH: Hush, Teusret.
  The stage grows dark.

MOSES: Seti
May see better without the light of day.
The hand of God has gone across his eyes
And closed all life upon itself. Egypt

Goes inward, by a gate which shuts more heavily than
    sunset,
Leaving man alone with his baffled brain.
Only Seti can let the sun free again.

ANATH: It is here! The darkness!

MOSES: Tell him, tell Seti
That I wait for his answer.

Curtain to Act Two

ACT THREE

SCENE ONE: MIRIAM's *tent at night.* AARON. *Enter* MIRIAM.

AARON: Everything has been done, I think. I have daubed
  The lamb's blood three times over the entry
  And all that remained of the meat has been burned.—
  Miriam! You; not Moses! What do you want
  Here at close on midnight?

MIRIAM: Must I want something
To come into my own tent?

AARON: Tell me; what is it?
  There's no time left. Has the news got past our silence?
  Do they know? That's why you've come in the night.
    The Egyptians
  Are one ahead of us!

MIRIAM: News? I've got no news.
Is there any news at midnight? I've come to sleep.

AARON: Why not sleep, as you did, in the city with
  Shendi?

MIRIAM: Do I have to stand and be catechized in my
  own tent?
If you want to ferret in unlighted places

Penetrate into the mind of Moses, and let me
Sleep.

AARON: His mind will be our history
Before the morning. Whatever is about to happen—
I cannot doubt that something is about to happen—
Will divulge him to us at last. I have become
Almost docile to his darkness. By what providence
I wonder, did you come back? There was no way
Of getting word to you, but you came, thank God.
Whatever is wrong for you, to make you walk
So far to sleep, this midnight of Moses
(I call it to myself his midnight) will clarify
Into right.

MIRIAM: Wrong things and right things!
So you still talk of those, those things that are catches
To make us lose heart. Take evil by the tail
And you find you are holding good head-downwards.
Let me go to sleep.

AARON: Something that Shendi has done
Has brought you back.

MIRIAM: Shendi, Shendi to blame!
To you Shendi is always blameable.
Because at last he can have ambitions,
Because he's ripping up the bare boards
His boyhood lay on, to make himself a fire
Which will warm his manhood, we turn on him—yes,
I also, as much as you—I stormed so.
I? The right to blame him? The wrong to have borne
    him
To that childhood. Why shouldn't he be finished with
    the lot of us?

AARON: So he turned you out: he sent you away.

MIRIAM: I left him.
I came away from him. I couldn't watch him
Live what is now his life.

AARON: I won't think of him.

MIRIAM: He'll succeed without your thoughts.

AARON: Look at me, Miriam.

MIRIAM: You're going away.

AARON: And so is all Israel.
We all have staves in our hands and our feet shod
For travelling; Moses' orders. He also gave
Other orders; they were very curious.
We have all had to eat lambs' flesh, seasoned
With bitter herbs. As I see it, Miriam,
That is his characteristic way of achieving
Unity among us, before the event,
That we should all fill this waiting time by doing
The same thing, however trivial. And then
We have splashed the blood three times over the doorways.
That is quite inexplicable. It is drying in the night air,
At this moment, while I speak. What happens, I ask myself,
When it is dry? It means our freedom. He has told me so.
To-night we're to go free. And when I look at him
I have to permit myself a wonderful hope.

MIRIAM: He came back from Midian a madman.

AARON: His madness seems to be a kind of extended sanity.
But he tells me nothing, nothing is discussed or planned
Even with me, his lieutenant. And this closeness
Has hurt me, I won't try to deny it. And yet
He has me by the scruff of the heart and I ask
No questions. I've begun to believe that the reasonable
Is an invention of man, altogether in opposition
To the facts of creation, though I wish it hadn't
Occurred to me. I've been with Moses, watching
How in tent after tent he manipulated
Man upon man into consciousness. Though perhaps
They don't know of what they're conscious, any more than I do.
Except of the night; of the night, Miriam! I would swear
The night is dedicated to our cause.

You must have seen it: there's such a brightness,
Such a swingeing stillness, the sky has transfixed itself;
As though it hung with every vigorous star
On some action to be done before daybreak.
Is it my nerves? A sort of high apprehensive fever?
I can't discuss myself. To-morrow this glitter
And piercing peace may be something of our own.

MIRIAM: Peace! Give it to me, for God's sake.
All I could see was the peace of the crouching creature
Hanging upon its pounce.

    Enter SHENDI.

SHENDI: Why must he be here?
I have something to say to you, mother.

MIRIAM: Not any more
To-night; nothing more said to-night. Go back
To your bed.

SHENDI: Yes, you must listen!

AARON: Listen to your tongue
Or your brotherly whip?

MIRIAM: He knows already what we feel.
Now let him alone.

SHENDI: Let him think what he likes; I have come
To you, not to him. We've taken so long to get
What at last we have: why must you spoil it? I know;
It was the spate of our tempers, gone again now.
If you go away from me, more than half the triumph
Is lost. You haven't been my mother for nothing.
I mean to see you happy.

MIRIAM: I shall stay alone.

SHENDI: Oh, it's fantastic. What did you expect
My work to be? And how can we be scrupulous
In a life which, from birth onwards, is so determined
To wring us dry of any serenity at all?

MIRIAM: You must do as you must.

AARON: But in the morning
He may wish he had chosen otherwise.

SHENDI: What do you mean?
Let me hear what you mean by that. Have you

And your brother done some dirtiness against me
To put me wrong with the Pharaoh? I know you'd founder me
If you had the chance—

Enter MOSES.

MOSES: Get ready. Miriam. And you,
Shendi. Get together all that you value.
You won't come to this tent again.

MIRIAM: Get ready?
All that I value? What would that be, I wonder?
Tell your delirium to be precise.

AARON: This midnight is his. For pity's sake believe it,
Miriam. Then all our wills resolved into
One Will—

SHENDI: His, of course! The stupendous mischief
Of the man! I beg your pardon if he no longer
Rates himself as a man after living through
The pestilences as though he owned them.
You can blame him, not me, for the punishment
I give the labourers. He makes them undisciplined
With his raving of freedom which they'll never get.
It's he, not I, who knits the darker and darker
Frowns for Pharaoh—it's he who's the one for you
To abominate, if anybody.

MOSES: Be ready for journey.
The time is prepared for us. What we were is sinking
Under the disposition of what will be.
Let it so dispose; let us not fondle our wrongs
Because they're familiar. Now, as the night turns,
A different life, pitched above our experience
Or imagining, is moving about its business.
To-night—Aaron, Miriam, Shendi—our slavery
Will be gone.

AARON: Do you hear what he says?

MIRIAM: What is he hiding?
There's something he knows.

AARON: Something known by the night;
That was how it felt to me.

SHENDI: Come out of this,
  Mother. They need more room to foam and splutter in.
  If you come back with me you know you can be sure
  Of a rational world of pleasant men and women.
  Isn't that so? You don't want to stay here.

MIRIAM: I want to know why he's standing there, so cer-
    tain
  That something will happen to-night. What does he
    know?

SHENDI: The shape of his own mouth.

AARON: Confidence
  In what he knows, but not in us, alas;
  Not in me. The advance begins, and I am in command
  Of my perfect ignorance. Moses, tell me, is that
  How it is to be?

MIRIAM: What is it you know?

MOSES: The sound
  Of God. It comes; after all, it comes. It made
  The crucial interchange of earth with everlasting;
  Found and parted the stone lips of this
  Egyptian twilight in the speech of souls,
  Moulding the air of all the world, and desiring
  Into that shell of shadow, a man's mind—
  Into my own. Only now, only
  Now, Aaron, as it moves away,
  Can I try to form it to you. Miriam,
  This is what I know, and how I know what comes
  To-night.

MIRIAM: Am I to believe it? Isn't this no more
  Than I thought it would be: the thumping of the
    frenzy in him?

AARON: What was told? What was said?

SHENDI: Oh, leave them
  To excite each other. I'm going if you're not. Perhaps
  By to-morrow you'll see reason. I'll come back then.

MOSES: Stay where you are. Can you comprehend
  That we're sometimes hoisted by the unbelievable
  On to the shoulders of truth? Our custom is

To live backward of reality. When it turns its face
How can it be recognized? But a refusal
Of recognition is like a cancellation
Of our existence. Do you deny voice
To that power, the whirler of suns and moons, when
even
Dust can speak, as it does in Moses now?
It comes. And by the welding of what loved me
And what harmed me, I have amazingly been brought
To that stature which has heard. To-night, at midnight,
God will unfasten the hawk of death from his
Grave wrist, to let it rake our world,
Descend and obliterate the firstborn of Egypt,
All the firstborn, cattle, flocks, and men:
Mortality lunging in the midnight fields
And briding in the beds: a sombre visit
Such as no nation has known before. Upon
All Egypt! Only we who have the darkness
Here in our blood, under the symbol of blood
Over our doors, only we of Israel
Standing ready for the morning will be unvisited.

AARON: So this is what you know.

SHENDI: What he wants, what he fondly
Imagines. Is he so dull he can't see the risk
Of heaving this up in front of me? An officer
Of Egypt. He may have forgotten it.

AARON: I should say this is no night to be an Egyptian.

MIRIAM: There will never be this midnight! It will still
Stop short of us!

SHENDI: Why did I follow you here
To get drawn into this? That fox has his tail on fire
And someone should know about it. For the last time,
Are you coming?

MIRIAM: Don't go back—not just
Within a pace of this midnight; Shendi, not now
When I've lost the knack of knowing sense from non-
sense.

The city, for my peace of mind, can find its way
Over midnight without you.

SHENDI: I can see
What's been thought out between you. Were you the
    decoy
To fetch me here? And now that you have me away
You think you'll keep me: here, dropped back in the
    pit.
What a chance of it! Must I tell you that I'm an Egyp-
    tian?
An Egyptian! I'm an Egyptian! Now what becomes
Of your craftiness and your birdlime?

MIRIAM: No! No!
The midnight is in us before it comes; it comes to us
Out of ourselves! I didn't know that you would follow
    me.
You're scoring your own heart for nothing, for nothing,
Shendi. I only ask you to wait until midnight
Is safely past us.

AARON: Soon enough now; before
We know where we are.

SHENDI: Do you think you can make a fool of me?
Do I look so very credulous? Don't I know
How he's waited for me to slip up, because he
Slipped up?

MOSES: Break and finish that! With every ram
Of your intelligence, break that jealous, bitter
And scheming puppet you have dubbed with my name.
Are you going to let the non-existing
Dog and destroy your existence? That Moses in your
    head
Is a lie.

SHENDI: What does it matter whether he is
Or he isn't? You want to bring Egypt down,
To fell her with the weight of her own achievement.
What else but Egypt is able to make birth
A proposition? You aim to destroy excellence

For what you call a justice. Justice
Is the greatness that comes to the great!

MOSES: It's the crossing of mind
With mind. How can I make you see me, clear
Of what you want to believe?

SHENDI: I see you well enough.
You've taken ten years looking for the logic of your
     murder
And now you think you've found it.

AARON: Midnight, midnight!
Have you both forgotten it? No doubt the timing of
     God
Will be extremely exact. But in fact we realize
Nothing. If it comes, how completely
Shall we realize it then? And does nothing, no presen-
     timent,
Creep on the heart of Pharaoh at this moment?
I wonder, does nothing make him fetch his firstborn
Beside him—

MOSES: Aaron!

MIRIAM: Shendi, let me keep you here
For one hour only, to protect me from panic.

MOSES: Aaron!
Do you see the ambush I have blundered into?
I heard God, as though hearing were understanding.
But he kept his hands hidden from me. He spoke,
But while he spoke he pointed. Aaron, he pointed
At Ramases, and I couldn't see!

AARON: The boy
Pays for the father, as though we bred in order
To redeem ourselves.

MOSES: Why had I not thought of him?
I had such tremendous heart. It seemed at last
As though we had reached the breaking of the seals,
When we no longer should be set down blindfold
To build upon light. I saw the passion of bewilderment
Drawing off from the earth. But can we go forward
Only by the ravage of what we value? Surely

I who have been the go-between for God
Can say that this is not part of my intention
And be heard?

AARON: What, at this point? Is this how you fought
Your other wars? There were boys then who put
Eager toes into fatal stirrups, who were young
And out of life altogether in the same
Almighty and unthinkable moment. You learnt
Then to grieve and advance, uninterrupted.
And so it has to be now.

MOSES: If it were the same!
But I am stealing Ramases without warning
And handing him to oblivion. Look what it is.
God is putting me back with the assassins.
Is that how he sees me? Does one deed
Become our immortal shape? And Egypt! Egypt!
He was meant for Egypt. If I have any freedom
More than the freedom of my thoughts, I must make
Providence mutual with my world of sense,
Or else I shall become wandering in my soul.
Ramases must be dragged clear of this runaway
Misconceiving miracle of God.
It isn't he that I shall be forced to spend
To get the fulfilment of what I do! Aaron,
You are here in my place until I come again.
Keep Shendi with you.

AARON: Where are you going?

MOSES: To the palace.

AARON: What will you do? Am I to be left midstream
Of a miracle, not even knowing what it portends?

MOSES: Do nothing but watch the night become day. All
happens.
I have to know what I am. Keep Shendi with you.
(*He goes*)

AARON: He is in a space somewhere between
The human and inhuman. That's a terrible
Neighbourhood.

SHENDI: Did you see how he looked? He believes
What he said. He looked a ghost haunting his face.
He believes it all—like a child.

MIRIAM: Shut us in. He has gone.
Can't we forget the man?

SHENDI: I won't stay here!
The place is putrid with childishness. I won't stay!
Thank goodness I can go where things are healthier,
Where I can wake a few men and get myself back
To normal.

MIRIAM: You know I was born to be uneasy;
I kindle dragons. Shendi, come away
From that questionable air outside.

AARON: It's midnight.
Wasn't that the winding of the city's horn,
The sound of twelve? I think so. I have to delay you,
Shendi.

SHENDI (*at the tent-opening*): Nobody will delay me.

MIRIAM: Stay in the tent!

AARON: The hour may go past and leave us knowing
It was unremarkable. But wait till the light,
Wait, Shendi, keep yourself unseen
By that inquisition of stars out there.
Wait for Moses to return.

SHENDI: Who?

MIRIAM: What is it? What have you seen?

SHENDI: I've lost the city,
I can't reach it! You trapped me!

MIRIAM: What do you see?

SHENDI: The sand is rising and living! Do not let it
Happen. It can't, it can't rise without a wind.
Is an invisible nation going through to the north?
Or what is it the sand can feel? I can't go back,
God, God, I can't go!

MIRIAM: Come inside,
Shendi, come into the tent.

AARON: Happening,
You see, happening. Why try to go back?

SHENDI: Some of the men will still be awake. We could light

The lights in the barrack-room. If only some of them

Would come out to look for me! But who'd come now?

Do you see how the sand is wavering upright, disturbed—

Disturbed in God's name by what? It's by the passing

Of a trance of eagles! Can you hear it, the noise,

The rending apart and shuddering-to of wings?

Where can I get away from this? Nowhere

Except into the ground.

MIRIAM: Shendi, here, in the tent.

In the tent: it will pass the tent.

AARON (*dragging him in*):   Are you trying to die?

SHENDI: Let me go, death; death, let me go!

AARON: It is I

Not death.

SHENDI: It isn't only you.

The wings were right over me and I was wrenched by a hand

That came spinning out of them. I'll not be sent into a grave.

I'll be what I was. I am Shendi, a Jew.

How can my blood alter and make me Egyptian?

I only wanted to be free! (*He tears off the insignia of Egypt.*)

Look: Egypt comes away—it's no part of me,

It's easily off. This body is all I am—

It is Shendi, the Jew, Shendi, Shendi, a Jew,

A Jew! Isn't it so? Then why am I dying?

MIRIAM: You are not, Shendi; it's gone past us. There's nothing more.

AARON: Look, you're with us.

SHENDI: Only free to die?

This wasn't a world. It was death from the beginning.

Here's my name, without a man to it. My name!

Let me go. It's a chance! I'll make them see me. Wings,

He breaks away into the dark.

Shadows, eagles! I am Shendi, Shendi, the Jew!
I am Shendi the Jew! Shendi the Jew!

MIRIAM: Shendi!
He has gone behind the sand. Son! (*She runs into the
dark.*)

AARON: The night
Of deliverance. To-night we all go free.
And Miriam too. He said she would go free.

The voice of MIRIAM *is heard crying out her last
desperate "Shendi!"*

Curtain

SCENE TWO: *The Palace.* ANATH. TEUSRET.

TEUSRET: Are you casting about in the night for sleep?
Try well beyond the terrace. Here there isn't
Even the swimming of minnow drowsiness.
I have to be stark awake, tired or not.

ANATH: One restless spirit in the house is enough.
What is the matter?

TEUSRET: If you could tell me that
Perhaps I might sleep. Listen to those men
Singing in the streets, and two women, or one?
"I'm waiting where you left me."—Are all the souls
In the city looking for sleep? Can there be nights
When sleep doesn't exist at all? Please hold me.
It is only that I've lost my way in myself.

ANATH: There come those times—maybe this is one of
them—
When, as though we were trespassing on the credible,
We're driven off from the blind poise of custom
And see the unnerving, profound chasm
Between ourselves and creation: we, human,
(That singular expense of nature) lapped

And perpetuated by a universe
Of inhumanity. So, to befriend ourselves,
We give limbs to our thoughts of the gods. I find
It is easier believing the gods exist.
Than believing that men do. A living body is stranger
Than a spirit. How shall we comfort ourselves? We can
    only
Sound our curious notes, without expecting
Any mating answer from any world,
Content to be a snatch of ambiguity,
Disturbing eternity with a kind of music.

TEUSRET: If only my life would speak lower, or more
    Deliberately and yet still be bright, more like
    That routine of fire up there, the night's
    Commonplace of stars.

ANATH: How they have taken
    Possession of the sky to-night.

TEUSRET: Occasion,
    Dear Aunt. Phipa is coming, the magnitude
    Out of Syria.

ANATH: To-morrow.

TEUSRET: No; now they say to-night.
    Very soon, for Ramases. Messengers were here
    Half an hour ago, sweating in the cool yard.
    She's already at Hahiroth, with her romantic nature
    Plying the spurs and waking all the poor villages
    With the interminable jingle-jangle of what father calls
    Her considerable means. We shall see her
    To-night.

ANATH: How do we welcome her? Nothing has been said
    To me.

TEUSRET: Who says anything in this palace now
    Except good morning or good night? Father
    Waits for each moment to come and touch him, and
    then
    It has gone before he can use it.

ANATH: Is it Phipa's
    Coming that made sleep impossible?

TEUSRET: Will you believe me? I'm praying her here. I
fetch her
To Ramases, with prayers like the grip of a moon
On the long tide of her caravan. Don't you see?
She will bring solid and gay Syria
Among the fiends that sway the walls here. Aunt,
She'll bedizen nightmare until it sinks, will she not?

ANATH: I haven't weighed the power of the blandishment
Of diamonds.

    Enter SETI.

TEUSRET: Who is that?

SETI: I. Is there something
To be seen?

ANATH: We're watching the dark for bridles.

TEUSRET: And the dark
Watches us. I know you dislike me to be afraid of it.
Are we all to meet her in the jumping shadows,
Aunts, owls, flame, sisters and all?
Or will she go quietly to bed and wait for to-morrow?

SETI: To-night. She must dismount into a light
Of welcome. Where's your brother? Turn this way;
Are you handsome? Well, the years of my life
Conveyed in a woman, perhaps safely. Remember to
love me
For everything you become, particularly
For the worship of the male sunrise which will stand
Over your maturity.

TEUSRET: What is it, father?
What is it?

SETI: How many thousand thousand years
Are being nursed in your body, my young daughter?
And under a secure lock, away from the eyes

TEUSRET: What eyes?

SETI: The envy; confusion. Do you know
Where to look for Ramases?

TEUSRET: He was trying to sleep.
What is it that is wrong?

SETI: The world's constitution.
Otherwise everything is much as we would wish it.
I'll tell you what is wrong. The world is a wonder
Married to some deformity; but we'll fetch them
Apart. Where is Ramases?

TEUSRET: In bed.

SETI: He can go to bed to-morrow.

ANATH: Precious heart,
That was a wild cry that ripped the darkness
From somewhere down in the city. Did you hear it?

SETI: He will have dreams in a host after to-night;
I'm giving them to him with both my hands. Where is
    he?
Fetch him.

RAMASES (*in the doorway*): I am here, sir.

SETI: You're the Pharaoh.

ANATH: Seti!

SETI: Egypt is a child again.
Have I been as young as this? You have slept
Into a throne and an empire, while time has begun
To heap age over me with a bony spade
To make me like the rest, Ramases, like
The poor rest.

RAMASES: Has Syria come?

ANATH: Tell the boy
What you mean: and me. What are you pulling down
    now?

SETI: Myself. It seems that I have grown too tall
And keep out the sun. I overbranch the light.
I am giving you the throne, Ramases.
It gives itself. The wind has hurled it under you,
A biting wind, the hatred that has turned me
Into storm, decay and grub in my own garden.
You may have luckier hands. You have at least
Hands less calloused with enemies. You will be able
To hold the sceptre perhaps without such pain.

ANATH: Abdication!

RAMASES: Is that what you mean? The throne.
  Earth's ruin is to become my region.
SETI: What? Come out of your sleep. Are you going to
    mope
  Good gold away as though it were sand in glass?
  We're in time. Aren't you myself again? Listen to me:
  This is how we distract them: under my seal
  Affixed in the morning, Moses shall be given the per-
    mission
  He has raged for: and then, with the sun somewhat
    higher,
  Under my final seal you shall take Egypt.
  I drown myself in my own wave: I am not,
  But I am always. And when they come, the factions,
  The whorers and devourers, roaring over
  The rocks of the dynasty, they'll only find
  Perpetual Egypt.
ANATH: Like a haven of sand.
  But that's for me, not for these two children.
  For them I'll believe in hope, or the hope of hope.
SETI: Hope? What has Egypt to do with hope,
  That dwindled and dingy prayer? You long ago
  Drove yourself out of your rights, and made yourself
  Servile in some thankless kingdom of your head.
  Is my abjuration of the bright
  Wrists of the world, on which the centuries
  Are bracelets, expected to fetch us only hope?
  I am delivering Egypt up to my son.
  Shouldn't that buy off apprehension for ever?
  Do none of you understand what I'm sacrificing?
RAMASES: Yes: whatever was prefigured in time
  To be my life. I'm to inherit the kingdom
  Of desperate measures, to be not a self
  But a glove disguising your hand. Is there nowhere
  Where I can come upon my own shape
  Between these overbearing ends of Egypt?
  Where am I to look for life?
SETI: But what

Am I shaking over you if not a wealth
Of life? Do you comprehend, this land of cities
Lying dazed with time's faithfulness
Is yours? And the heart of beauty out of Syria.
Teusret, watch; is there anything to be seen?
Any sound yet?—Stupidity, what would you have?
Love is the dominant of life, to which all our changes
Of key are subdued in the end. You will be able
To wander the winding and coitous passages
Of the heart, and be more than you could have prophesied
For yourself.

TEUSRET: The singing in the street has stopped;
But now, something else—

SETI: Well, what? Is it the girl?

ANATH: Listen!

TEUSRET: A tortured gale, a gale of crying
Moving up through the streets! Oh no! no!

SETI: Crying of what?

ANATH: Has the earth found voice
At last to bring compassion to the nail-thrusts
Of those glaring stars?

TEUSRET: It's the noise of breaking lives!
Isn't it so?

ANATH: As though the roots of faith
Were being dragged out of the live flesh of the land.

TEUSRET: We're together, Ramases, some way, or is no
one
Ever with another? Your hand feels wise. And now
Mine is part of it. So much for fear!
We're locked against whatever is there in the city.

RAMASES: Teusret, what is there may be ourselves
Coming to find us; we have to listen to it.

SETI: What is it now? Has evil so many rat-holes
We can't stop them up? In the name of the soul,
How can we caulk a world which is such a sieve
To darkness?

RAMASES: What is it, Darkness?

ANATH: Oh, make the city
   Silent! Did you see that? The shape of a man
   Leaping for the terrace?

SETI: Get back into the room!
   Back! Here is treachery's shadow in the shadow.

RAMASES: Let it come to me, then. If I'm to have Egypt
   I'll have its treachery as well. Keep
   Away from the window. Who goes there? Stand.
   Who goes there? Who is it?

     MOSES *comes breathlessly on to the terrace.*

MOSES: Shut all your doors!
   Nothing will wait for us, we are at war
   With this moment, draw yourselves like swords. It is
   For Ramases: Put your lives round him.

ANATH: My life? Who has my life? Find it.

RAMASES: For me?

SETI: Have you come out of the city? What is there?
   Show your hand, even with the ace of terror.
   What is on its way to us?

MOSES: Death, death, deliberately
   Aimed, falling on all your firstborn sons,
   All Egypt's firstborn, Seti, cattle and men;
   Death particular and infallible, mounting
   With an increasing terrible wake of cries
   To your window, to come to Ramases. I know—
   It was I that loosed it. Can I deflect it now?
   Can we so rope our lives together that we
   Can be a miracle against death?

SETI: Go back
   Into your night! I don't believe in you.
   You are a figment of the insupportable,
   Face of a lie. Go back out of belief.

ANATH: He can't, can't, can't! He is caught with us,
   Like us, in the falling tower of time. He is true;
   And I give him my desperation to do what he may
     with.
   Will that save Ramases?

TEUSRET: But who has condemned him?

What has he done? Has he made too much love
In the world? What guilt do you want us to clear him
of?
Oh we can, easily, easily!

RAMASES: My own death
Is near to me. I hear what you all say
But all I can feel is that the night will be heavy,
Awkward with goodbyes. Death, it appears,
Tells nothing upon its beaches, has no breeze
Explaining to the land, nor even a kiss
Of warning salt, or frail disposal of spray
To hint at such huge water. Can it rise
So darkly over the sand without a sound?
Perhaps this is its hand that seems to be passing
Through my hair, feeling for the skull.
An utter end of all the neighbourhood
Of light and yet there is nothing I understand.
Is it my action? Or an action done to me?
And do I live by this, because of this,
For this only?

TEUSRET: Ramases, you're believing
It will come! Then if it does, life is wicked,
Life will deserve death.

SETI: But I have changed
The channel that evil was running in. The boy
Is the Pharaoh. What has set humanity tolling
Now? It has no reason to.

MOSES: The Pharaoh?

RAMASES: Is it too late, no use after all?

MOSES: We'll hold you
With our lives, if our lives will hold, and if before mid-
night
We can only pass to each other safely. In life's
Name, what are we? Five worlds of separation?
Or can we be five fingers to close into
A hand, to strike this night clean away from us?
There must be no thin place left for death
To arrow through to him.

ANATH: How can we be in time?
  Are we all as lost within ourselves
  As this?

TEUSRET: Father, the crying-out! Quickly, quickly,
  It is so near!

SETI: I will do anything.
  But all direction is gone.

RAMASES: Perhaps it is
  My own deed after all. Then no one can change it.

MOSES: All was right, except this, all, the reason,
  The purpose, the justice, except this culmination.
  God, now good has turned on itself and become
  Its own enemy. Have we to say that truth is only
  Punishment? What *must* we say to be free
  Of the bewildering mesh of God?

ANATH: What do you want from us?

MOSES: Power of life, to beat death out of this house.

ANATH: Say what it is! Say what is my life?
  It went to be your shadow. For fifteen years
  It has been nothing but a level of darkness
  Cast on the world by you. I was the cheat
  Of my own heart, who made myself your mother
  And then loved you and desired you, until you became
  The world's bruise and ease, the blessing and torment,
  The water that kept me alive to thirst.
  Is this the power you can use against death?

MOSES: This isn't what we must say—not now!

ANATH: What else?
  Ramases must live! At last, at last
  You need something of me. Ramases must live.
  Can the power of my unsleeping madness—
  That burning beauty and insidious worm
  Of hunger—can my love for you get him
  From death? If it will, let it enrich itself
  On that; but what power has it that can never know
  If you could have loved me? Merely to have known
  How little or much I strangled, how near I was
  To peace? But fear shapes and changes us

And becomes our only courage, and I was afraid
For you to know you were not my son, for then
I should have lost even that right in you.
And so the world has been one thing and I another
And the life in me has kept me out of life.

MOSES: Anath—

ANATH: I loved you until I longed to hear
That you were dead.

MOSES: What can we make
Of the old circling peewit of our past
That whimpers for the breast of the dry moon
And keeps a querulous twilight, year and year?
More life! The dark is already pacing us.
Must we be agents of this deadly visit
Of God? Give me greater life, for the boy's sake!

RAMASES: But how should I wear life now? It has become
Something too large to put on. If I'm to live
Shall I know how?

SETI: Yes, ask, son of myself,
Ask that! There's life in questions. But pray
With your soul that you receive no answers.
My branch, my Ramases, on to your knees.
Truth will be the finish, the disaster.
Our power and progress is our being free
Of truth. Do you think I haven't known
That it's the immortal lying of our spirits
Gives the unpromising earth the look of excellence?
Am I to deride myself away
Into what I am, futility?
Sufficient illusion is sufficient life.
No one will persuade me
That I must break my heart with truth.

RAMASES: And in your prime of illusion I was begotten.
It's fair enough I should be dispelled. Gods,
I'm tired of thinking. If it were here and quick
I should stop trembling.

MOSES: Has none of us the life

To keep him living? Pain of man, iron
Of nature without record, sacrifice, faith,
Storm-riding souls and rearing spirit,
Are we the way through, letting in destruction?
Affirm and succeed into my strength to lock me
Equally with this wrestler rising out of midnight.

TEUSRET: Look, look—the torches in the gateway.
She is here! We shall be alive again.
Phipa has come to us, and the shawms have begun
To wind their welcome in the towers. Come on,
Ramases, come to meet her.

SETI: Anath, all of you,
We meet her as though Egypt were in high health.
No anxiety in your faces as of ambassadors
Of a haunted country. Is it the main body
Or only the advance riders?

TEUSRET: Ramases,
Are we going? The dark's not dangerous now.

RAMASES: But still dark. And we have to enact a daylight
For this unsuspecting beauty. How easy is that?
Well, for the stairs, then. We'll meet her.

ANATH: No,
Don't go, don't look! Moses, it is now
That you must break in on to your powers.
Now, now! What strength have you? I saw—

MOSES: I am nothing!

ANATH: There were men, opening the gates,
Who fell and still are lying there, and an owl
In mid-air wrenched itself upward screaming and
    smashed
Down on to the yard—there's another! Oh,
The bat that flew by me now, has dropped from
    sight!—
Are these the flowers we throw to a bride? Of the birds
The shouts and neighing wakened, many are falling
Dead; one has struck a torch from a man's
Hand. It is here!

MOSES: The shadows are too many.
  Where is my hand to go to? Ramases,
  There's no more of me than this. This is all.
  I followed a light into a blindness.

TEUSRET: Come away, Ramases, Ramases
  Come now, now. You must meet her and love her.
  Isn't it in love that life is strongest?
  I want you to love her. Already we're late.

RAMASES: Why is she sighing, Teusret? Such great sighs.
  They have taken all the air. Now there will be
  Nowhere to breath. Come with me. (*He crumples and
    falls.*)

TEUSRET: Ramases!
  I don't know the way!

RAMASES: I am finding it for you.

MOSES: Ramases, can you forget life
  So quickly? This is my hand, a living hand;
  Do you remember? Still be as this hand is,
  Like this and this.

RAMASES: Stoop, Teusret. You see?
  You cannot lose me. Here I am. (*He dies.*)

TEUSRET: Oh, help me to take him to her, make him see
  her
  Ramases, we're to go to the stairs. Listen,
  That shouting is in Syrian. How can he hear,
  With his head so? I had a secret to bring you
  When you marry. Ramases! I'll meet her alone, then.
  Coming in she'll reach you—must, must.
  She came so far. (*She runs to the courtyard.*)

MOSES: This is how it is
  To make time your friend. The earth has come and
    gone.
  For him the earth has gone. But for us it still
  Hangs in the air, like a smell of burning
  Which must be searched for, so slight, but we cannot
    rest
  Until, like this, we have put it out.

SETI: What's that movement? The light touching his ring.
Is that all the life you have for me now?
Light, there are his eyes. Go to them again.
Why will you waste on a stone? A stone. Stone.

ANATH: Is death the last illusion, Ramases,
Pharaoh of sleep? O darling hope,
You have become my promise. Keep it, unbroken.
You have the one possession of the world.

MOSES: An end? Why should he die again in us?
Live in us, Ramases, in what years we can have for you.

SETI (*turning on* MOSES): You have done what you re-
turned for. You came in the morning.
Leave us with what remains of the night.
No man in Egypt will prevent you. The day
You found us in is over.

ANATH: You have the freedom of the darkness, Moses.
Why do you wait? Haven't you recognized
The triumph of your purpose? Your twelve hundred
Thousand souls, out there in the dungeon of the night,
Are waiting to hear the long bolts grate back.
Ramases has died, and the air stands
Ready in the wilderness to take you in.
Ramases has died. To-morrow the lizards
Will be sparkling on the rocks. Why aren't you dancing
With such liberty for such starving souls?

MOSES: I do not know why the necessity of God
Should feed on grief; but it seems so. And to know it
Is not to grieve less, but to see grief grow big
With what has died, and in some spirit differently
Bear it back to life. The blame could impale me
For ever; I could be so sick of heart
That who asked for my life should have it; I could
believe
Creation to be no more than a weight of stone
Quarried for the chisel of doom; or I could see
Man's life go forward only by guilt and guilt.
Then we should always watch Ramases dying,
Whereas he had such life his death can only

Take him for a moment, to undo his mortality,
And he is here pursuing the ends of the world.
There is a wilderness between my blood and peace.
But what does eternity bear witness to
If not at last to hope? Eternal failure
Would make creation void before the void
Had seen creation. Anath—Egypt—
Why should it have been I that had to be
Disaster to you? Now, always unknown
To each other, we must force the arduous, damnable
Pass of time. Farewell.

ANATH: You were wrong, wrong!
You will have nothing now except the wilderness.
It's all your future and your old age. Oh, take
Your shadow off me. I shall remember only
What I have loved and make to-morrow of that.

MOSES: Somehow the pulse of living mustn't falter.
Is that enough to carry into the wilderness?
We must each find our separate meaning
In the persuasion of our days
Before we meet in the meaning of the world.
Until that time.

          He goes. Re-enter TEUSRET.

TEUSRET: I have seen her. How can she be
Too late? Is beauty not a wand? Then
We shall live again. Oh Ramases,
I'm Teusret. Are you so taken with the dark
That what has dazzled me won't open your eyes?
I have whispered into your sleep at other times
And you've heard me.—Ramases,
She has come so gifted for you, possessing
A fable of rubies, and pearls like seeds of the moon,
With metal and strange horns, ebon and ivory,
Spilling chalcedonyx and male sapphires.
Doesn't their brightness come to you? Do they glimmer
Nowhere into the cupboards of your sleep?

SETI: She need bring nothing, except the hour that has
    gone.

MOSES: Death and life are moving to a call.
　I turn from Egypt.

ANATH:　　　　　　　What is left
　To call to me?

MOSES:　　　　　The morning, which still comes
　To Egypt as to Israel, the round of light
　Which will not wheel in vain.
　We must each find our separate meaning
　In the persuasion of our days
　Until we meet in the meaning of the world.
　Until that time.

He goes. The early light reaches RAMASES.

THE CURTAIN FALLS

THE PLAY ENDS

DAVID

A Play

D. H. LAWRENCE

CHARACTERS

DAVID, *son of Jesse.*
SAUL, *King of Israel.*
SAMUEL, *Prophet of God.*
JONATHAN, *son of Saul.*
ABNER, *leader of Saul's host.*
AGAG, *King of Amalek.*

MERAB, *daughter of Saul.*
MICHAL, *daughter of Saul.*
WOMAN-SERVANT.
MAIDENS.

JESSE, *father of David.*
ELIAB, ABINADAB, SHAMMAH, *brothers of David.*
FOURTH, FIFTH, SIXTH, AND SEVENTH BROTHERS *of David.*
ADRIEL THE MEHOLATHITE.

CAPTAINS, FIGHTING-MEN, HERALD, ARMOUR-BEARER, ELDERS, NEIGHBOURS, PROPHETS, HERDSMEN, AND LAD.

SCENE I: *Courtyard of* SAUL's *house in Gilgal: sort of compound with an adobe house beyond.* AGAG, *bound, seated on the ground, and fastened by a rope to a post of the shed. Men with spears. Enter* MERAB *and* MICHAL, *daughters of* SAUL, *with tambourines.* MAIDENS.

MERAB (*running and dancing*): Saul came home with the spoil of the Amalekite.

MAIDENS: Hie! Amalekite! Hie! Amalekite!

MICHAL: Saul threw his spear into the desert of Shur, through the heart of the Amalekite.

MAIDENS: Stuck the Amalekite, pierced him to the ground.

MICHAL: Wind of the desert blows between the ribs of Amalek, only the jackal is fat on that land. Who smote the Amalekite, as a sand-storm smites the desert?

MAIDENS: Saul! Saul! Saul is the slayer and the death of Amalek.

MERAB (*before* AGAG): What is this dog with a string round his neck?

MAIDENS: What dog is this?

MICHAL: I know this dog, men used to call it King!

MAIDENS: Look at this King!

MERAB: Agag, Agag, King of the Amalekites! Dog on a string at the heel of mighty Saul!

MICHAL (*speaking to* AGAG): Are you the King of the Amalekites?

AGAG: I am he, maiden!

MICHAL: I thought it was a dog my father had brought home, and tied to a post.

MERAB: Why are you alone, Agag? Where are all your armed men, that ran like lions round the road to Egypt? Where are your women, with gold on their foreheads? Let us hear the tinkle of the bracelets of your women, O King, King Agag, King of mighty Amalek!

167

MAIDENS (*laughing—shaking tambourines in* AGAG's *face— spitting on him*): Dog! Dog! Dog of an Amalekite!

MICHAL: Who hung on the heels of Israel when they journeyed out of the wilderness of Shur, coming from Egypt, in the days of our fathers, in the day of Moses our great deliverer?

MAIDENS: Ay! Ay! Who threw their spears in the backs of the wandering Israelites?

MICHAL: Who killed our women, and the weary ones, and the heavy-footed, in the bitter days of wandering, when we came up out of Egypt?

MERAB: Who among our enemies was accursed like the Amalekite? When Moses held the rod of God uplifted in his hand, Joshua smote the Amalekite till the sun went down. But even when the sun was gone, came the voice of the Almighty: *War, and war with Amalek, till Amalek is put out from under heaven.*

MICHAL: Dog! Son of dogs that lay in wait for us as we passed by! Dog! Why has Saul left you eyes to see, and ears to hear!

SAUL (*coming from house*): Agag is among the maidens!

MICHAL: See, Father, is *this* a king?

SAUL: Even so.

MICHAL: It is a dog that cannot scratch his own fleas.

SAUL: Even so, it is a king: King of rich Amalek. Have you seen the presents he has brought for the household of Saul?

MICHAL: For the daughters of Saul, Father?

SAUL: Surely for Merab and Michal, daughters of Saul. (*To a man.*) Ho! Bring the basket of spoils for the daughters of the King.

MICHAL: Listen! Listen! King Agag seeks a wife in Gilgal! Oh, Father, I do not like him! He looks like a crow the dogs have played with. Merab, here is a King for your hand!

MERAB: Death is his portion, the Amalekite.

MICHAL: Will you put him to death, Father? Let us laugh a little longer at his Amalek nose.

Enter man with basket—also JONATHAN *and* ABNER.

SAUL: See the gifts of Agag, King of Amalek, to the daughters of Saul! Tissue from Egypt, head-veils from Pharaoh's house! And see, red robes from Tyre, and yellow from Sidon.

MICHAL (*screams*): That for *me*, Father, that for me! Give the other to Merab.—Ah! Ah! Ah!—Thank you, King Agag; thank you, King of Amalek.

SAUL: Goldsmith's work for arms and ankles, gold and dropping silver, for the ears.

MICHAL: Give me those! Give me those! Give the others to Merab! Ay! Ay! Maidens! How am I?—See, Agag, noble Agag, how am I now? Listen! (*She dances, the ornaments clink.*) They say: *Noble Agag!—King of Givers!* Poor draggled crow that had gold in its nest! Caw! King Agag! Caw! It's a daughter of Saul, of long-limbed Saul, smiter of Amalek, who tinkles with joys of the Amalekite.

JONATHAN: Peace, maiden! Go in and spin wool with the women. You are too much among the men.

MICHAL: Art thou speaking, O Jonathan, full of thy own manhood?

JONATHAN: Take in these spoils from the eye of men, and the light of day. Father, there came one saying that Samuel sought you in Carmel.

SAUL: Let him find me in Gilgal.

ABNER: They are calling even now at the gate.

Moves to gate.

SAUL (*to girls*): Go to the house and hide your spoil, for if this prophet of prophets finds the treasure of the Amalekite upon you, he will tear it away, and curse your youth.

MICHAL: That he shall not! Oh, Merab, you got the blue shawl from me! Run! Maidens! Run! Farewell, King Agag, your servant thanks your lordship!—Caw!—Nay, he cannot even say caw!

*Exit—running—*MICHAL, *and other* MAIDENS *follow.*

ABNER: It is so, my lord. Samuel even now has passed the stone of directions, seeking Saul in Gilgal.

SAUL: It is well. He has come to bless our triumph.

JONATHAN: Father, will you leave that man in the sight of Samuel?

SAUL: No! Go you quickly into the house, O Agag! Take him quickly, men, and let no mouth speak his name.
Exeunt AGAG *and men.*

JONATHAN: I have a misgiving, Father, that Samuel comes not in peace, after Saul in Gilgal.

SAUL: Has Saul laid low the Amalekite, to fear the coming of an old prophet?

ABNER: Samuel is a jealous man, full of the tyranny of prophecy. Shall we wait him here, or go into the house and be seated on the mats? Or shall we go forth from the gate towards him?

SAUL: I will stay here, and brighten my sword-edge in the waiting.

ABNER (*at the gate—calling*): He is coming across the field; an old man in a mantle, alone, followed by two of his prophets.

JONATHAN (*joining* ABNER): It is he. And coming in anger.

ABNER: In anger against whom?

JONATHAN: Against my father. Because we have not destroyed the Amalekite utterly, but have saved the best spoil.

ABNER: Nay, but it is a foolish thing, to throw fine linen into the fire, and fat young oxen down a dry well.

JONATHAN: It was the commandment.

ABNER: Why should the maidens not rejoice in their ornaments, and the God of the Unknown Name enjoy the scent of blood-sacrifice?

> *They retreat from the gate;* SAUL *sharpens his sword. After a pause, enter* SAMUEL, *followed by the prophets.*

SAUL (*laying down his sword*): Blessed be thou of the Lord! I have performed the commandment of the Lord.

SAMUEL: What meaneth the bleating of the sheep in my ears, and the lowing of the oxen which I hear?

SAUL: They have brought them from the Amalekites. The people spared the best of the sheep, and of the oxen, to sacrifice unto thy God, but the rest we have utterly destroyed.

SAMUEL: Stay, and I will tell thee what I have heard out of the inner darkness, this night.

SAUL: Say on.

SAMUEL: When thou wast little in thine own sight, wast thou not made the chieftain of the tribes of Israel, and the Deep poured his power over thee, to anoint thee King? And the Voice out of the deeps sent thee on a journey, saying: Go, and utterly destroy the sinners the Amalekites, and fight against them until they be consumed.—Why then did you not obey the Voice, instead of flying upon the spoil, and doing evil in the sight of the Unclosing Eyes?

SAUL: Yea, I have obeyed the Voice from the beyond. I have gone the way which the Great One sent me, and have brought Agag the King of Amalek prisoner, and have utterly destroyed the Amalekites. But the people took the spoil, sheep and oxen, the chief of the things which should have been utterly destroyed, to sacrifice in Gilgal unto the Lord thy God.

SAMUEL: Does the Breather of the skies take as great delight in sacrifice and burnt offerings as in obedience to the Voice that spoke on the breath of the night? Behold, to obey is better than sacrifice, and to hearken than the fat of rams.

SAUL: Is not God the sender of life, and the bread of life? And shall we deny the meat and destroy the bread that is sent?

SAMUEL: Behold, is the Lord my God a sutler, to stock the larders of Saul? Lo, He heeds not the fat beef nor the fine raiment, but threshes out His anger in the firmament. Amalek has defied the living Breath, and cried mockery on the Voice of the Beyond. Therefore the living Wrath will wipe out the Amalekite, by the hand of His servant, Israel. And if the Nameless is without compunction, whence the compunction of Saul?

SAUL: I feared the people, and obeyed their voice.

SAMUEL: Yea, that was bravely done! Thou didst not fear the Great Lord, thou fearest the people, smaller than thyself. Thou didst not obey the Cry from the midst of the dark, but the voice of the people!—I tell thee, rebellion is as the sin of witchcraft, and stubbornness is as iniquity and idolatry. Because thou hast rejected the word of the Lord, the Lord hath also rejected thee from being King.

SAUL: Shall a King not hearken to the voice of his people?

SAMUEL: The people cried for a King, in the frowardness of their hearts. But can they make a King out of one of themselves? Can they whistle a lion forth from a litter of dogs? The people cried for a King, and the Lord gave to them. Even thee, Saul. But why art thou King! Because of the voice of the people?

SAUL: Thou didst choose me out.

SAMUEL: The finger of the Thunder pointed me to thee, and the Wind of Strength blew me in thy way. And thou art King because from out of the middle world the great Wish settled upon thee. And thou art King because the Lord poured the oil of His might over thee. But thou art disobedient, and shuttest thine ears to the Voice. Thou hearest the barkings of dogs and the crying of the people, and the Voice of the Midmost is nothing to thee. Therefore thou hast become as nothing unto the Lord, and He that chose thee rejecteth thee again. The power of the Lord shall fall away from thee, and thou shalt become again a common man, and a little thing, as when the Lord first found thee.

SAUL: I have sinned. For I have transgressed the commandments of the Lord, which thou didst hear out of the deeps of the night. Because I feared the people, and obeyed their voice. But now, I pray thee, pardon

my sin, and turn again with me, that I may find the
Lord, to worship Him.

SAMUEL: I will not return with thee: for thou hast rejected
the word of the Lord, and the Lord hath rejected thee
from being King over Israel. (*Samuel turns away.* SAUL
catches hold of the hem of SAMUEL's *garment and it
tears in his hand.*) The Lord hath rent the Kingdom of
Israel away from thee this day, and hath given it to a
neighbour of thine, that is better than thou (*pause*);—
and the Mighty One that moveth Israel will not lie, nor
repent towards thee again: for He is not a man that He
should repent.

SAUL: I have sinned, I have sinned, I have turned my face
the wrong way. Yet honour me now, I pray thee! Honour
me before the elders of my people, and before Israel,
and turn again with me, that I may find the Lord thy
God, and worship Him.

SAMUEL (*turning*): Thou hast turned away from the Hidden Sun, and the gleam is dying from out of thy face.
Thou hast disowned the Power that made thee, and the
glow is leaving thy limbs, the glisten of oil is waning on
thy brow, and the vision is dying in thy breast. Yet because thou art the Lord's anointed I will bless thee again
in the sight of the elders. Yet if the Lord hath decided
against thee, what avails an old man's blessing?

SAUL: Yet bless me, my Father.

SAMUEL (*lifting his hand*): The Lord be with thee! The
Lord's strength strengthen thee! The power and the
might of the Lord brighten thine eyes and light thy
face: the Lord's life lift thy limbs and gladden the walls
of thy breast, and put power in thy belly and thy hips!
The Lord's haste strengthen thy knees and quicken thy
feet!

SAUL (*lifting both hands to heaven*): Lo, I have sinned,
and lost myself, I have been mine own undoing. But I
turn again to Innermost, where the flame is, and the
wings are throbbing. Hear me, take me back! Brush me
again with the wings of life, breathe on me with the

breath of Thy desire, come in unto me, and be with me, and dwell in me. For without the presence of the awful Lord, I am an empty shell. Turn to me, and fill my heart, and forgive my transgression. For I will wash myself clean of Amalek, to the last speck, and remove the source of my sinning (*drops his hands—turns to* SAMUEL). Is it well, O Samuel!

SAMUEL: May it be well! Bring me hither Agag, King of the Amalekites.

SAUL: Ho, Jonathan, send here Agag the Amalekite. And send thou the chief of the herdsmen, O Abner, for we must wipe away the stain of Amalek swiftly, out of Gilgal.

    Exeunt JONATHAN *and* ABNER.

SAUL (*to* SAMUEL): The Lord shall be with me again this day, that the Kingdom be not rent from me.

SAMUEL: Who knoweth the ways of the Deep? I will entreat, ah! for thee in the night-time, and in the day. But if He hath turned His face away, what am I but an old man crying like an infant in the night!

    Enter AGAG—*coming forward delicately.*

AGAG: Surely the bitterness of death is past.

SAMUEL (*seizing* SAUL's *sword*): As thy sword hath made women childless, so shall thy mother be childless among women. *Rushes on* AGAG *with sword*—AGAG *steps behind a wall,* SAMUEL *upon him.*

    Enter HERDSMAN.

JONATHAN: Better it had been in battle, on the field of the fight.

ABNER: It is a sacrifice.

SAUL (*to* HERDSMAN): Gather together the cattle of the Amalekite which came as spoil, and fasten them in a pen. Leave out no sheep and no calf, nor any goat, but put them all in.

HERDSMAN: It shall be as Saul says.

    Exit.

SAMUEL (*entering with red sword*): I have hewed him in pieces before the Lord, and his blood has gone up to the

Most High; it is in the nostrils of the God of Wrath.

SAUL: Come now, I pray thee, within the house, and let them bring water for thy feet and food to gladden thine heart.

SAMUEL: It may not be. But I must go to Ramah to entreat for thee before the Lord, and even now must I go. And may the Might be with thee.

Curtain

SCENE II: *A room in Ramah. Night.* SAMUEL *in prayer.*

SAMUEL: Speak to me out of the whirlwind, come to me from behind the sun, listen to me where the winds are hastening. When the power of the whirlwind moves away from me, I am a worthless old man. Out of the deep of deeps comes a breath upon me, and my old flesh freshens like a flower. I know no age. Oh, upon the wings of distance turn to me, send the fanning strength into my hips. I am sore for Saul, and my old bones are weary for the King. My heart is like a fledgling in a nest, abandoned by its mother. My heart opens its mouth with vain cries, weak and meaningless, and the Mover of the deeps will not stoop to me. My bowels are twisted in a knot of grief, in a knot of anguish for my son, for him whom I anointed beneath the firmament of might. On earth move men and beasts, they nourish themselves and know not how they are alive. But in all the places moves Unseen Almighty, like a breath among the stars, or the moon, like the sea turning herself over. I eat bread, but my soul faints, and wine will not heal my bones. Nothing is good for me but God. Like waters He moves through the world, like a fish I swim in the flood of God Himself. Answer me,

Mover of the waters, speak to me as waves speak without mouths. Saul has fallen off, as a ripe fig falls and bursts. He, anointed, he moved in the flood of power, he was God's, he was not his own. Now he is cast up like a fish among the dry stones, he beats himself against the sun-licked pebbles. He jumped out from the deeps of the Lord, the sea of God has seen him depart. He will die within the smell of his own violence. Lord, Lord, Ocean and Mover of oceans, lick him into the flood of Thyself. Wilt Thou not reach for him with the arm of a long wave, and catch him back into the deeps of living God? Is he lost from the sway of the tide for ever and for ever? When the rain wets him, will it wet him Godless, and will the wind blow on him without God in it? Lord, wilt Thou not reach for him, he is Thine anointed? Bitter are the waters of old age, and tears fall inward on the heart. Saul is the son whom I anointed, and Saul has crawled away from God, he creeps up the rocks in vanity, the stink of him will rise up like a dead crab. Lord, is it verily so with Saul, is he gone out from Thee for ever, like a creeping thing crawled in vanity from the element of elements? I am old, and my tears run inward, they deaden my heart because of Saul. For Saul has crawled away from the Fountain of Days, and the Ancient of Days will know him no more. I hear the voice of the Lord like waters washing through the night, saying: *Saul has fallen away and is no more in the way of the power of God.* Yea, what is love, that I should love him! He is fallen away, and stinketh like a dead crab, and my love stinks with him. I must wash myself because of Saul, and strip myself of him again, and go down into the deeps of God. Speak, Lord, and I will obey. Tell me, and I will do it. I sink like a stone in the sea, and nothing of my own is left me. I am gone away from myself, I disappear in the deeps of God. And the oracle of the Lord stirs me, as the fountains of the deep. Lo! I am not mine own. The flood has covered me and the waters of the beginning sound in the shell of my heart. And I will find another King for Israel, I shall know him by the whispers of my heart. Lo, I will fill the horn with oil again, with the oil from the body of Him, and I will go into the hills of Judah. I will find out one, in whom the power sleeps. And I will pour potency over his head and anoint him with God's fecundity, and place him beyond forgetting. I will go into the hills of Judah, where the sheep feed among the rocks, and find a man fresh in the morning of God. And he shall be King. On the morrow I will gather myself and go, silently, carrying the kingship away from Saul, because the virtue is gone out of him. And Saul will kill me with a spear, in one stroke, for rage he will kill me, if I tell him. But I shall not tell him. I shall say: I must away to the land of Judah, it is the time to sacrifice in the place of Bethlehem, the appointed time is at hand.—So I shall go away from Saul for ever, and never shall I see his face again. I shall hide myself away from his face, lest he hurt himself, slaying me. I shall go in the morning with sure feet, but the shell of my heart will be weary. For I am the Lord's and the servant of the Lord, and I go in obedience, even with the alacrity of willingness. But alas, that I should have loved Saul, and had pride in him! I am old.

Curtain

SCENE III: *Bethlehem: an open place in the village. An old man on a roof calling aloud and kindling a signal fire.*

1ST ELDER (*calling, on the roof*): Come in! Come in! Come in! Come all men in! Come all in to the place of counsel! Gather into the place of counsel, all men gather now. Come in! Come in!

2ND ELDER (*on the plaza*): What now?

3RD ELDER: The watchman on the fourth hill saw a host of prophets coming, even Samuel among them.

2ND ELDER: Yea! What does this bode?

JESSE: What have we done wrong, that Samuel comes down upon us? If he curses us we are dead men.

4TH ELDER: Dread is on me. The sun looks darkened.

3RD ELDER: Nay, let us wait. It may be he comes in peace.

ELIAB (*brother of* DAVID): Why do we, who are men that fear not the lion nor the bear, nor even the Philistine, tremble before the raging of these prophets?

2ND ELDER: Hush then! For the Bolt is above us, and can strike out of a clear sky. Canst thou hear His meaning, or know His vision, Who is secret save to the prophets? Peace then, hush thy mouth.

JESSE: Verily, there is no open vision, and the word of One is precious. Without Samuel, we should stare with the stare of deaf men, and the fixed eyes of the blind. We should run our faces against the wall, and fall with our feet into a hole. We should not hear the lion roaring upon us.

ELIAB: Not so, my Father. Without a prophet I seek the lion when he roars about the herd, I slay him without advice from the Lord. We live our lives as men, by the strength of our right hand. Why heed the howlings of priests in linen ephods, one or many!

JESSE: My son, shut thy teeth on such words. Seal thy heart to silence. The strength of a man lasts for a little time, and wastes like the oil in a lamp. You are young, and your lamp is unbroken. But those that live long needs must renew their strength again, and have their vessel replenished. And only from the middle-middle of all the worlds, where God stirs amid His waters, can strength come to us.

ELIAB: Will it not come without Samuel?

JESSE: There is a path that the gazelle cannot follow, and the lion knows not, nor can the eagle fly it. Rare is the soul of the prophet, that can find the hidden path of the

Lord. There is no open vision, and we, who can see the lion in the thicket, cannot see the Lord in the darkness, nor hear Him out of the cloud. But the word of One is precious, and we perish without it.

ELIAB: *I* cannot bow my heart to Samuel. Is he a King to lead us into battle, and share the spoil with us? Why should we fare worse without him?

JESSE: My son, day follows day, and night travels between the days. But the heart of man cannot wander among the years like a wild ass in the wilderness, running hither and thither. The heart at last stands still, crying: *Whither? Whither?* Like a lost foal whinnying for his dam, the heart cries and nickers for God, and will not be comforted. Then comes the prophet with the other vision in his eyes, and the inner hearing in his ears, and he uncovers the secret path of the Lord, Who is at the middlemost place of all. And when the heart is in the way of God, it runs softly and joyously, without weariness.

ELIAB: I would sooner follow the King, with spear and shield.

JESSE: Samuel is more precious than the King, and more to be obeyed. As God is to Samuel, Samuel to the King is God. The King is as a boy awaiting his father's bidding, uneasy till he is told what he shall do. Even so Samuel speaks to Saul, with the mouth of authority, to be obeyed. For he is the lips of God.

ELIAB: For me, give me the right arm of Saul.

SAMUEL *enters—followed by wild prophets. The* ELDERS *go to meet him.*

1ST ELDER: The Lord be with thee!

SAMUEL: The Lord keep this people!

1ST ELDER: Comest thou in peace?

SAMUEL: In peace. I come to sacrifice unto the Lord. Sanctify yourselves and come to sacrifice, according to your families. Renew your clothes and purify yourselves.

1ST ELDER: Into which house will you go?

SAMUEL: Into the house of Jesse.

JESSE: I am here, my lord.

SAMUEL: Call your household together, and sanctify yourselves, for we will sacrifice a heifer to the Lord this day,
in your house. And it shall be a feast unto you.

Curtain

SCENE IV: JESSE'S *house. A small inner courtyard: a rude
altar smoking, and blood sprinkled round:* SAMUEL *before
the altar, hands bloody. In another part a large red fire
with a great pot seething, and pieces of meat roasting on
spits.* JESSE *turning the spits. It is evening, sun going down.*

SAMUEL: Call your sons. Call them one by one to pass
before me. For I will look on them, before we sit around
to the feast of the sacrifice.

JESSE: They are in the house, waiting. I will call the firstborn first. (*Calling.*) Eliab, come forth! Samuel asks for
thee!

ELIAB (*entering*): The Lord be with you.

SAMUEL (*aside*): Surely the Lord's anointed is before Him!
(*Gazes at* ELIAB *who is big and handsome.*)

SAMUEL (*aside*): I shall not look on his countenance, nor
on the height of his stature. For the voice of my soul
tells me he is rejected. The Lord sees not as men see.
For man looketh on the outward appearance, but the
Lord looketh on the heart.

SAMUEL (*to* JESSE): Him hath the Lord not chosen. Call
thy other son.

JESSE: Ha! Abinadab! And Eliab, gather all thy brothers
together, for the feast shall be set forth.

    Exit ELIAB.

ABINADAB (*entering*): The Lord be with you.

SAMUEL (*gazing on* ABINADAB): Neither hath the Lord chosen this.

JESSE: Go thou, Abinadab! Be all thy brethren ready in the house?

ABINADAB: They be all there, waiting for the sacrifice meat.

JESSE (*calling*): Come, Shammah! And when I call, come you others in your order, one by one.

SHAMMAH (*entering*): The Lord be with you.

SAMUEL (*slowly*): Neither hath the Lord chosen this.

JESSE: Go thou! Nay! Rather go to the fire and turn the spitted meat.

SHAMMAH: Yea! For it should not singe.

JESSE (*calling*): Ho! Son! Come forward!

FOURTH SON: The Lord be with you!

SAMUEL: Neither hath the Lord chosen this.

JESSE: Go thou hence, and wait yet a while.

FOURTH SON: What wouldst thou then with me?

JESSE (*calling*): Ho! Son! (*To him who waits.*) Nay, go or stay, as thou wilt. But stand aside. (*He stands aside.*)

FIFTH SON: The Lord be with you.

JESSE: Turn thy face to the sun, that it may be seen.

SAMUEL: Neither hath the Lord chosen this.

JESSE: Thou art not he, whom Samuel seeks. Stand thou aside. (*Calling.*) Ho! Son! (*To him who waits.*) Bring in thy brother.

> Enter SIXTH SON: *all the other brothers edge in after him.*

SIXTH SON: The Lord be with you!

SAMUEL: Neither hath the Lord chosen this.

SIXTH SON: Wherefore hast thou called me, my Father?

JESSE: Samuel would look on the faces of all my sons. Go now! Who then was not called? Who among you has not come forward?

SEVENTH SON: I! Wilt thou me?

JESSE: Nay, but come into the light before the prophet of God.

SAMUEL: Neither hath the Lord chosen this.

JESSE: Nay, then it is finished, for there be no more.

SAMUEL: Are here all thy children?

JESSE: Yea, verily, there remaineth yet the youngest. And behold, he keepeth the sheep.

SAMUEL: Send and fetch him. For we will not sit down till he come hither.

JESSE: Go thou, Shammah, for he will be coming in now. I will see——!

Exit JESSE, *also* SHAMMAH.

ELIAB: My lord, will the Lord of Hosts anoint a King, while Saul yet liveth?

SAMUEL: My son, out of the deep cloud the lightning cometh, and toucheth its own. Even so, from the whirlwind of the whole world's middle, leaneth out the Wonderful and toucheth His own, but whether the anointing be for prophecy or priesthood, or for a leader or a King over Israel, the Mover of all hath it in His own deeps.

ELIAB: Yea! But if the Lord anoint a man to be King, can the Lord again take back the anointing, and wipe out the oil, and remove the gift, and undo the man He has made?

SAMUEL: The power is beyond us, both before and after. Am I not anointed before the people? But if I should say: *The power is my own; I will even do my own bidding,* then this is the sin of witchcraft, which stealeth the power of the whirlwind for its own. And the power will be taken from me, and I shall fall into a pit.

ELIAB: It is a hard thing, to be the Lord's anointed.

SAMUEL: For the froward and irreverent spirit, it is a thing well-nigh impossible.

Enter JESSE *with* DAVID.

JESSE: This is David, the last of the sons of Jesse.

Enter SHAMMAH.

SAMUEL (*aside*): I shall arise and anoint him. For this is he. (*Aloud.*) The Lord hath chosen this one. (*Takes the horn of oil and holds it over* DAVID'S *head.*) The skies will anoint thee with their glory, the oil of the Sun is poured over thee, and the strength of His power. Thou shalt be a master of the happenings among men. Answer then. Does thy soul go forth to the Deep, does the Wonderer move in thy soul?

DAVID: Yea, my lord. Surely my soul leaps with God!

SAMUEL (*anointing* DAVID): The Glory pours Himself out on thee. The Chooser chooseth thee. Thou shalt be no more thine own, for the chosen belongs to the Chooser. When thou goeth in, it shall be at the whisper of the Mover, and when thou comest out, it shall be the Lord. Thy strength is at the heart of the world, and thy desires are from thence. The walls of thy breast are the front of the Lord, thy loins are the Deep's, and the fire within them is His. The Lord looketh out of thy eyes and sits on thy lips. Thou closest thy fist on the Deep, and thy knees smile with His strength. He holdeth the bow of thy body erect, and thy thighs are the pillars of His presence. Henceforward thou art not thine own. The Lord is upon thee, and thou art His.

DAVID (*making an obeisance*): I am thy servant, my lord.

SAMUEL: Ye shall sit around, and divide the meat, and eat of the feast, and bid the neighbours to your feast of sacrifice this night.

> *They move around, fetching trenchers of wood, and a huge dish, and a heap of flat bread. They begin to take the meat from the fire, and with a cry lift down the pot.*

JESSE: David is a child, and the Lord hath chosen him. What shall become of him? Make it plain to us, O Samuel, this night!

SAMUEL: Ask not, for none knoweth. Let him live till such time as the Unseen stretcheth out His hands upon him. When the time is fulfilled, then we shall know. Beforehand no man knoweth. And now the meat is ready from the fire, and the feast of sacrifice is prepared, and I have done. Eat you of the feast, and live before the Lord, and be blessed. Speak nothing of this hour, lest mischance

befall you. I go my way. Do not seek to stay me. Call
whom ye will to meat, eat then what is before you, for
this is your hour.

JESSE: The sun has gone down, and it is night. Wilt thou
verily go forth?

    Exit SAMUEL.

ELIAB: He has anointed the youngest, and the oldest he
has passed over.

JESSE: It is the Lord. Go, Abinadab, and bid in the neighbours to the feast.

ELIAB: Nay, it is Samuel, who envies a strong man his
strength, and settles on the weak.

JESSE: These things, at this hour, thou shalt not say. Is
my son David chosen beneath the heavens, and shall
Eliab his brother cast it up a reproach to him? Yea!
pile up the dish from the pot, that it may cool, and not
burn the hand of him that tasteth.

ELIAB (*to* DAVID): Wilt thou be a priest in a blue ephod?

DAVID: I know not. To-day and to-morrow I shall keep my
father's sheep. More I know not.

ELIAB: Canst thou see the Bolt within the cloud? Canst
thou hear His voice out of the ground?

DAVID: I know not. I wish the Lord be with me.

ELIAB: Is He nearer thee, than thine own father?

DAVID: My father sits before me and I see his face. But
the Lord is in my limbs as a wind in a tree, and the
tree is shaken.

ELIAB: Is not the Lord also in me, thou stripling? Is thine
the only body that is visited?

DAVID: I know not. My own heart I know. Thou knowest
thine own. I wish the Lord be with me.

ELIAB: Yea, I know my own heart indeed. Neither is it
the heart of a whelp that minds the sheep, but the heart
of a man that holds a spear. Canst thou draw my bow,
or wield my sword?

DAVID: My day is not yet come.

JESSE: It is enough. The guests we have bidden are here!
O David, my son, even carry out their portion to the

womenfolk, for they may not come here. And think thou no more of this day. The Lord will move in His own time, thou canst not hasten Him. (*To the* NEIGHBORS.) Nay, come! And sit ye to meat! For we will eat this night of the sacrifice that Samuel hath slain before the Lord.

NEIGHBOURS: Peace be to this house! And is Samuel at once gone forth? Yea! Good seemeth thy feast, O Jesse!

JESSE: An heifer, of the first year, fat and goodly! Reach forth thy hand.

> *They all sit around the huge, smoking platter.* JESSE *dips in his hand, and carries the mess to his mouth.*

NEIGHBOUR: Yea! Good is the feast! And blessed be Samuel, who came to Bethlehem this day! (*Re-enter* DAVID: *sits down and eats. They all dip their hands in the great platter, and eat in silence.*) Verily, this is a great feast! Surely the Lord hath visited thy house this day, O Jesse!

Curtain

SCENE V: SAUL'S *house in Gilgal.* MERAB *and* MICHAL *in the courtyard, spinning wool, with their maidens. They are laughing and giggling.*

1ST MAIDEN: Now I'll ask one! I'll ask one.

MERAB: Ask then!

3RD MAIDEN: Why does a cow look over a wall?

MICHAL: Yah! Yah! We know that old one. We all know it.

MERAB: Who knows the answer? Hold your hand up.

> *Only* MICHAL *holds up her hand.*

3RD MAIDEN: There! There! They don't know it! Why does a cow look over a wall?

1ST MAIDEN: To see what's on the other side.

MICHAL: Wrong! Wrong! How silly! (*Laughter.*)

2ND MAIDEN: Because it wants to get out.

MICHAL: Wrong! And it's such an easy one.

3RD MAIDEN: Why does a cow look over a wall?

4TH MAIDEN: To scratch its neck. (*Much laughter.*)

3RD MAIDEN: Wrong! Wrong! All wrong! Give it up!

MICHAL: No! No! Let them guess again. Why does a cow look over a wall?

1ST MAIDEN: To see if David's coming to drive her to pasture. (*Wild laughter.*)

MICHAL: That's wrong! That's not the answer!

MERAB: Give it up?

3RD MAIDEN (*laughing wildly*): *To see if David's coming to drive her to pasture!*

MICHAL: That's not the answer, *Stupid!*

1ST MAIDEN: Why not, say I? It's as good as the real answer.—The cows of Jesse will have to look a long time over a wall. (*Much laughter.*) No doubt they're looking at this moment. (*Shrieks of laughter.*) Mooo-oo! Moo-oo! David, come home. (*Hysterical laughter.*)

MICHAL: Fool! Fool! That's not the answer.

1ST MAIDEN: Yes. That's the answer in Bethlehem. Why does a Bethlehem cow look over a wall?—Because David's come to Gilgal. (*Much laughter.*)

MICHAL: That's wrong! That's wrong!

2ND MAIDEN: It's not wrong for a Bethlehem cow.

MICHAL: But it's not a Bethlehem cow. (*Much laughter.*)

1ST MAIDEN: Is it the heifers of Gilgal? (*Wild laughter.*)

4TH MAIDEN: Why do the heifers of King Saul look over the wall in Gilgal?

1ST MAIDEN: Listening to the music. (*Wild laughter.*)

MERAB (*amid her laughter*): If my father hears us!

MICHAL: You are all fools! You don't know the right answer. You can't guess it! You can't guess it.

2ND MAIDEN: Well, what is it then? Only Michal knows what the cow is looking for! (*Laughter.*)

MAIDENS: Go on! Go on! Tell us, Michal!

MICHAL: Because she can't see through it. (*Laughter.*)

1ST MAIDEN: See through what? (*Wild laughter.*)

MAIDENS: See through what? (*All laughing.*)

2ND MAIDEN: Because who can't see through what? (*Shrieks of laughter.*)

1ST MAIDEN: What a senseless answer! *Because she can't see through it!* (*Shrieks of laughter.*)

MICHAL: You are all fools! fools! fools! You know *nothing.* You don't know *anything.*

 Enter SAUL—*angry.*

SAUL: Enough! Enough! What is all this? Is there a madness among the women? Silence, I say!

MICHAL: We are but telling riddles.

SAUL: It shall not be! What! am I to hear the shrieks of my daughters' folly spoiling the morning? I will riddle you a riddle you shall not care for. (MAIDENS *steal away.*)

MERAB: We had thought my father was abroad among the men.

SAUL: You had thought, had you! And your father's being abroad was timely to let loose your ribaldry!

MICHAL: Nay, Father, there was no ribaldry. The maid did only ask, Why does a cow look over a wall?

SAUL (*shouting*): Be still! Or I will run this spear through your body. Am I to wrestle with the Lord and fail because of the wantoning of my daughters among their maidens! Oh! cursed in my offspring as in all things! (MERAB *steals away.*) Cursed above all in my women-folk!

MICHAL: Could we not help you, Father, to strive with the Lord? They say the wise women can command the spirits of the deep.

SAUL: Art thou then a seeress? art thou amongst the witches?

MICHAL: Not so. But Saul my father is among the wondrous. Should not his daughter be as wise as the wise women who can see into the mysteries?

SAUL (*groaning*): This is the sin of witchcraft! The hand of my children is against me!

MICHAL: Nay, Father, we would indeed be for you, and not against you.

SAUL: I have sworn to wipe out the sin of witchcraft from the land, I have sworn the death of all who lure the people with spirits and with wizardry. I have killed the soothsayers in the towns and the villages.

MICHAL: But, Father, might I not see the Bolt in a cloud, or call the Spirits out of the earth! I am your daughter, is that to be a witch?

SAUL: Thou art a spawn of evil, and I will run thee through.

MICHAL: But why! Oh why!

SAUL: Thy soul is a soul of a witch that workest against thy father. I call on the Lord, and my heart foams, because He will not hear me. I know it now. It is thee, thou witch! (*Wanting to strike her with the spear.*)

MICHAL (*weeping*): It is not so! It is not so! The people say of thee, the Lord has departed from thee, and I would only help thee with the Lord, as Jonathan helps thee against the Philistines.

SAUL (*horrified*): Is the Deep a Philistine! Nay, now I know thou art the brood of witches, who catch the powers of the earth by cunning. Now I will surely pierce thee through, that my house may be pure, and the Fire may look on me again.

MICHAL (*screams*): My lord! My lord!

SAUL: I will pierce thee through. For I have sworn the death of all witches, and such as steal the powers of earth and sky by their cunning. It will be as good a deed in the sight of the Lord, as when the prophet of God slew Agag, and Samuel will turn to me again. For I am empty when the Lord abandons me. And evil spirits break into my empty place, and torture me.—I will surely slay this witch, though she were seven times my youngest. For she lifts the latch to the evil spirit that gets into my soul unawares.

MICHAL: My lord! My lord! I am no witch! I am not!

SAUL: Thou art a witch, and thy hand worketh against me, even when thou knowest not. Nay, thou art a witch and

thy soul worketh witchcraft even when thou sleepest.
Therefore I will pierce thee through. And I will say
unto the people: Saul hath slain the witch that gnawed
nearest into his heart.

MICHAL: I will not be slain! (*Shrieks.*)

> *Enter* JONATHAN *and* DAVID, *running.*

JONATHAN: My Father!

DAVID: O King!

SAUL: This is the witch that hinders me with the Lord!

JONATHAN: This, Father! Why, Michal is a child, what
can she know of witchcraft?

SAUL: It is in her will. My soul tells me that women with
their evil intentions are playing against me, with the
Lord. And this is she. She shall die as the others, seer-
esses, died, to cleanse the land before the Lord God.

DAVID: But yet, O King, thy servant has heard it is a hard
thing to be a witch, a work of silent labour and of years.
And this maiden your daughter is not silent, I think, nor
does she seem to waste her young brows in secret
labours.

JONATHAN: That is true enough. She is a feather-brain.

SAUL: Yet is her spirit against her father's.

MICHAL (*still weeping*): No! No! I would help him.

DAVID: If some spirit of evil hinder King Saul with the
Lord of Hosts, it will be more than the whims of a girl.
The spirits that hamper the soul of the King cannot be
children and girls.

SAUL: It may be so. Yet though I wrestle, the spirit of the
Deep will not come to me. And the wound is greater
than a wound in battle, bleeding inwardly. I am a
strange man unto myself.

DAVID: Yet Saul is King, comely in his pride, and a great
leader in battle. His *deeds* cry unto the whirlwind and
are heard. Why should Saul wrestle with the Lord? Saul
speaks in actions, and in the time of action the spirit of
God comes upon him, and he is King in the sight of all
men.

SAUL: It is even so. Yet my soul does not cease to ache,

like the soul of a scorned woman, because the Lord will not descend upon me and give me peace in strength.

DAVID: Who is strong like Saul, in Israel?

SAUL: Yet his strength is as a drunken man's—great with despair.

DAVID: Nay, O King! These are fancies. How can my lord speak of despair, when victory is with him, and the light is on his brow in the sight of all Israel!

SAUL: Can I so deceive myself?

DAVID: Surely the King deceives himself.

JONATHAN: Surely, Father, it is a strange self-deception you put on yourself.

SAUL: Can it be so? Yet if so, why does Samuel visit me no more, and withhold his blessing? And why do I feel the ache in me, and the void, where the Full should be? I cannot get at the Lord.

MICHAL: May I speak, my Father?

SAUL: Yea!

MICHAL: Why not laugh as you used to laugh, Father, and throw the spear in sport, at a mark, not grip it in anger? Saul is beautiful among men, to make women weep for joy if he smile at them. Yet his face is heavy with a frown.

SAUL: Why should I smile at thee, witch?

MICHAL: To gladden me, Father. For I am no witch.

SAUL: And when dost thou need gladdening, say?

MICHAL: Now, Father, even here!

SAUL: Thy sorrows are deep, I warrant me.
Touches her cheek with his fingers.

MICHAL: Yea! Did not this strange young man—indeed he is but a boy—find me chidden and disgraced and in tears before the King?

SAUL: And what then?

MICHAL: Who is this boy from the sheepfolds of Bethlehem, that he should think lightly of the King's daughter in Gilgal?

DAVID: Nay! What man could think lightly of Michal, the

daughter of Saul? Her eyes are like the stars shining through a tree at midnight.

MICHAL: Why through a tree?

SAUL (*laughing suddenly*): Thou bird of the pert whistle! Run! Run, quail! Get thee among the maidens! Thou hast piped long enough before the men.

MICHAL: Even if I run my thoughts run with me.

SAUL: What thoughts, bird of mischief?

MICHAL: That this boy, ruddy with the shepherd's sun, has seen my tears and my disgrace.

DAVID: Surely the tears of Michal are like falling stars in the lonely midnight.

MICHAL: Why, again, in the night?

SAUL (*laughing aloud*): Be gone! Be gone! No more!
    Exit MICHAL.

SAUL: She is a chick of the King's nest! Think not of her, David!

DAVID: But she is pleasant to think of.

SAUL: Even when she mocks thee?

DAVID: Very pleasant.

SAUL: The young men flee from a mocking woman.

DAVID: Not when the voice is sweet.

SAUL: Is Michal's voice sweet? To me at times it is snarling and bad in my ears.

DAVID: That is only when the harp-strings of the King's ears are unstrung.

SAUL: It may be. Yet I think I am cursed in my women-folk. Was not the mother of Jonathan a thorn in my heart? What dost thou prescribe for a thorn in the heart, young wiseling?

DAVID: Pluck it out, O King, and throw it aside, and it is forgotten.

SAUL: But is it easy to pluck out a rancorous woman from the heart?

DAVID: I have no certain knowledge. Yet it should not be hard, I think.

SAUL: How?

DAVID: A man asks in his heart: *Lord, Who fannest the fire of my soul into strength, does the woman cast fuel on the Lord's fire within me, or does she cast wet sand?* Then if the Lord says: *She casts wet sand;* she departs for ever from a man's presence, and a man will go nigh unto her no more, because she seeks to quench the proper fire which is within him.

SAUL: Thou art wiser than if thou hadst been many times wived. Thou art a cocksure stripling.

DAVID: My brothers say of me, I am a cocksure malapert. Yet I do not wish to be! Why am I so, my lord?

SAUL (*laughing*): It must be the Lord made thee so.

DAVID: My brother has struck me in the face, before now, for words in which I saw no harm.

SAUL (*laughing*): Didst see the harm afterwards?

DAVID: Not I. I had a bruised mouth, and that was harm enough. But I thought still the words were wise.

SAUL (*laughing*): Dost think so even yet?

DAVID: Yea, they were wise words. But unwisely spoken.

SAUL (*laughing heartily*): The Lord sends the wisdom, and leaves thee to spend it! You offer a tit-bit to a wolf, and he takes your fingers as well.

DAVID: I shall learn in the King's household.

SAUL: Among the wolves?

DAVID: Nay, the lion is nobler than the wolf.

SAUL: He will not grudge thee thy callow wisdom.—I go to speak with Abner.

DAVID: Can I serve the King in anything?

SAUL: Not now.

    Exit.

DAVID: He has gone in good humour.

JONATHAN: We found him in an evil one.

DAVID: Evil spirits out of the earth possess him, and laughter from a maiden sounds to him as the voice of a hyena sounds to a wounded man stricken in the feet.

JONATHAN: It is so. He rails at his daughter, and at the mother who bore me, till my heart swells with anger. Yet he was not always so. Why is it?

DAVID: He has lost the Lord, he says.

JONATHAN: But how? Have I lost the Lord, too?

DAVID: Nay! You are good.

JONATHAN: I wish I knew how my father had lost the Lord.—You David, the Dawn is with you. It is in your face.—Do you wrestle before the Lord?

DAVID: Who am I, that I should wrestle before the Lord? But when I feel the Glory is with me, my heart leaps like a young kid, and bounds in my bosom, and my limbs swell like boughs that put forth buds.—Yet I would not be vainglorious.

JONATHAN: Do you dwell willingly here in Gilgal?

DAVID: I am strange here, and I miss my father, and the hills where the sheep are, in Bethlehem. Yet I comfort myself, turning my soul to the Nameless; and the flame flares up in my heart, and dries my tears, and I am glad.

JONATHAN: And when my father has been bitter and violent, and you go alone in tears, in a strange place—I have seen the tears, and my heart has been sad—then do you yearn for Bethlehem, and your own?

DAVID: I am weak still.—But when I see the stars, and the Lord in darkness alive between them, I am at home, and Bethlehem or Gilgal is the same to me.

JONATHAN: When I lie alone in camp, and see the stars, I think of my mother, and my father, and Michal, and the home place.—You, the Lord becomes a home to you, wherever you are.

DAVID: It is so. I had not thought of it.

JONATHAN: I fear you would never love man nor woman, nor wife nor child, dearly.

DAVID: Nay! I love my father dearly, and my brothers and my mother.

JONATHAN: But when the Lord enters your soul, father or mother or friend is as nothing to you.

DAVID: Why do you say so?—They are the same. But when the Lord is there, all the branches are hidden in blossom.

JONATHAN: Yea!—I, alas, love man or woman with the heart's tenderness, and even the Lord cannot make me forget.

DAVID: But nor do I forget.—It is as if all caught fire at once, in the flame of the Hope.

JONATHAN: Sometimes I think the Lord takes from me the flame I have. I love my father. And my father lifts the short spear at me, in wild anger, because, he says, the Fire has left him, and I am undutiful.

DAVID: The King is the Lord's anointed. The King has known, as none know, the strong gladness of the Lord's presence in his limbs. And then the pain of wanting the Lord, when He cometh not, passes the pain of a woman moaning for the man she loves, who has abandoned her.

JONATHAN: Yet we love the King. The people look up to him. Abner, the chief captain, is faithful to him unto death. Is this nothing to a man?

DAVID: To a man, it is much. To the Lord's anointed, it is much riches. But to the King whom the Lord hath rejected, even love is a hurt.

JONATHAN: Is my father truly rejected from being King, as Samuel said? And merely that he spared Agag and a few Amalekite cattle? I would not willingly have drawn the sword on naked Agag.

DAVID: Who knows? I know not.—When a people choose a King, then the will of the people is as God to the King. But when the Lord of All chooses a King, then the King must answer to the Lord of All.

JONATHAN: And the Lord of All required the death of defenceless Agag?

DAVID: Amalek has set his will against the Whirlwind. There are two motions in the world. The will of man for himself, and the desire that moves the Whirlwind. When the two are one, all is well, but when the will of man is against the Whirlwind, all is ill, at last. So all is decreed ill, that is Amalek. And Amalek must die, for he obstructs the desire of the breathing God.

JONATHAN: And my father?

DAVID: He is King, and the Lord's anointed.

JONATHAN: But his will is the will of a man, and he cannot bend it with the Lord's desire?

DAVID: It seems he cannot. Yet I know nothing.

JONATHAN: It grieves me for my father. Why is it you can soothe him? Why cannot I?

DAVID: I know not. It is the Lord.

JONATHAN: And why do I love thee?

DAVID: It is the Lord.

JONATHAN: But do you love me again, David?

DAVID: If a man from the sheep dare love the King's son, then I love Jonathan. But hold it not against me for presumption.

JONATHAN: Of a surety, lovest thou me, David?

DAVID: As the Lord liveth.

JONATHAN: And it shall be well between us, for ever?

DAVID: Thou art the King's son. But as the Lord liveth and keepeth us, it shall be well between me and thee. And I will serve thee.

JONATHAN: Nay, but love my soul.

DAVID: Thy soul is dear to my soul, dear as life.

They embrace silently.

JONATHAN: And if my father sends thee away, never forget me.

DAVID: Not while my heart lives, can I forget thee.—But David will easily pass from the mind of the son of the King.

JONATHAN: Ah never! For my heart is sorrowful, with my father, and thou art my comfort. I would thou wert King's son, and I shepherd in Bethlehem.

DAVID: Say not so, lest thine anger rise on me at last, to destroy me.

JONATHAN: Nay, it will not.

Curtain

SCENE VI: *Yard of* SAUL's *house in Gilgal.* MICHAL *with tambourine, singing or talking to herself.*

MICHAL: As for me, I am sad, I am sad, I am sad, and why should I not be sad? All things together want to make me sad. I hate the house when the men are gone to war. All the men are gone out against the Philistine. Gone these many days. And never a victory. No one coming home with spoil, and no occasion to dance. I am sad, I am sad, my life is useless to me. Even when they come, they will not bring David. My father looked pleasantly on him for a while, then sent him away. So are men! Such is a king! Sent him away again! And I know, some day when the Lord has left Saul, he will marry me to some old sheik.—Unless he dies in the war. Anyhow, everybody is gone, and I am dull, dull. They say it is the Lord. But why should the Lord make the house of Saul dreary? As for me, I don't know whether the Lord is with me, or whether He is not with me. How should I know? Why should I care! A woman looks with different eyes into her heart, and, Lord or no Lord, I want what I want. I wish I had a sure charm to call back David, son of Jesse. The spells I have tried were no good. I shall try again with the sand and the bones. (*She puts a little sand, and three small white bones, in her tambourine—mutters and bends—tosses her tambourine softly and drops it on the ground. Kneels and gazes intently.*) Bones, bones, show me the ways in the sand. Sand, lie still, sand lie still and speak. Now then, I see the hills of Judah, where Bethlehem is. But David is not there, he is gone. At least I don't see him. In the sand is a road to Gilgal, by the white crown-bone. But he is not coming this way, that I can see. Where else? Where else? This must be Elah in the sand, where my father is. And there is Shochoh, opposite, where the Philistines are. Ah yes, two hills, and a valley between, with a brook in the bottom. And my father with our men on one slope, the Philistines on the other. Ah yes, that will be my father among our men; at least that is his black tent. But Jonathan is not there. O woe, if Jonathan were killed! My heart is afraid for Jonathan. Though how should I know Jonathan as a speck of sand, anyhow? There is nothing in the sand. I am no wise woman, nor a seeress, even though I would like to be. How dull it is! How dull it is here! How dull it is to be a woman! (*Throws away her tambourine.*) Why do they sit in front of the Philistines without defeating them!

WATCHMAN (*entering from the gate*): Men are coming, from the host of Saul. They come with a litter.

SOLDIER (*entering*): The Lord strengthen you.

MICHAL: Who comes? Is it news of victory?

SOLDIER: No, lady! Jonathan is wounded in the knee, and comes home to rest.

MICHAL: Wounded in the knee? And what else?

SOLDIER: How, else?

MICHAL: Oh, slow-witted! What other news? Are the Philistines defeated and slaughtered?

SOLDIER: Nay, they are not.

MICHAL: Then what has happened?

SOLDIER: Naught has happened.

MICHAL: Where is the King? Is all well with him?

SOLDIER: The King is with the host at Elah, and all is well with him.

MICHAL: Then where are the Philistines?

SOLDIER: The Philistines are arranged over against us, on the opposite hill at Shochoh.

MICHAL: And what has happened? Do Israel and the Philistines sing songs to one another?

SOLDIER: Nay! A portion of the men go forth to fight, well-nigh each day. And the champion of the Philistines comes each day to challenge us.

MICHAL: And who answers out of Israel?

SOLDIER: None answers

MICHAL: None answers! Yea, that is news to hear! Has Israel never a champion? Is my father, the King, sick?

SOLDIER: Many champions have we, forsooth. But we are men. And this Philistine is huge: he is out of the old days, before the Flood. He is a huge giant, whose great voice alone shakes the tents.

MICHAL: And not one man answers his challenge?

SOLDIER: Nay, where shall we find a huge giant among us, to answer him?

MICHAL: If he were a mountain, I would prick him with my needle.

SOLDIER: Yes; and would you might prick the eyeballs of him!

Enter litter-bearers with JONATHAN.

MICHAL: This is most strange!—Ah, Jonathan, and art thou wounded in the knee?

JONATHAN: Yea!

MICHAL: The Lord be praised it is not in the calf!

JONATHAN: Hush, shrew!

MICHAL: Did the Philistine giant wound thee in the knee, O Jonathan?

JONATHAN: A Philistine wounded me.

MICHAL: But I hear they boast a giant, a champion.

JONATHAN: Yea, verily.

MICHAL: A huge unheard-of giant.

JONATHAN: Huge enough: and heard daily.

MICHAL: What does he say, daily?

JONATHAN: Oh—he asks that we send down a man to fight with him. And if he, the Philistine of Gath, slay our man, then shall all Israel be servant to the Philistines. But if our man slay this Goliath, then the Philistines shall be our servants. And seeing that this giant be so large, no ordinary man can get past his sword to attack him, therefore the King is not willing that the fight be settled between champions, lest we lose our freedom in a moment.

MICHAL: And dare no man go up against this huge one?

JONATHAN: Nay, many dare. And many a man seeks to go.

I myself would willingly go. Though I know I should die. But what would I care about dying, if the Philistine died first? Yet I doubt *I* should die first, and Israel be delivered into bondage. Hence the King will accept no champion from our midst. But we shall sally forth in daily companies, and defeat the Philistines at length.

MICHAL: At great length.

JONATHAN: Hast thou wounds or pain, to find it so?

MICHAL: Yea, the wound of shame, that Israel, challenged, is dumb. Israel has no champion! What wound of shame for the woman!

JONATHAN: Why risk the nation in a fight between champions? We are all champions, and we all fight the Philistine.

MICHAL: Only not this big one.

JONATHAN: In single combat, with the fate of the nation hanging in the issue, no! But if Goliath mingle in the battle ranks, then every man of Benjamin will have at him.

MICHAL: And mingles he not in the battle ranks?

JONATHAN: Ah no! He saves himself for the single combat, for this bawling of the challenge and the rattling of the oversized shield.

MICHAL: Some man should think of a way.

JONATHAN: Think thou! I must rest, and recover, and return to the field of battle.

Curtain

SCENE VII: *The camp of the Israelites at Elah. In the background, black tents of worsted. Morning. Men assembling in arms, to battle. Much shouting of war-cries—much noise of war-like anticipation.* DAVID *entering, carrying a staff.*

DAVID: Is yon the tent of Eliab of Bethlehem?

SOLDIER: The tent of the sons of Jesse.

SHAMMAH (*coming armed from the tent*): Is not this our brother David? (*Calling.*) Ho! David is here! (*Embracing* DAVID.) And art thou also come to the fight?

ELIAB (*also armed*): What, David! Hast thou left the sheep to come among the men-at-arms?

They embrace.

DAVID: My father sent me here to inquire of you, and to bring you bread, and the cheeses for the captain of your thousand. The loaves and the parched corn and the cheeses have I left with the keeper of the victuals. But where is Abinadab?

ELIAB: With the host, where we must form to battle.

(*The men are forming in loose array,* ABINADAB *comes and embraces* DAVID.)

ABINADAB: Hast thou come from Bethlehem? And how is our father, and all the homestead?

DAVID: Yea, all are well. My father sent me with victual, and to see how you fare, and to take your pledge.

ELIAB: The pledge we will give you after the fight. And how fares my young son at home?

CAPTAIN (*calling*): The thousand of Judah, get you to your hundreds: get you to your places. (*Bustle of men falling into rank.*)

DAVID (*following his brothers*): Your son was bitten by a hound, but all is well.

ELIAB: What hound, forsooth? And lives the dog yet?

SAUL (*passing*): Five hundred of Benjamin, lead into the valley!

SOLDIERS: Ah! Ah! The five hundred are moving forth!

Loud shouting of SOLDIERS.

DAVID: And how goes the fight?

SHAMMAH: Wellah, this way and that, as wind bloweth!

DAVID: The days are many, that you are afield. My father grew uneasy, and could stay no longer. Long days and no news are ill to live, said he.

ELIAB: Tell my father, this is no folding of sheep, out here.

DAVID: And has no weighty blow been struck, on either side?

SOLDIERS (*calling*): Ha! Ha! The five hundred are near the brook! And behold, the Philistine champion cometh forth from the ranks, to meet them.

Hush in the camp.

MIGHTY VOICE OF GOLIATH: Ho! Ho, there! Israel! Why are ye come to set your battle array? Am I not a Philistine, and ye servants to Saul? Choose you a man for you, and let him come down to me.

DAVID (*in the hush*): But who is this?

SOLDIERS: Ha! Ha! The five hundred are fleeing back from him! They are sore afraid.

A hush.

SHAMMAH: This is Goliath, their champion.

VOICE OF GOLIATH: Ha! ha! Why run ye? Choose you a man for you, and let him come down to me. If he can fight with me, and kill me, then will we be your servants. But if I prevail against him, and kill him, then shall ye be our servants, and serve us. It is fairly said. Choose you a man for you!

DAVID (*in the hush*): Surely he is a huge man! Goeth no man forth to meet him?

SOLDIER: Have you seen this man! Surely, forty days has he come up to defy Israel. And it shall be, that the man who killeth him, the King will enrich him with great riches, and will give him his daughter, and make his father's house free in Israel.

DAVID: What will the King do to the man that killeth this Philistine and taketh away the reproach from Israel? Will he surely give him his daughter? The daughter of his house in Gilgal?

SOLDIER: Ay, surely he will. And much riches. And make his father's house free in Israel.

DAVID: Who is this uncircumcised Philistine, that he should defy the armies of the living God?

SOLDIERS: Ah! He is what thou seest.

DAVID: As the Lord liveth, there shall be an end to him.

SOLDIERS: Would that it were so! But who shall do it?

DAVID: Is the Lord naught in the reckoning? The Lord is with me, and I will do it.

SOLDIERS: Thou? How canst thou kill this great giant?

DAVID: I can do it. I will kill him, as the Lord liveth in me, were his name six times Goliath.

SOLDIER: Nay, but how?

DAVID: The Lord will show you how. I, I will kill him.

ELIAB (coming forward): What art thou doing here? Why camest thou hither, and with whom hast thou left those few sheep in the wilderness? I know thy pride, and the naughtiness of thy heart. For thou art come down that thou mightest see the battle.

DAVID: What have I now done? Was I not sent by my father, for a cause?

ELIAB (turning away in anger): Thou didst persuade him, in the vanity of thy mind.

SOLDIER: Shall we say to Saul of thee, that thou art minded to kill the giant?

DAVID: Say so to him. For the Lord is with me.

ANOTHER SOLDIER: Verily, feelest thou in the power to kill this mighty man?

DAVID: Verily! And is it sooth the King will give his daughter to him that slayeth the roaring Philistine?

SOLDIER: Yea, it is sooth, for it is so proclaimed. But tell us how thou wilt come nigh him, to slay him.

DAVID: The Lord will show you.

SOLDIERS: Saul is coming.

SAUL (approaching): Which is this man will go forth against the Philistine?

DAVID: Let no man's heart fail because of the giant, for thy servant will go out and fight with him.

SAUL: Thou? Thou art not able to go against this Philistine to fight with him, for thou art but a youth, and he is a man of war from his youth.

DAVID: Thy servant slew both the lion and the bear; and

this uncircumcised Philistine shall be as one of them, seeing he hath defied the armies of the living God.

SAUL: But neither lion nor bear came against thee in greaves of brass nor armed with sword a man's length. How shallst thou fight with this giant in panoply?

DAVID: The Lord that delivered me out of the paw of the lion, and out of the paw of the bear, He will deliver me out of the hand of the Philistine.

SAUL: Thou shalt go. And the Lord be with thee. (*To* ARMOUR-BEARER.) Fetch hither my armour, and another sword. For we will put them on him.

    Exit ARMOUR-BEARER.

DAVID: Shall thy servant go in armour clad?

SAUL: How else canst thou keep thy life?

VOICE OF GOLIATH: Ho! men of Saul! Is there no man among you, to answer when a fighter calls? Are you all maidens, combing your hair? Where is Saul, the slayer of foemen? Is he crying like a quail to his God? Call to Baal, and call to Astaroth, for the God of Israel is a pigeon in a box.

DAVID: Ha! Lord God! Deliver him into my hand this day!

SAUL: Yea! (*Enter* ARMOUR-BEARER.) Put the coat of proof upon him, and the helmet of brass.

    They put the armour of the KING *on* DAVID.

DAVID: I am not used to it.

SAUL (*unbuckling his sword*): Take thou my sword.

DAVID (*girding it on*): Thy servant hath honour beyond his lot. Lo! I am strange in this array! The Lord hath not intended it for me.

    Takes shield.

SAUL: Now thou art ready. A man shall bear thy shield.

DAVID: Then let me go. But let me assay this sword and battle harness that is on me. (*Sets forth. Tries his sword; goes a little way. Turns suddenly back.*) I cannot go with these, for I have not proved them.

    Drops his shield. Hastily unbuckles sword, and gives it to SAUL. *Unfastens the helmet. The* ARMOUR-BEARER *disarms* DAVID.

SAUL: Then thou goest not! Uncovered thou canst not go.

DAVID: As the Lord liveth, I will go with naught but God upon me.

VOICE OF GOLIATH: The God of Israel is a blue pigeon in a box, and the men of Israel are quails in the net of the Philistine. Baal is laughing aloud, and Astarte smiles behind her sleeve, for Israel is no more than worms in a dung-hill.

DAVID: I shall go. Sound the trumpet!

He picks up his staff, recrosses hastily to the back of the stage, downwards as to a valley. Stoops in the distance: meanwhile trumpet sounds, and the voice of the HERALD *is heard, crying.*

HERALD: Come down, Goliath! Come forward, Philistine! For Israel sendeth a champion against thee.

Noise of shouting in both camps.

SHAMMAH: See, David is picking smooth stones from the brook bed.

ABINADAB: He has put them in his leather pouch, and taken his sling in his hand. Surely he will go after the Philistine as after a wolf.

SAUL: The Philistine cometh down, with his shield-bearer before him.—Yea, but the youth is naked and unafraid.

VOICE OF GOLIATH: Where art thou, champion of Israel? I see thee not. Hast thou already perished, of thy dread?

VOICE OF DAVID (*small*): Yea, I am coming.

VOICE OF GOLIATH: Thou!

SAUL: How he disdains the youth! If we have lost all on this throw!

VOICE OF GOLIATH: Am I a dog, that thou comest to me with staves? Now shall Astaroth slay thee with spittle, and Baal shall break thy bones with a loud laugh.

VOICE OF DAVID: Thou comest to me with a sword, and with a spear, and with a shield: but I come to thee in the name of the Lord of Hosts, the God of the armies of Israel, Whom thou hast defied.

VOICE OF GOLIATH: Come! Ha-ha! Come to me, and I will

give thy flesh to the fowls of the air, and to the wild beasts of the hills.

Meanwhile the bystanders, SHAMMAH, ABINADAB, SOLDIERS, *all save the* ARMOUR-BEARER *and* SAUL, *have been running to the far background, to look closer.*

VOICE OF DAVID: This day will the Lord deliver thee into my hand; and I will smite thee, and take thy head from thee.

VOICE OF GOLIATH: Ha! Ha! Canst thou chirp? Come over, thou egg, that they see me swallow thee.

Loud yelling from Philistines.

VOICE OF DAVID: I will give the carcass of the host of the Philistines this day to the fowls of the air, and to the beasts of the earth. That all the earth may know there is a God in Israel.

Loud yelling of Israel.

VOICE OF GOLIATH: Come, thou whistling bird! Come! Seest thou this sword?

Loud yelling of Philistines.

VOICE OF DAVID: Yea! and all this people shall know that the Lord saveth not with sword and spear: for the battle is the Lord's, and He will deliver you into our hands.

Great defiance heard in Israel.

VOICE OF GOLIATH: Must we die of thy talking? And wilt thou not come forth? Then must I fetch thee. . . .

Tumult in Philistia.

ARMOUR-BEARER: The Philistine is hastening down!—Oh, and behold, the youth is running at him fast! Ha-a-a!

ARMOUR-BEARER *rushes away, leaving* SAUL *alone.*

SAUL (*in a pause*): Ah! Ah!—Lord, my Lord!—Is he down? (*Great shouting heard—men running.*) What? Yea, the Philistine has fallen! The boy but slang a stone at him! It is the Lord! Nay, he riseth not!—Ah God! was it so easy a thing? Why had I not done it! See, see, Saul, see, thou King of Israel, see this nameless boy who hath run upon the fallen Philistine, and seized his sword

from his hand, and stands upon his body hewing at the
neck of the giant! Ah, sight for the King of Israel, who
stands alone, in safety, far off, and watches this thing
done for him! Yea, they may shout! It is not for me. It
is for that boy, whom I know not. How should I know
him, with his young beard on his lip! It is a hard thing
to hack off the head of such a giant, and he cannot find
the neck joint. I see him stooping! (*A great wild shout
is heard.*) Ah! Even so! Even so!

ABNER (*entering running*): The youth hath slain the Philistine with a stone from a sling, and even now has hewn
his head loose, and is holding it up before the armies.

SAUL: Even so!

ABNER: Yea! He stands upon the body of that which was
Goliath, and holds up the head to Israel! The Lord has
prevailed.

    Loud shouting.

SOLDIERS (*running past*): The host of the Philistines is in
flight! After them! After them!

ABNER: Shall we not pursue? Will not the King lead the
pursuit? Lo! they flee in abandon, flinging away their
spears in their haste.

SAUL: This needs no leader. Any man can strike in the
back of a running enemy. What of the youth?

ABNER: He hath stripped the Philistine of his gear. Yea,
I can see the body of the giant naked in blood upon the
ground.

SAUL: Who is this youth? Whose son is he?

ABNER: As thy soul liveth, O King, I cannot tell.

SAUL: Enquire thou whose son the stripling is.

ABNER: He is coming towards the brook. I will bring him
hither.

    Exit.

SAUL: Yea, he is coming! And alone up the slope, for the
men have gone like hounds after the Philistine, and to
the stripping of the tents. Yea, as bees swarm in upon
the sweetmeats, when the window is opened. This is a
day to make songs for. But not in the name of Saul.

Whom will the maidens sing to? To him yonder, coming up the hill slowly, with the swinging head, and the bright brass armour of the Philistine. To that ruddy-faced fair youth, with a young beard on his mouth. It seems I should know him, if I would. Yea, I shall know him in my hour. Ah the blithe thing! Ah the blithe boy! Ah God! God! was I not blithe? Where is it gone? Yea, where! Blitheness in a man is the Lord in his body. Nay, boy, boy! I would not envy thee the head of the Philistine. Nay, I would not envy thee the Kingdom itself. But the blitheness of thy body, that is thy Lord in thee, I envy it thee with a sore envy. For once my body too was blithe. But it hath left me. It hath left me. Not because I am old. And were I ancient as Samuel is, I could still have the alertness of God in me, and the blithe bearing of the living God upon me. I have lost the best. I had it, and have let it go. Ha! whither is he going? He turns aside, among the tents. Aha! Aha! So it is. Among the tents of Judah, and to the booth of the Bethlehemite! So, he has gone in to lay down his spoil, the helmet of brass, and the greaves of brass, the coat, the great sword, and the shirt fringed with scarlet. Lay them by, they are thine. Yea, they are thine, lay them in thy tent. No need to bring them unto the King. They are no king's spoil. Yea, lead him hither, Abner! Lead him hither! He is bringing the head in his hand. Oh yes, the champion, the victor! He is bringing the head in his hand, to swing it under the nose of the King. But the sword, the great sword, and the greaves of brass and the body-spoil he has e'en laid by in his own tent, where no man may lay a hand on it. Oh! it is a shrewd youth, and a canny youth, cunning as the Lord makes them.

Enter DAVID, *with head of* GOLIATH—*and* ABNER.

SAUL: So! Comest thou again?

DAVID: Even so! To lay the head of thine enemy before thee, O King!

SAUL: Whose son art thou, thou young man?

DAVID: I am the son of thy servant Jesse the Bethlehemite.

SAUL: Art thou so! Ay, thou art David! And brother to Eliab, and Abinadab, and Shammah, three men of war! —Thou hast put cunning in thy skill, and slain thine enemy as he were a hare among the bushes.

ABNER: See! The place where the stone sunk in, in the side of the forehead bone! It lies still there, the stone of David.

SAUL: Yea, that was death without weapons meeting, indeed.

ABNER: Surely the Lord was in that round stone, that digged the pit in Goliath's head-bone!

DAVID: Except the Lord had been with me, I had not done it.

SOLDIERS (*standing round*): Yea, the Lord sped the hand of David. The Lord is with this young man.

SAUL: Praise we must give to the Lord, and to David the promised reward. Seekest thou thy reward at the King's hand, thou young man?

DAVID: It is as the King willeth. Yet what should the reward be?

SAUL: Hast thou not heard it proclaimed?

DAVID: Nay, I arrived but in the dawn, with provender from my father to my brethren.

SAUL: Didst thou not set forth even now against the Philistine, hoping big for the reward?

DAVID: Not so, O King. But the Lord moved me to go, to take off the shame and the reproach from the army of the living God.

SAUL: Thou hast done well! Yet claimest thou thy reward?

DAVID: Shall I not hear from the King's mouth, what the reward should be?

SAUL: How was it said, Abner? Recallest thou?

ABNER: Yea, O King! Riches and the King's daughter, and freedom for his father's house, to the man that should slay Goliath in the single combat.

SAUL: Single-handed hath David slain Goliath, indeed! Even without any combat at all. But how likest thou thy reward, thou young man?

DAVID: Were it mine, O King, I should rejoice for my father's sake, and fall to the ground beneath the honour put upon me, being son-in-law to the King.

SAUL: Even so! Now thou shalt stay with me, and live in my house, and return no more to thy father's house. And all shall be done to thee, as was said.—For surely thou hast brought much honour upon Israel. And we will make much of thee. For thou art champion of Israel in the sight of all the people. And thou shalt sit at the King's right hand, that all men may delight in thee. Yet, since thou art young, and fresh from the sheepfold, we will not hasten thee to thy confusion. But thou shalt dwell as a son among us, and rise in degree as a son rises, sitting at the King's meat. And behold, my elder daughter Merab, her will I give thee to wife. Only be thou valiant for me, and fight the Lord's battles.

DAVID: Let but thy servant serve thee, O King, in the sight of the Lord. And Saul will take the head of this Philistine, to put it on a pole?

SAUL: Nay! Thou thyself shalt bring it before the people, in Jerusalem of Judah.

Curtain

SCENE VIII: *The* KING's *tent at Elah: a square tent of dark worsted, with the wide front open. Heaps of panoply and spoil without. Within, in the public part of the tent,* SAUL, *with* DAVID *on his right hand,* JONATHAN *on his left, and sitting around, the* CAPTAINS *of the armies of Israel.*

SAUL: We have numbered the armies in tens, in hundreds, and in thousands. And now are all men returned from pursuing after the Philistine, and the spoil is all brought in. And the wounded of the Philistine have fallen by the way, even to the valley of Ekron and the gates of Gath, their dead are more than their living. Yet are their princes within the land, holding on to strong places. Therefore we will rejoice not yet, nor go home to the feasting. But while his heart is sunk low, we will follow up the Philistine in every place where he holds out. Is it sooth?

CAPTAIN: It is good, O King.

ABNER: The blow that was struck with a pebble, we will follow up with swords and spears, till in the Lord's name not one uncircumcised remains in the land.

CAPTAIN: It is good! It is good!

They strike their shields.

SAUL (*presenting* DAVID): This is David, that slew Goliath the Philistine, and delivered Israel from reproach. Sits not David high in the heart of every man in Israel, this day?

CAPTAINS: Yea! David! David!

Striking shields.

SAUL: Who is first among the men of war this day? Is it not David, my son David?

CAPTAINS: David! David! It is David!

SAUL: Yea, Captains! Your King is but captain of the captains! Whom shall we set over the men of war this day? Shall it not be David? This time, shall not David lead the hosts? Is he not the first against the Philistine? Yea, in this foray of triumph and this campaign of victory, should any man lead but David?

CAPTAINS: It is good! David shall command, till we return home this time from smiting the Philistine.

They clash shields with martial noise.

SAUL (*to* DAVID): Hearest thou, David, son of my delight?

DAVID: O King, I am no leader of men of war. I have no skill in arts of battle. Honour me not to my confusion.

SAUL: Nay, this time shalt thou take the charge. For in *this* fight art thou the first man among the men of war in Israel. Answer, Captains! Is it not so?

CAPTAINS: Verily! This time we will have David.

ABNER: Verily, save David lead us, we will not go.

> *The* CAPTAINS *rise, and lift locked shields before* DAVID *as if to raise him up.*

SAUL: If we go not now, we lose the golden hour. The choice is upon thee, David.

DAVID: Thy servant will do according to thy will, O King, and according to the will of Abner, and of the Captains. (*He rises before the* CAPTAINS.) But I am young, and not brought up to war. And the Captains and the strong men will laugh at me, seeing my inexperience and my presumption.

ABNER: Nay! No man shall find occasion to laugh at thee, for the fight is in thee as in a young eagle. Leading to war shalt thou learn war.

DAVID: It is as the King and the Captains shall bid me.

SAUL (*rising*): We will make ready, and send out the news through the camp: *In this is David our leader!* Then David shall choose his men, and go forth. He shall give his orders, and the Captains shall march at his bidding. David, the day is thine!

> *Salutes. The* CAPTAINS *again salute* DAVID *with spear on shield, then they go out.*

CAPTAINS: To thee, David!

> *Exeunt.*

DAVID (*to* JONATHAN): How shall I bring this to a pass?

JONATHAN: Thy soul will not fail thee. Thou art the young lion of Judah, thou art the young eagle of the Lord. O David, is it well between me and thee, and hast thou verily not forgotten me?

DAVID: Verily, thou hast not left my soul. But how shall I go before these men?

JONATHAN: We have sworn a covenant, is it not between us? Wilt thou not swear with me, that our souls shall be as brothers, closer even than blood? O David, my heart hath no peace save all be well between thy soul and mine, and thy blood and mine.

DAVID: As the Lord liveth, the soul of Jonathan is dearer to me than a brother's.—O brother, if I were but come out of this pass, and we might live before the Lord, together!

JONATHAN: What fearest thou then?

DAVID: In the Lord, I fear nothing. But before the faces of men, my heart misgives me.

JONATHAN: Sittest thou not high in the hearts of Israel?

DAVID: Yea, but who am I, to be suddenly lifted up! Will they not throw me as suddenly down?

JONATHAN: Who would throw thee down, that art strong as a young eagle, and subtle as the leopard?

DAVID: I will rest in the Lord.

JONATHAN: And in me wilt thou not trust?

DAVID: I will trust thee, Jonathan, and cleave to thee till the sun sets on me. Thou art good to me as man never before was good to me, and I have not deserved it. Say thou wilt not repent of thy kindness towards me!

JONATHAN: O brother, give me the oath, that naught shall sunder our souls, for ever.

DAVID: As the Lord liveth, my soul shall not part for ever from the soul of my brother Jonathan; but shall go with him up the steeps of heaven, or down the sides of the pit. And between his house and my house the covenant shall be everlasting. For as the hearts of men are made on earth, the heart of Jonathan is gentlest and most great.

JONATHAN: The covenant is between us.

Covers his face.

DAVID (*after a pause*): But how shall I go before these captains, O my brother? Comest thou not with me? Wilt thou not stand by me? Oh, come!

JONATHAN: I am limping still in the knee, and how shall I lead a foray? But thou art mine and I am thine. And I will clothe thee in my clothes, and give thee my sword and my bow, and so shall my spirit be added to thy spirit, and thou shalt be as the King's son and the eagle of the Lord, in the eyes of the people.

Takes off striped coat, or wide-sleeved tunic.

DAVID: But can I do this thing?

JONATHAN: Yea! That all men know thou art as the King's son in the world. For the eagle hath gold in his feathers and the young lion is bright. So shall David be seen in Israel.

> DAVID *slowly pulls off his loose robe, a herdsman's tunic cut off at the knee.* JONATHAN *takes off his sleeveless shirt, and is seen in his leather loin-strap. From his upper arm he takes a metal bracelet.*

JONATHAN: Even all my garments thou shalt take, even the armlet that should not leave me till I die. And thou shalt wear it for ever. And thy garments will I take upon me, so the honour shall be mine.

> DAVID *pulls off his shirt, and is seen in the leather loin-strap,* JONATHAN *puts his bracelet on* DAVID'S *arm, then his own shirt over* DAVID'S *head, and holds up his coloured robe.* DAVID *robed,* JONATHAN *brings him a coloured head-kerchief and girdle, then his sword and his bow and quiver and shoes.* JONATHAN *puts on* DAVID'S *clothes.*

DAVID: How do I appear?

JONATHAN: Even as the eagle in his own plumage. It is said, David, that thou art anointed of Samuel, before the Lord. Is it so?

DAVID: Yea.

JONATHAN: Thou hast the sun within thee, who shall deny thee?

DAVID: Why speakest thou sadly, Jonathan, brother?

JONATHAN: Lest thou go beyond me, and be lost to me.

DAVID: Lord! Lord! Let not my soul part from the soul of Jonathan for ever, for all that man can be to man on earth, is he to me.

JONATHAN: Would I could give thee more!

SAUL (*entering*): Yea! And which now is the King's son, and which the shepherd?

DAVID: Thy son would have it so, O King.

JONATHAN: It is well, Father! Shall not the leader shine forth?

SAUL: Even so. And the young King-bird shall moult his feathers in the same hour.

JONATHAN: The robe of David honours the shoulders of Jonathan.

SAUL: Art thou ready, thou brave young man?

DAVID: I am ready, O King.

SAUL: The host is in array, awaiting thy coming.

DAVID: I will come where the King leads me.

SAUL (*to* JONATHAN): Put another robe upon thee, ere thou come forth.

JONATHAN: I will not come forth. (*Turns abruptly.*)

> DAVID *follows* SAUL *from the tent—loud shouting of the army.*

JONATHAN (*alone*): If the Lord hath anointed him for the kingdom, Jonathan will not quarrel with the Lord. My father knoweth. Yet Saul will strain against God. The Lord hath not revealed Himself unto me: save that once I saw the glisten in my father that now I see in David. My life belongs to my father, but my soul is David's. I cannot help it. The Lord sees fit to split me between King and King-to-be, and already I am torn asunder as between two wild horses straining opposite ways. Yet my blood is my father's. And my soul is David's. And the right hand and the left hand are strangers on me.

Curtain

SCENE IX: *Outside the courtyard of* SAUL's *house in Gilgal. Doorway of courtyard seen open.* MAIDENS *running forth with instruments of music. Men-servants gazing into the distance. People waiting.*

MAIDENS: Lu-lu-a-li-lu-lu-lu! Lu-lu-lu-li-a-li-lu-lu! A-li-lu-lu-lu-a-li-lu! Lu-al-li-lu! Lu-al-li-lu-a!

MERAB: Out of Judah Saul comes in.

MICHAL: David slew the Philistine.

MERAB AND HER MAIDENS: Out of Judah Saul comes in!

MICHAL AND HER MAIDENS: David slew the Philistine.

ALL (*repeat several times*): A-li-lu-lu! A-li-lu-lu-lu! Lu! lu! lu! lu! li! lu! lu! a! li! lu! lu! lu! lu!

MERAB: All the Philistine has fled.

MICHAL: By the roadside fell their dead.

MERAB: Wounded fell down in the path.

MICHAL: Beyond Ekron unto Gath.

MERAB AND MAIDENS: All the Philistine has fled.

MICHAL AND MAIDENS: By the roadside fell their dead.

MERAB AND MAIDENS: Wounded fell down in the path.

MICHAL AND MAIDENS: Beyond Ekron unto Gath.

ALL (*repeat continuously*): Lu-li-lu-lu-lu! Lu-lu-li-a-lu-lu! Li-a-li-lu-lu-lu? Lu! Lu! Lu! A! li! Lu! Lu! Lu! Lu! Li! A! Lu! Lu! Li! Lu! A! Li! Lu! Lu! Lu! Lu! u!

MERAB: Saul in thousands slew their men!

MICHAL: David slew his thousands ten!

MERAB AND MAIDENS: Saul in thousands slew their men!

MICHAL AND MAIDENS: David slew his thousands ten! Oh! Lu! Lu! Lu! Lu! Lu! Lu! A! Li! Lu! Lu! Lu!

ALL: Lu! Lu! Lu! Li! Lu! Lu! Lu!—A-li-lu-lu-a-li-lu-lu! Lu-a-li-lu-lu-lu! Lu-lu-lu!

MERAB: Out of Judah Saul comes in.

MICHAL: David slew the Philistine.

MERAB AND MAIDENS: Out of Judah Saul comes in.

MICHAL AND MAIDENS: David slew the Philistine.

ALL: Lu-li-lu-lu-lu-li-lu! Lu-lu-a-li-lu-lu-lu!

> *They continue the repetition of the simple rhymes, as* SAUL *draws near, followed by* DAVID, JONATHAN, ABNER *and the armed men. The* MAIDENS *keep up the singing, all the time dancing;* MERAB *with her* MAIDENS *on one side of the men,* MICHAL *and her* MAIDENS *on the other, singing loudly back and forth all the time. The men pass slowly into the gate, without response. The* MAIDENS *run peering at the*

spoil the servant-men are carrying in. All pass in at the gate.

Curtain

SCENE X: *Courtyard of* SAUL's *house in Gilgal. Confusion of people and men just come in—*MAIDENS *still singing outside.*

ABNER: The King is returned to his own house once more full of victory. When shall we slay the sacrifice?

SAUL: To-night I will slay a bull calf for my house, and an ox will I sacrifice for my household. And for the men will we slay oxen and sheep and goats.

ABNER: Yea! For this is a great day before the Lord in Israel! And we will sprinkle the spoil with the sacrifice.

SAUL: Hast thou heard the song of the women? Nay, hearest thou? Hark!

In the distance is heard the singing.

MERAB: *Saul in thousands slew his men.*

MICHAL: *David slew his thousands ten.*

ALL: *Lu-lu-lu-li-lu-lu-a! A li-lu-lu-a-li-lu!*

ABNER: Ay!

SAUL: May such mouths be bruised!

ABNER: Nay! Nay! King Saul! In this hour!

SAUL: In this instant! They have ascribed to David ten thousands, and to me they have ascribed but thousands. And what can he have more, but the Kingdom?

ABNER: Nay, nay, O Saul! It is but the light words of women. Ay, let them sing! For as vain women they fancy naught but that head of Goliath, with the round stone sunken in. But the King is King.

SAUL: Shall that shepherd oust me, even from the mouths of the maidens?

ABNER: Nay, this is folly, and less than kingly.

MICHAL (*followed by* MERAB—*running round the* KING *with their tambourines*): Lu-li-lu-lu-a-li-lu! A-li-lu-lu-a-li-lu-lu-lu!

SAUL: Away!

MERAB AND MICHAL: Lu-lu-lu-lu! Saul, the King! Lu-lu-lu-lu-al-li-lu-lu! Saul! Saul! Lu-lu-lu! Saul! Saul! Lu-lulu!

SAUL: Peace, I say!

Exit, passing into house.

MERAB AND MICHAL: Jonathan and David. Lu-lu-lu! Here they come, the friendly two! Lu-lu-lu-lu-a-li-lu! Lu-lu-a-li-lu-lu-lu!

MERAB: Jonathan is kingly bred.

MICHAL: David took Goliath's head.

BOTH: Jonathan and David! Lu-lu-lu!—a! Here they come the loving two-a!

MICHAL (*to* DAVID): Where is the giant's head?

DAVID: It is in Jerusalem of Judah, O Maiden.

MICHAL: Why did you not bring it here, that we might see it?

DAVID: I am of Judah, and they would have it there.

MICHAL: But Saul is King, and could have it where he would.

DAVID: Saul would leave it in Jerusalem.

MICHAL: And the armour, and the greaves of brass, and the shield, and the sword? The coat of brass that weighs five thousand shekels. Where are these? I want to see them, O David!

DAVID: The armour is in my father's house, and in Jerusalem. The sword lies before the Lord in Ramah, with Samuel, O Maiden!

MICHAL: Why take it to Samuel? Do you not know my name, O David!

DAVID: You are Michal.

MICHAL: I am she. And this is Merab! Look at him, Merab, and see if you like him. Is it true, O my brother Jonathan, that the King will give Merab his daughter to the slayer of the Philistine?

JONATHAN: He hath said so.

MICHAL: To us he has not said one word. O Merab! Look at thy man! How likest thou him?

MERAB: I will not look at him yet.

MICHAL: Oh, thou! Thou hast spied out every hair in his beard. Is he not fox-red? I think the beard of a man should be raven-black. O Merab, thy David is very ruddy.

MERAB: Nay! He is not yet mine, nor I his.

MICHAL: Thou wouldst it were so! Aiee! Thou art hasty and beforehand with the red youth! Shame on thee, that art a King's daughter.

MERAB: Nay, now, I have said naught.

MICHAL: Thou shouldst have said somewhat, to cover thy unmaidenly longing.—O David, this Merab sighs in her soul for you. How like you her?

DAVID: She is fair and a modest maiden.

MICHAL: As am not I! Oh, but I am Saul's very daughter, and a hawk that soars king high. And what has David brought, to lay before Merab?

DAVID: All I have is laid before the King.

MICHAL: But naught of the Philistine Goliath! All that spoil you took home to your father's house, as the fox brings his prey to his own hole. Ah, David, the wary one!

MERAB: It was his own! Where should he take it, but to his father's house!

MICHAL: Is not the King his father! Why should he not bring it here? Is Merab not worth the bride-money?

JONATHAN: Oh, peace! Thou art all mischief, Michal. Thou shouldst be married to a Philistine, for his undoing.

MICHAL: Ayeee! This David has come back to trouble us! Why didst not *thou* slay the Philistine, Jonathan?

JONATHAN: Peace! Let us go in, David! These maidens are too forward. My father did never succeed in ruling his household of women.

MICHAL: Ayee! His household of women! Thou, Jonathan! Go in, David! They shall not put poison in your meat.

As DAVID *and* JONATHAN *depart she sings:*
Empty-handed David came!

Merab saw him full of shame!
Lu-lu-lu-lu-lu-li-lu! A-li-lu-a! A-li-lu!
Empty-handed David came!
Merab saw him full of shame!
A-li-lu-lu! A-li-lu-li! Li-lu-li-lu-a!

(*To* MERAB.) So he has come!

MERAB: Even so! Yet his brow says: *Have a care!*

MICHAL: Have a care, Merab! Have a care, David! Have a care, Michal! Have a care, Jonathan! Have a care, King Saul! I do not like his brow, it is too studied.

MERAB: Nay, it is manly, and grave.

MICHAL: Ayee! Ayee! He did not laugh. He did not once laugh. It will not be well, Merab.

MERAB: What will not be well?

MICHAL: The King will not give thee to him.

MERAB: But the King hath spoken.

MICHAL: I have read the brow of Saul, and it was black. I have looked at David's brow, and it was heavy and secret. The King will not give thee to David, Merab. I know it, I know it.

MERAB: A King should keep his word!

MICHAL: What! Art thou hot with anger against thy father, lest he give thee not to this shepherd boy! David hath cast a spell on Merab! The ruddy herdsman out of Judah has thrown a net over the King's daughter! Oh, poor quail! poor partridge!

MERAB: I am not caught! I am not!

MICHAL: Thou art caught! And not by some chieftain, nor by some owner of great herds. But by a sheep-tending boy! Oh, fie!

MERAB: Nay, I do not want him.

MICHAL: Yea, thou dost. And if some man of great substance came, and my father would give thee to him, thou wouldst cry: *Nay! Nay! Nay! I am David's!*

MERAB: Never would I cry this that thou sayest. For I am not his.—And am I not first daughter of the King!

MICHAL: Thou waitest and pantest after that red David. And he will climb high in the sight of Israel, upon the mound of Merab. I tell thee, he is a climber who would climb above our heads.

MERAB: Above my head he shall not climb.

MICHAL:

> Empty-handed David came!
> Merab saw him full of shame!
> Lu-li-lu-li! Lu-li-lu-lu-li! A-li-lu-lu!

Curtain

SCENE XI: *Room in* KING's *house at Gilgal. Bare adobe room, mats on the floor.* SAUL, ABNER *and* ADRIEL *reclining around a little open hearth.*

SAUL: And how is the slayer of Goliath looked upon, in Gilgal?

ABNER: Yea! he is a wise young man, he brings no disfavour upon himself.

SAUL: May Baal finish him! And how looks he on the King's daughter? Does he eye Merab as a fox eyes a young lamb?

ABNER: Nay, he is wise, a young man full of discretion, watching well his steps.

SAUL: Ay is he! Smooth-faced and soft-footed, as Joseph in the house of Pharaoh! I tell you, I like not this weasel.

ABNER: Nay, he is no enemy of the King. His eyes are clear, with the light of the Lord God. But he is alone and shy, as a rude young shepherd.

SAUL: Thou art his uncle, surely. I tell you, I will send him back to Bethlehem, to the sheep-cotes.

ABNER: He is grown beyond the sheep-cotes, O King! And wilt thou send him back into Judah, while the giant's head still blackens above the gates of Jerusalem, and David is darling of all Judea, in the hearts of the men of

Judah? Better keep him here, where the King alone can honour him.

SAUL: I know him! Should I send him away, he will have them name him King in Judah, and Samuel will give testimony. Yea, when he carried the sword of the giant before Samuel in Ramah, did not Samuel bless him in the sight of all men, saying: Thou art chosen of the Lord out of Israel!

ABNER: If it be so, O King, we cannot put back the sun in heaven. Yet is David faithful servant to the King, and full of love for Jonathan. I find in him no presumption.

SAUL: My household is against me. Ah, this is the curse upon me! My children love my chief enemy, him who hath supplanted me before the Lord. Yea, my children pay court to David, and my daughters languish for him. But he shall not rise upon me. I say he shall not! Nor shall he marry my elder daughter Merab. Wellah, and he shall not.

ABNER: Yet Saul has given his word.

SAUL: And Saul shall take it back. What man should keep his word with a supplanter? Abner, have we not appointed him captain over a thousand? Captain over a thousand in the army of Saul shall he be. Oh yes! And to-morrow I will say to him, I will even say it again: *Behold Merab, my elder daughter, her will I give thee to wife: only be thou valiant for me, and fight the Lord's battles.* And then he shall go forth with his thousand again, quickly, against the Philistine. Let not my hand be upon him, but let the hand of the Philistine be upon him.

ABNER: But if the Lord be with him, and he fall not, but come back once more with spoil, wilt thou then withhold the hand of thy daughter Merab from him?

SAUL: He shall not have her! Nay, I know not. When the day comes that he returns back to this house, then Saul will answer him. We will not tempt the Thunderer.

ADRIEL: I have it sure, from Eliab his brother, that David was anointed by Samuel to be King over Israel, secretly, in the house of his father Jesse. And Eliab liketh not the youngster, saying he was ever heady, naughty-hearted, full of a youngling's naughty pride, and the conceit of the father's favourite. Now the tale is out in Judah, and many would have him King, saying: Why should Judah look to a King out of Benjamin? Is there no horn-anointed among the men of Judah?

SAUL: So is it! So is it!—To-morrow he shall go forth with his men, and the hand of the Philistine shall be upon him. I will not lift my hand upon him, for fear of the Dark! Yet where is he now? What is he conniving at this moment, in the house of Saul? Go, see what he is about, O Adriel!

Exit ADRIEL.

ABNER: It is a bad thing, O Saul, to let this jealous worm eat into a King's heart, that always was noble!

SAUL: I cannot help it. The worm is there. And since the women sang—nay, in all the cities they sang the same—*Saul hath slain his thousands, but David hath slain his tens of thousands,* it gnaws me, Abner, and I feel I am no longer King in the sight of the Lord.

ABNER: Canst thou not speak with the Morning Wind? And if the Lord of Days have chosen David to be king over Israel after thee, canst thou not answer the great Wish of the Heavens, saying: *It is well!*

SAUL: I cannot! I cannot deny my house, and my blood! I cannot cast down my own seed, for the seed of Jesse to sprout. I cannot! Wellah, and I will not! Speak not to me of this!

ABNER: Yet wert *thou* chosen of God! And always hast thou been a man of the bright horn.

SAUL: Yea, and am I brought to this pass! Yea, and must I cut myself off? Almost will I rather be a man of Belial, and call on Baal. Surely Astaroth were better to me. For I have kept the faith, yet must I cut myself off! Wellah, is there no other strength?

ABNER: I know not. Thou knowest, who hast heard the thunder and hast felt the Thunderer.

SAUL: I hear It no more, for It hath closed Its lips to me. But other voices hear I in the night—other voices!

    Enter ADRIEL.

SAUL: Well, and where is he?

ADRIEL: He is sitting in the house of Jonathan, and they make music together, so the women listen.

SAUL: Ah! And sings the bird of Bethlehem? What songs now?

ADRIEL: Even to the Lord: *How excellent is thy name in all the earth.* And men and women listen diligently, to learn as it droppeth from his mouth. And Jonathan, for very love, writes it down.

SAUL: Nay, canst thou not remember?

ADRIEL: I cannot, O King. Hark!

    A man is heard in the courtyard, singing loud and manly, from Psalm viii.

Voice of singer: What is man, that thou art mindful of him? and the son of man, that thou visitest him?

For thou hast made him a little lower than the angels, and hast crowned him with glory and honour.

Thou madest him to have dominion over the works of thy hands;

Thou hast put all things under his feet:

All sheep and oxen, yea, and the beasts of the field;

The fowl of the air, and the fish of the sea, and whatsoever passeth through the paths of the seas.

O Lord our Lord, how excellent is thy name in all the earth!

    SAUL *listens moodily.*

SAUL: I hear him! Yea, they sing after him! He will set all Israel singing after him, and all men in all lands. All the world will sing what he sings. And I shall be dumb. Yea, I shall be dumb, and the lips of my house will be dust! What, am I naught; and set at naught! What do I know? Shall I go down into the grave silenced, and like one mute with ignorance? Ha! Ha! There are wells in the desert that go deep. And even there we water the sheep, when our faces are blackened with drought. Hath Saul no sight into the unseen? Ha, look! look down the deep well, how the black water is troubled.—Yea, and I see death, death, death! I see a sword through my body, and the body of Jonathan gaping wounds, and my son Abinadab, and my son Melchishua, and my son Ishbosheth lying in blood. Nay, I see the small pale issue of my house creeping on broken feet, as a lamed worm. Yea, yea, what an end! And the seed of David rising up and covering the earth, many, with a glory about them, and the wind of the Lord in their hair. Nay, then they wheel against the sun, and are dark, like the locusts sweeping in heaven, like the pillars of locusts moving, yea, as a tall, dark cloud upon the land. Till they drop in drops of blood, like thunder-rain, and the land is red. Then they turn again into the glory of the Lord. Yea, as a flight of birds down all the ages, now shedding sun and the gleam of God, now shedding shadow and the fall of blood, now as quails chirping in the spring, now as the locust pillars of cloud, as death upon the land. And they thicken and thicken, till the world's air grates and clicks as with the wings of locusts. And man is his own devourer, and the Deep turns away, without wish to look on him further. So the earth is a desert, and manless, yet covered with houses and iron. Yea, David, the pits are digged even under the feet of thy God, and thy God shall fall in. Oh, their God shall fall into the pit, that the sons of David have digged. Oh, men can dig a pit for the most high God, and He falls in—as they say of the huge elephant in the lands beyond the desert. And the world shall be Godless, there shall no God walk on the mountains, no whirlwind shall stir like a heart in the deeps of the blue firmament. And God shall be gone from the world. Only men there shall be, in myriads, like locusts, clicking and grating upon one another, and crawling over one another. The smell of them shall be as smoke, but it shall rise up into the air, without finding the nostrils of God. For God shall be gone! gone! gone! And men shall inherit the earth! Yea, like locusts and whirring on wings like locusts. To this the seed of David shall come, and this is their triumph, when the house of Saul has been swept up, long, long ago into the body of God. Godless the world! Godless the men in myriads even like locusts. No God in the air! No God on the mountains! Even out of the deeps of the sky they lured Him, into their pit! So the world is empty of God, empty, empty, like a blown egg-shell bunged with wax and floating meaningless. God shall fall Himself into the pit these men shall dig for Him! Ha! Ha! O David's Almighty, even He knows not the depth of the dark wells in the desert, where men may still water their flocks! Ha! Ha! Lord God of Judah, thou peepest not down the pit where the black water twinkles. Ha-ha! Saul peeps and sees the fate that wells up from below! Ha! Lo! Death and blood, what is this Almighty that sees not the pits digged for Him by the children of men? Ha! Ha! saith Saul. Look in the black mirror! Ha!

ABNER: It is not well, O King.

SAUL: Ha! It is very well! It is very well. Let them lay their trap for his Lord. For his Lord will fall into it. Aha! Aha! Give them length of days. I do not ask it.

ABNER: My lord, the darkness is over your heart.

SAUL: And over my eyes! Ha! And on the swim of the dark are visions. What? Are the demons not under all the works of God, as worms are under the roots of the vine? Look! (*Stares transfixed.*)

ABNER (*to* ADRIEL): Go quickly and bring Jonathan, and David, for the King is prophesying with the spirit of the under-earth.

Exit ADRIEL.

SAUL: The room is full of demons! I have known it filled with the breath of Might. The glisten of the dark, old movers that first got the world into shape. They say the god was once as a beetle, but vast and dark. And he rolled the earth into a ball, and laid his seed in it. Then he crept clicking away to hide for ever, while the earth brought forth after him. He went down a deep pit. The gods do not die. They go down a deep pit, and live on at the bottom of oblivion. And when a man staggers, he stumbles and falls backwards down the pit—down the pit, down through oblivion after oblivion, where the gods of the past live on. And they laugh, and eat his soul. And the time will come when even the God of David will fall down the endless pit, till He passes the place where the serpent lies living under oblivion, on to where the Beetle of the Beginning lives under many layers of dark. I see it! Aha! I see the Beetle clambering upon Him, Who was the Lord of Hosts.

ABNER: I cannot hear thee, O King. I would e'en be deaf in this hour. Peace! I bid thee! Peace!

SAUL: What? Did someone speak within the shadow? Come thou forth then from the shadow, if thou hast aught to say.

ABNER: I say Peace! Peace, thou! Say thou no more!

SAUL: What? Peace! saith the voice? And what is peace? Hath the Beetle of the Beginning peace, under many layers of oblivion? Or the great serpent coiled for ever, is he coiled upon his own peace?

Enter JONATHAN, DAVID, *and* MEN.

SAUL (*continuing*): I tell you, till the end of time, unrest will come upon the serpent of serpents, and he will lift his head and hiss against the children of men—thus will he hiss! (SAUL *hisses.*) *Hiss! Hiss!* and he will strike the children of men—thus——

SAUL *strikes as a serpent, and with his javelin.*

JONATHAN: Father, shall we sound music?

SAUL: Father! Who is father? Know ye not, the vast, dark, shining beetle was the first father, who laid his eggs in a dead ball of the dust of forgotten gods? And out of the egg the serpent of gold, who was great Lord of Life, came forth.

JONATHAN (*to* DAVID): Now sing, that peace may come back upon us.

DAVID: If he heed me. (*Sings Psalm viii.*)

SAUL *meanwhile raves—then sinks into gloom, staring fixedly.*

SAUL: And the serpent was golden with life. But he said to himself: I will lay an egg. So he laid the egg of his own undoing. And the Great White Bird came forth. Some say a dove, some say an eagle, some say a swan, some say a goose—all say a bird. And the serpent of the sun's life turned dark, as all the gods turn dark. Yea, and the Great White Bird beat wings in the firmament, so the dragon slid into a hole, the serpent crawled out of sight, down to the oblivion of oblivion, yet above the oblivion of the Beetle.

DAVID *meanwhile sings.*

SAUL (*striking with his hands as if at a wasp*): Na-a! But What is this sound that comes like a hornet at my ears, and will not let me prophesy! Away! Away!

JONATHAN: My Father, it is a new song to sing.

SAUL: What art thou, Jonathan, thy father's enemy?

JONATHAN: Listen to the new song, Father.

SAUL: What? (*Hearkens a moment.*) I will not hear it! What! I say I will not hear it! Trouble me not, nor stop the dark fountain of my prophecy! I will not hearken! (*Listens.*)

DAVID (*singing*): When I consider thy heavens, the work of thy fingers, the moon and the stars, which thou hast ordained.

SAUL: What! art thou there, thou brown hornet, thou stealer of life's honey! What, shalt thou stay in my sight! (*Suddenly hurls his javelin at* DAVID. DAVID *leaps aside.*)

JONATHAN: My Father, this shall not be!

SAUL: What! art thou there? Bring me here my dart.

JONATHAN (*picking up the javelin*): Look then at the hole in the wall! Is not that a reproach against the house of the King for ever? (*Gives the javelin to* SAUL.)

SAUL *sinks into moody silence, staring.* DAVID *begins to sing very softly.*

DAVID (*singing*): O Lord our Lord, how excellent is thy

name in all the earth! Who hast set thy glory above the heavens.

> SAUL *very softly, with the soft, swift suddenness of a great cat, leaps round and hurls the javelin again.* DAVID *as swiftly leaps aside.*

SAUL: I will smite David even to the wall.

ABNER: Go hence, David! Swiftly hence!

JONATHAN: Twice, Father!

> *Exit* DAVID.

ABNER (*seizing javelin*): The evil spirits upon thee have done this. O Saul! They have not prevailed.

SAUL: Have I pierced him? Is he down with the dead? Can we lay him in the sides of the pit?

ABNER: He is not dead! He is gone forth.

SAUL (*wearily*): Gone forth! Ay! He is gone forth!—What, did I seek to slay him?

JONATHAN: Yea, twice.

SAUL: It was out of myself. I was then beside myself.

ABNER: Yea, the evil spirits were upon thee.

SAUL: Tell him, O Jonathan, Saul seeks not his life. Nay! Nay! Do I not love him, even as thou dost, but more, even as a father! O David! David! I have loved thee. Oh, I have loved thee and the Lord in thee.—And now the evil days have come upon me, and I have thrown the dart against thee, and against the Lord. I am a man given over to trouble, and tossed between two winds. Lo, how can I walk before the faces of men! (*Covers his face with his mantle.*)

ABNER: The evil spirits have left him. Peace comes with sorrow.

JONATHAN: And only then.

SAUL: Bring David hither to me, for I will make my peace with him, for my heart is very sore.

JONATHAN: Verily, shall it be peace?

SAUL: Yea! For I fear the Night. (*Exit* JONATHAN.) Surely now will David publish it in Judah: *Saul hath lifted his hand to slay me.*

ABNER: He will not publish it in Judah.

SAUL: And wherefore not? Is he not as the apple of their eyes to the men of Judah, who love not over-much the tribe of Benjamin?

ABNER: But David is the King's man.

SAUL: Ah, would it were verily so.

Enter JONATHAN *and* DAVID.

DAVID: The Lord strengthen the King!

SAUL: Ah, David, my son, come, and come in peace. For my hands are bare and my heart is washed and my eyes are no longer deluded. May the Lord be with thee, David, and hold it not against me, what I have done. Spirits of the earth possess me, and I am not my own. Thou shalt not cherish it in thy heart, what Saul did against thee, in the season of his bewilderment?

DAVID: Naught has the King done against me. And the heart of thy servant knoweth no ill.

SAUL: Hatest thou me not, David?

DAVID: Let the word be unspoken, my Father!

SAUL: Ah, David! David! Why can I not love thee untroubled?—But I will right the wrong.—Thou shalt henceforth be captain of the thousand of Hebron, and dwell in thine own house, by the men. And behold, Merab, my elder daughter, I will give thee to wife.

DAVID: Who am I, and what is my life, or my father's family in Israel, that I should be son-in-law to the King?

SAUL: Nay, thou art of mine own heart, and the Lord is thy great strength. Only be valiant for me, and fight the Lord's battles.

DAVID: All my life is the King's, and my strength is to serve.

SAUL: It shall be well. And with thy thousand shalt thou succour Israel.

Curtain

SCENE XII: *The well at Gilgal:* MAIDENS *coming with water-jars.* Two HERDSMEN *filling the trough—one below, at the water, one on the steps. They swing the leathern bucket back and forth with a rough chant: the lower shepherd swinging the load to the upper, who swings it to the trough, and hands it back.* DAVID *approaching.*

1ST HERDSMAN: Ya! David missed her.

2ND HERDSMAN: Let him get her sister—Oh! Oh-oh-h!

1ST HERDSMAN: Ya! David missed her.

2ND HERDSMAN: Let him get her sister—Oh-h-h-h! (*Continue several times.*)

1ST MAIDEN: How long, O Herdsman!

2ND HERDSMAN: Ho-o-o! Enough!

1ST HERDSMAN (*coming up*): Ya! David missed her!
> MAIDENS *run away from him.*

1ST MAIDEN: Ho, thou! Seest thou not David?

1ST HERDSMAN: Yea, he is there! Ho! David! And hast thou missed her?
> MAIDENS *laugh.*

DAVID: What sayest thou, O Man?

1ST HERDSMAN: Thou hast missed her—say!—am I not right?

DAVID: And whom have I missed?

1ST HERDSMAN: Wellah! And knowest thou not?

DAVID: Nay!

1ST HERDSMAN: Wellah! But Merab, the King's elder daughter! Wellah! We feasted her week half a moon ago, whilst you and your men were gone forth against the Philistines. Wellah, man, and didst thou not know?

DAVID: Sayest thou so?

1ST HERDSMAN: Wellah! And is it not so? Say, Maidens, hath not Adriel the Meholathite got Merab, Saul's daughter, to wife? And hath he not spent his week with her? Wellah, thou art ousted from that bed, O David.

DAVID: And hath the King given his daughter Merab unto

Adriel the Meholathite! Wellah, shall he not do as he choose, with his own?

1ST HERDSMAN: Ay, wellah, shall he! But thou wert promised. And in thy stead, another hath gone in unto her. Is it not so, O Maidens? Sleeps not Merab in the tent of Adriel the Meholathite?

1ST MAIDEN: Yea, the King hath married her to the man.

DAVID: And sings she as she shakes his butter-skin?

1ST MAIDEN: Nay, as yet she sings not. But if David sits here beneath the tree, she will come with her jar. Nay, is that not Adriel the Meholathite himself, coming forth? O Herdsman, drive not the cattle as yet to the drinking troughs!

Goes down and fills her pitcher.

2ND MAIDEN: Will David sit awhile beneath the tree?

DAVID: Yea!

2ND MAIDEN: Then shall Michal, daughter of Saul, come hither with her water-jar. Is it well, O David?

DAVID: Yea, it is very well.

MAIDEN *goes down with her pitcher.*

ADRIEL: Ha, David! And art thou returned? I have not seen thee before the King.

DAVID: I returned but yesterday. And I saw the King at the dawn. Now art thou become a great man in Israel, O Adriel, and son-in-law to the King. How fareth Merab in the tents of the Meholathite?

ADRIEL: Yea, and blithely. And to-morrow even in the early day will I set her on an ass, and we will get us to my father's house. For he is old, and the charge of his possessions is heavy upon him, and he fain would see his daughter Merab, who shall bring him sons—sons to gladden him. And she shall have her hand-maidens about her, and her store-barns of wool, and corn, and clotted figs, and bunches of raisins, all her wealth she shall see in store!

DAVID: May she live content, and bring thee sons, even males of worth.

ADRIEL: The Lord grant it! And thou hast come home

once more with spoil! How thou chastenest the Philistine! Yea, and behold, the King hath delight in thee, and all his servants love thee! Lo! I am the King's son-in-law, of Merab. Now, therefore, be thou also the King's son-in-law, for there is yet a daughter.

DAVID: Seemeth it to you a light thing, to be the King's son-in-law, seeing that I am a poor man, and lightly esteemed?

ADRIEL: By my beard, the King delighteth in thee, and all his servants love thee. There is no man in Israel more fit to take a daughter of the King.

DAVID: Yea, there be men of mighty substance such as thou, whose flocks have not been counted, and who send men-at-arms pricking with iron lance-points, to the King's service. But what have I, save the bare hands and heart of a faithful servant?

ADRIEL: Nay, thy name is high among men. But lo! here cometh Saul, as he hath promised. He is coming out to my tents. I will go forward to bring him in. Come thou?

DAVID: Nay! Leave me here.

Exit ADRIEL.

1ST HERDSMAN: I have heard the mouth of Adriel, O David! Surely he is the King's listener.

DAVID: And thou! Who made *thee* a listener?

1ST HERDSMAN: Nay, I must guard the water-troughs till the cattle have drunk. Adriel hath flocks and men-servants, but David hath the Lord, and the hearts of all Israel! Better a brave and bright man, with a face that shines to the heart, than a great owner of troops and herds, who struts with arms akimbo. As I plant this driving-stick in the soft earth, so hath the Lord planted David in the heart of Israel. I say: Stick, may thou flourish! May thou bud and blossom and be a great tree. For thou art not as the javelin of Saul, levelled at David's bosom.

DAVID: Peace! Saul cometh.

1ST HERDSMAN: Wellah! And I will go down to the water.

Goes to the well.

DAVID: The Lord strengthen the King.

SAUL: Art thou my son, David? Yea, David, have they told thee, I have married my daughter Merab unto Adriel the Meholathite, even to him who stands here?

DAVID: Yea, O Saul! They told me the King's pleasure. May the Lord bless thy house for ever!

SAUL: Have I not promised my daughter unto thee? But my servants tell me the heart of Michal goes forth wishful unto David. Say now, is she fair in thine eyes?

DAVID: Yea! Yea, O King, yea!

SAUL: When the new moon shows her tender horns above the west, thou shalt this day be my son-in-law in one of the twain.

DAVID: Let thy servant but serve the King!

SAUL: Yea, an thou serve me, it shall be on the day of the new moon.

DAVID: Yea, will I serve without fail.

SAUL: So be it!

    Exit with ADRIEL.

HERDSMAN (*coming up*): Now is David the richest man in Israel—in promises! Wilt thou not sell me a King's promise, for this my camel-stick?

DAVID: It is well.

HERDSMAN: Sayest thou? Then it is a bargain? Wellah! Take my stick. It is worth the word of a King.

DAVID: Peace!

HERDSMAN: Thou meanest *war!*

DAVID: How?

HERDSMAN: If thou get her, it is war. If thou get her not, it is more war. Sayest thou peace?

MAIDENS (*running*): Oh, master David, hath Saul passed with Adriel?

HERDSMAN: They have passed, letting fall promises as the goat droppeth pills.

DAVID: Peace, O Man!

MAIDEN: Oh, master David, shall Michal come forth to fill her water-jar? For Merab is setting meats before the

King, in the booth of Adriel. Oh, David, shall Michal bring her jar to the well?

HERDSMAN: Ay, wellah, shall she! And I will hold back the cattle this little while, for I hear their voices.

Exit.

DAVID: Run back quickly and let her come.

Exit MAIDEN.

DAVID (*alone*): Lord! dost Thou send this maiden to me? My entrails strain in me, for Michal, daughter of Saul. Lord God of my Salvation, my wanting of this maiden is next to my wanting Thee. My body is a strong-strung bow. Lord, let me shoot mine arrow unto this mark. Thou fillest me with desire as with thunder, Thy lightning is in my loins, and my breast like a cloud leans forward for her. Lord! Lord! Thy left hand is about her middle, and Thy right hand grasps my life. So Thou bringest us together in Thy secret self, that it may be fulfilled for Thee in us. Lord of the Great Wish, I will not let her go.

MICHAL (*entering—covering her chin and throat with her kerchief*): Wilt thou let me pass to fill my jar, O thou stranger?

DAVID: Come, Michal, and I will fill thy jar.

She comes forward—he takes her jar and goes down the steps. Returning he sets it on the ground at his feet.

MICHAL: Oh, David! And art thou still unslain?

DAVID: As the Lord wills, no man shall slay me. And livest thou in thine house lonely, without thy sister Merab?

MICHAL: Is thy heart sore in thee, David, that thou hast lost Merab? Her heart is gentle, and she sighed for thee. But e'en she obeyed.

DAVID: She hath a man of more substance than David. And my heart is very glad on her account.

MICHAL: It is well.

DAVID: O Michal, didst thou come willingly to the well, when the maiden told thee I waited here?

MICHAL: Yea, willingly.

DAVID: O Michal, my heart runs before me, when it sees thee far off, like one eager to come to his own place. Oh, thou with the great eyes of the wilderness, shall my heart leap to thee, and shall thou not say Nay! to it?

MICHAL: What said my father, O David, when he passed?

DAVID: He said: when the new moon showeth her horns in the west, on this day shalt thou surely be my son-in-law of one of the twain.

MICHAL: Yea, and is thy heart uplifted, to be a King's son-in-law?

DAVID: So she be Michal, my body is uplifted like the sail of a ship when the wind arouses.

MICHAL: Nay, thou art a seeker of honours! Merab had been just as well to thy liking.

DAVID: Ah, no! Ah! Ah! Merab is gentle and good, and my heart softened with kindness for her, as a man unto a woman. But thou art like the rising moon, that maketh the limbs of the mountain glisten. O Michal, we twain are upon the hillsides of the Lord, and surely He will bring our strength together!

MICHAL: And if the Lord God say thee nay!

DAVID: He will not. He hath thy life in His left hand, and my life He holdeth in His right hand. And surely He will lay us together in the secret of His desire, and I shall come unto thee by the Lord's doing.

MICHAL: But if He say thee nay, thou wilt let me go.

DAVID: Thou knowest not the Lord my God. The flame He kindles He will not blow out. He is not yea-and-nay! But my Lord my God loveth a bright desire and yearneth over a great Wish, for its fulfillment. Oh, the Lord my God is a glowing flame and he loveth all things that do glow. So loves He thee, Michal, O woman before me, for thou glowest like a young tree in full flower, with flowers of gold and scarlet, and dark leaves. O thou young pomegranate tree, flowers and fruit together show on thy body. And flame calleth to flame, for flame is the body of God, like flowers of flame. Oh, and God is a great Wish, and a great Desire, and a pure flame for ever. Thou art kindled of the Lord, O Michal, and He will not let thee go.

MICHAL: Yet the Lord Himself will not marry me.

DAVID: I will marry thee, for the Lord hath kindled me unto thee, and hath said: Go to her, for the fruits of the pomegranate are ripe.

MICHAL: Will thou not seek me for thyself?

DAVID: Yea, for my very self; and for my very self; and for the Lord's own self in me.

MICHAL: Ever thou puttest the Lord between me and thee.

DAVID: The Lord is a sweet wind that fills thy bosom and thy belly as the sail of a ship; so I see thee sailing delicately towards me, borne onwards by my Lord.

MICHAL: Oh, David, would the new moon were come! For I fear my father, and I misdoubt his hindrances.

DAVID: Thinkest thou, he would marry thee away, as Merab?

MICHAL: Nay, but thou must make a song, and sing it before all Israel, that Michal is thine by the King's promise, no man shall look on her but David.

DAVID: Yea! I will make a song. And yea, I will not let thee go. Thou shalt come to me as wife, and I will know thee, and thou shall lie in my bosom. Yea! As the Lord liveth!

MICHAL: And as the Lord liveth, not even my father shall constrain me, to give me to another man, before the new moon showeth her horns.

DAVID: It is well, O Michal! O Michal, wife of David, thou shalt sleep in my tent! In the tent of the men of war, beside the sword of David, Michal sleeps, and the hand of David is upon her hip. He has sealed her with his seal, and Michal of David is her name, and kingdoms shall he bring down to her. Michal of David shall blossom in the land, her name shall blossom in the mouths of soldiers as the rose of Sharon after rain. And men-at-arms shall shout her name, like a victory cry it shall be heard. And she shall be known in the land but as Michal of David; blossom of God, keeper of David's nakedness.

MICHAL: They shall not reive me from thee.—I see men coming.

DAVID: Wilt thou go?

MICHAL: I shall call my maidens. So ho! So ho! (*Waves the end of her kerchief.*)

HERDSMAN (*entering*): There are two captains, servants of Saul, coming even now from the booths of the Meholathite, where the King is.

MICHAL: Yea, let them come, and we will hear the words they put forth.

HERDSMAN: And the cattle are being driven round by the apricot garden. They will soon be here.

DAVID: In two words we shall have the mind of Saul from these captains.

MAIDENS (*entering—running*): O Michal, men are approaching!

MICHAL: Fill you your jar, and with one ear let us listen. David stays under the tree.

1ST MAIDEN: Stars are in thine eyes, O Michal, like a love night!

2ND MAIDEN: Oh! and the perfume of a new-opened flower! What sweetness has she heard?

3RD MAIDEN: Oh, say! what words like honey, and like new sweet dates of the Oasis, hath David the singer said to Michal? Oh, that we might have heard!

1ST CAPTAIN (*entering*): David is still at the well?

DAVID: Yea, after war and foray, happy is the homely passage at the well?

2ND CAPTAIN: Wilt thou return to the King's house with us, and we will tell thee what is toward: even the words of Saul concerning thee.

DAVID: Say on! For I must in the other way.

1ST CAPTAIN: The King delighteth in thee more than in any man of Israel. For no man layeth low the King's enemies like David, in the land.

DAVID: Sayest thou so?

1ST CAPTAIN: Yea! And when the new moon shows her horns shalt thou be son-in-law to Saul, in his daughter Michal.

DAVID: As the Lord, and the King, willeth. Saul hath said as much to me, even now. Yet I am a poor man, and how shall the King at last accept me?

2ND CAPTAIN: This too hath Saul considered. And he hath said: Tell my son David, the King desireth not any bride-money, nay, neither sheep nor oxen nor asses, nor any substance of his. But an hundred foreskins of the Philistines shall he bring to the King, to be avenged of his enemies.

1ST CAPTAIN: So said the King: Before the new moon, as she cometh, sets on her first night, shall David bring the foreskins of an hundred Philistines unto Saul. And that night shall Saul deliver Michal, his daughter, unto David, and she shall sleep in David's house.

2ND CAPTAIN: And Israel shall be avenged of her enemies.

DAVID: Hath the King verily sent this message to me?

1ST CAPTAIN: Yea, he hath sent it, and a ring from his own hand. Lo! here it is! For said Saul: Let David keep this for a pledge between me and him, in this matter. And when he returneth, he shall give me my ring again, and the foreskins of the Philistine, and I will give him my daughter Michal to wife.

DAVID: Yea! Then I must hence, and call my men, and go forth against the Philistine. For while the nights yet are moonless, and without point of moon, will I return with the tally.

    Exit.

2ND CAPTAIN: Yea, he is gone on the King's errand.

1ST CAPTAIN: Let him meet what the King wishes.

    Exeunt.

HERDSMAN: Yea, I know what ye would have. Ye would slay David with the sword of the Philistine. For who keeps promise with a dead man! (MICHAL *and* MAIDENS *edge in.*) Hast thou heard, O Michal? David is gone forth against the Philistine. For Saul asketh an hundred fore-skins of the enemy as thy bride-money. Is it not a tall dowry?

MICHAL: Yea! hath my father done this!

HERDSMAN: Wellah, hath he! For dead men marry no kings' daughters. And the spear of some Philistine shall beget death in the body of David. Thy father hath made thee dear!

MICHAL: Nay, he hath made my name cheap in all Israel.

2ND HERDSMAN (*entering*): Run, Maidens! The cattle are coming round the wall, athirst!

MAIDENS (*shouldering their jars*): Away! Away!

Exeunt.

Curtain

SCENE XIII: *A room in* DAVID'S *house in Gilgal. Almost dark.* DAVID *alone, speaking softly: an image in a corner.*

DAVID: Give ear to my words, O Lord, consider my medita-tion.

Hearken unto the voice of my cry, my King, and my God: for unto thee will I pray.

My voice shalt thou hear in the morning, O Lord; in the morning will I direct my prayer unto thee, and will look up.

For thou art not a God that hath pleasure in wickedness: neither shall evil dwell with thee.

The foolish shall not stand in thy sight: thou hatest all workers of iniquity.

Thou shalt destroy them that speak leasing: the Lord will abhor the bloody and deceitful man.

But as for me, I will come into thy house in the multitude

of thy mercy: and in thy fear will I worship toward thy holy temple.

Lead me, O Lord, in thy righteousness, because of mine enemies; make thy way straight before my face.

For there is no faithfulness in their mouth; their inward part is very wickedness; their throat is an open sepulchre: they flatter with their tongue.

Destroy thou them, O God; let them fall by their own counsels; cast them out in the multitude of their transgressions; for they have rebelled against thee.

But let all those that put their trust in thee rejoice: let them ever shout for joy, because thou defendest them: let them also that love thy name be joyful in thee.

For thou, Lord, wilt bless the righteous; with favour wilt thou compass him, as with a shield.

Pause.

Nay, Lord, I am Thy anointed, and Thy son. With the oil of anointment hast Thou begotten me. Oh, I am twice begotten: of Jesse, and of God! I go forth as a son of God, and the Lord is with me. Yet for this they hate me, and Saul seeks to destroy me. What can I do, O Lord, in this pass?

Enter MICHAL, *through curtain at side, with tray and lamp.*

MICHAL: The dawn is at hand. Art thou not faint with this long watching before the Lord? Oh! why wilt thou leave thy bed and thy pleasure of the night, to speak out into the empty, chill hour towards morning? Come then, eat of the food which I have brought.

DAVID: I will not eat now, for my soul still yearns away from me.

MICHAL: Art thou sick?

DAVID: Yea! My soul is sick.

MICHAL: Why?

DAVID: Nay, thou knowest. Thy father hates me beyond measure.

MICHAL: But I love you.

DAVID (*takes her hand*): Yea!

MICHAL: Is it nothing to you that Michal is your wife and loves you?

DAVID: Verily, it is not nothing. But, Michal, what will come to me at last? From moon to moon Saul's anger waxes. I shall lose my life at last. And what good shall I be to thee then?

MICHAL: Ah, no! Ah, no! Never shall I see thee dead. First thou shalt see me dead. Never, never shall I tear my hair for thee, as a widow. It shall not be. If thou go hence, it shall not be into death.

DAVID: Yet death is near. From month to month, since I came back with the foreskins of the Philistine, and got thee to wife, Saul has hated me more. Michal loves David, and Saul's hate waxes greater. Jonathan loves David, and the King commands Jonathan, saying: There, where thou seest him, there shalt thou slay David.

MICHAL: My father is no more a man. He is given over entirely to evil spirits. But Jonathan will save thee through it all.

DAVID: The Lord will save me. And Jonathan is dearer to me than a heart's brother.

MICHAL: Think, O husband, if Saul hateth thee, how Michal and Jonathan, who are children of Saul, do love thee.

DAVID: Yea, verily! It is like the rainbow in the sky unto me. But, O Michal, how shall we win through? I have loved Saul. And I have not it in me to hate him. Only his perpetual anger puts on me a surpassing heaviness, and a weariness, so my flesh wearies upon my bones.

MICHAL: But why? Why? Why does it matter to thee? I love thee, all the time.—Jonathan loves thee.—Thy men love thee. Why does the frenzy of one distracted man so trouble thee? Why? It is out of all measure.

DAVID: Nay, he is Saul, and the Lord's anointed. And he is King over all Israel.

MICHAL: And what then? He is no man among men any more. Evil possesses him. Why heed him, and wake in the night for him?

DAVID: Because he is the Lord's anointed, and one day he will kill me.

MICHAL: He will never kill thee. Thou sayest thyself, the Lord will prevent him. And if not the Lord, then I will prevent him—for I am not yet nothing in Gilgal. And Jonathan will prevent him. And the captains will prevent him. And art thou not also the Lord's anointed? And will not the Lord set thee King on the hill of Zion, in thine own Judah?

DAVID: O Michal! O Michal! That the hand of the Lord's anointed should be lifted against the Lord's anointed! What can I do? For Saul is the Lord's, and I may not even see an enemy in him. I cannot, verily! Yet he seeks to slay me. All these months since he gave thee to me, after I brought the foreskins of the Philistine for thy dowry, he has hated me more, and sought my life. Before the moon of our marriage was waned away thy father commanded his servants, and even Jonathan, to slay David on that spot where they should find him. So Jonathan came to me in haste and secret, and sent me away into the fields by night and hid me. Yea, before the month of our marriage was finished I had to flee from thee in the night, and leave my place cold.

MICHAL: But not for long. Not for long. Jonathan persuaded my father, so he took thee back. Even he loved thee again.

DAVID: Yea, he also loves me! But Saul is a man falling backward down a deep pit, that must e'en clutch what is nearest him, and drag it down along with him.

MICHAL: But Saul swore: As the Lord liveth, David shall not be slain.

DAVID: Ay, he swore. But before two moons were passed his brow was black again. And when the season of the year came, that the Kings of the Philistine go forth, I went up against them, and fought. The months of the fighting I fought with them, and all the people rejoiced. But I saw with a sinking heart the face of Saul blacken, blacken darker with greater hate! Yea, he hath loved me, as the Lord's anointed must love the Lord's anointed. But Saul is slipping backward down the pit of despair, away from God. And each time he strives to come forth, the loose earth yields beneath his feet, and he slides deeper. So the upreach of his love fails him, and the downslide of his hate is great and greater in weight. I cannot hate him—nor love him—but, O Michal, I am oppressed with a horror of him.

MICHAL: Nay, do not dwell on him.

DAVID: And the year went round its course, and once more there was war with the Philistine. And once more we prevailed, in the Lord. And once more the armies shouted my name. And once more I came home to thee—and thou didst sing. And my heart did sing above thee. But as a bird hushes when the shadow of the hawk dances upon him from heaven, my heart went hushed under the shadow of Saul. And my heart could not sing between thy breasts, as it wanted to, even the heart of a bridegroom. For the shadow of Saul was upon it.

MICHAL: Oh, why do you care? Why do you care? Why do you not love me and never care?

DAVID: It is not in me. I have been blithe of thy love and thy body. But now three days ago, even in the midst of my blitheness, Saul again threw his javelin at me—yea, even in the feast. And I am marked among all men. And the end draws nigh.—For scarce may I leave this house, lest at some corner they slay me.

MICHAL: What end, then? What end draws nigh?

DAVID: I must get me gone. I must go into the wilderness.

MICHAL (*weeping*): Oh, bitter! Bitter! My joy has been torn from me, as an eagle tears a lamb from the ewe. I have no joy in my life, nor in the body of my lord and my husband. A serpent is hid in my marriage bed, my joy is venomed. Oh, that they had wed me to a man that moved me not, rather than be moved to so much hurt.

DAVID: Nay, nay! Oh, nay, nay! Between me and thee is no bitterness, and between my body and thy body there is constant joy! Nay, nay! Thou art a flame to me of man's forgetting, and God's presence. Nay, nay! Thou shalt not weep for me, for thou art a delight to me, even a delight and a forgetting.

MICHAL: No! No! Thou leavest me in the night, to make prayers and moaning before the Lord. Oh, that thou hadst never married in thy body the daughter of thine enemy!

DAVID: Say not so, it is a wrong thing; thou art sweet to me, and all my desire.

MICHAL: It is not true! Thou moanest, and leavest me in the night, to fall before the Lord.

DAVID: Yea, trouble is come upon me. And I must take my trouble to the Lord. But thy breasts are my bliss and my forgetting. Oh, do not remember my complaining! But let thyself be sweet to me, and let me sleep among the lilies.

MICHAL: Thou wilt reproach me again with my father.

DAVID: Ah, no! Ah, never I reproach thee! But now I can forget, I can forget all but thee, and the blossom of thy sweetness. Oh, come with me, and let me know thee. For thou art ever again as new to me.

MICHAL (*rising as he takes her hand*): Nay, thou wilt turn the bitterness of thy spirit upon me again.

DAVID: Ah, no! I will not! But the gate of my life can I open to thee again, and the world of bitterness shall be gone under as in a flood.

MICHAL: And wilt thou not leave me?

DAVID: Nay, lift up thy voice no more, for the hour of speech has passed.

Exeunt through curtain at back.

SCENE XIV: *The same room, unchanged, an hour or so later: but the grey light of day. A* WOMAN-SERVANT *comes in. There is a wooden image in a corner.*

WOMAN-SERVANT: Yea, the lighted lamp, and the food! My lord David hath kept watch again before the Lord, and tears will fall on Michal's bosom, and darken her heart! Aiee! Aiee! That Saul should so hate the life of David! Surely the evil spirits are strong upon the King.

BOY (*entering*): Jonathan, the King's son, is below, knocking softly at the door.

WOMAN-SERVANT: Go! Open swiftly, and make fast again. Aiee! Aiee! My lord Jonathan comes too early for a pleasure visit. I will see if they sleep. (*Goes through the curtain.*)

    Enter JONATHAN. JONATHAN *stands silent, pensive. Goes to window. Re-enter* WOMAN-SERVANT. *She starts, seeing* JONATHAN—*then puts her hand on her mouth.*

WOMAN-SERVANT: O my lord Jonathan! Hush!

JONATHAN: They are sleeping still?

WOMAN-SERVANT: They are sleeping the marriage sleep. David hath even watched before the Lord, in the night. But now with Michal he sleeps the marriage sleep, in the lands of peace. Now grant a son shall come of it, to ease the gnawing of Michal's heart.

JONATHAN: What gnaws in Michal's heart?

WOMAN-SERVANT: Ah, my lord, her love even for David, that will not be appeased. If the Giver gave her a son, so should her love for David abate, and cease to gnaw in her.

JONATHAN: But why should it gnaw in her? Hath she not got him, and the joy of him?

WOMAN-SERVANT: O Jonathan, she is even as the house of Saul. What she hath cannot appease her.

JONATHAN: What then would she more?

WOMAN-SERVANT: She is of the house of Saul, and her very love is pain to her. Each cloud that crosses her is another death of her love. Ah, it is better to let love come and to let it go, even as the winds of the hills blow along the heavens. The sun shines, and is dulled, and shines again; it is the day, and its alterings; and after, it is night.

JONATHAN: David and Michal are asleep?

WOMAN-SERVANT: In the marriage sleep. Oh, break it not!

JONATHAN: The sun will soon rise. Lo! this house is upon the wall of the city, and the fields and the hills lie open.

WOMAN-SERVANT: Shall I bring food to Jonathan?

JONATHAN: Nay! Hark! Men are crying at the city's western gate, to open. The day is beginning.

WOMAN-SERVANT: May it bring good to this house!

JONATHAN: It is like to bring evil.

WOMAN-SERVANT: Ah, my lord!

DAVID (*appearing through the curtain at the back*): Jonathan!

JONATHAN: David! Thou art awake!

DAVID (*laughing*): Yea! Am I not? Thou art my brother Jonathan, art thou not? (*They embrace.*)

JONATHAN: O David, the darkness was upon my father in the night, and he hath again bid slay thee. Leave not the house. Unbar not the door! Watch! And be ready to flee! If armed men stand round the door (MICHAL *appears*), then let down the boy from the window, and send instantly to me. I will come with thy men and with mine, and we will withstand the hosts of Saul, if need be.

MICHAL: Is something new toward?

JONATHAN: My father bade his men take David, and slay him in the dawn. I must away, lest they see that I have warned thee. Farewell, O David!

DAVID: Farewell, my brother Jonathan! But I will come down the stair with thee.

    Exeunt.

MICHAL: Yea! Yea! So sure as it is well between me and him, so sure as we have peace in one another, so sure as we are together—comes this evil wind, and blows upon us! And oh, I am weary of my life, because of it!

WOMAN-SERVANT: Aiee! Aiee! Say not so, O Michal! For thy days are many before thee.

MICHAL: This time, an they take him, they will surely kill him.

WOMAN-SERVANT: Sayest thou so! Oh, why, in the Lord's name!

MICHAL: I know it. If they take him this time, he is lost.

WOMAN-SERVANT: Oh, then shall they surely not take him! Oh, but what shall we do?

MICHAL: Creep thou on the roof! Let no man see thee. And there lie: watch if armed men approach the house.

DAVID (*entering*): There is no one there.

MICHAL: They will come as the sun comes. (*To* WOMAN.) Go thou and watch.

WOMAN-SERVANT: Verily I will!

Exit.

MICHAL: O David! So sure as it is springtime in me, and my body blossoms like an almond-tree, comes this evil wind upon me, and withers my bud! Oh, how can I bring forth children to thee, when the spear of this vexation each time pierces my womb?

DAVID: Trouble not thyself, my flower. No wind shall wither thee.

MICHAL: Oh, but I know. This time, an they take thee, thou shalt lose thy life.—And Jonathan will not save thee.

DAVID: Nay! Be not afraid for me.

MICHAL: Yes! I am afraid! I am afraid! Ho! Ho, there! (*Claps her hands. Enter* BOY. *To* BOY.) Bring the water-skin for thy master, filled with water. And his pouch with bread—for he goeth on a journey.—O David! David! Now take thy cloak, and thy bow, and thy spear, and put on thy shoes. For thou must go! Jonathan cannot avail thee this time.

DAVID: Nay! Why shall I flee, when the sun is rising?

MICHAL: Yea! If thou go not before the sun is here, in the

morning shalt thou be slain. Oh, make ready! Thy shoes! Put them on! (DAVID *reluctantly obeys.*) Thy cloak, so they shall not know thee! (*He puts it on.*) Thy spear and bow!

BOY (*entering*): Here is the pouch and the water-flask.

MICHAL: Run, bring figs and dry curds. Dost thou hear aught at the door?

BOY: Naught!

Exit.

MICHAL: O David, art thou ready! Oh, that thou leavest me!

DAVID: I need not go! Yea, to comfort thee, I will go to the place that Jonathan knoweth of, and thou shalt send thither for me. Or wilt thou——

WOMAN-SERVANT (*re-entering*): O Michal! O David, master! There be men-at-arms approaching, under the wall, and walking by stealth. Oh, flee! Oh, flee! for they mean thy life.

MICHAL: Now must thou go by the window, into the fields. I see the sun's first glitter. Even for this hour have I kept the new rope ready. (*She fastens the rope to a stout stake, and flings the end from the window. To* DAVID.) Go! Go! Swiftly be gone!

DAVID: I will come again to thee. Sooner or later, as the Lord liveth, I will take thee again to me, unto my bed and my body.

MICHAL: Hark! They knock! Ha——a!

BOY (*entering*): There are men at the door!

MICHAL: Go! Call to them! Ask what they want! But touch thou not the door!

DAVID *meanwhile climbs through the window—the stake holds the rope.*

WOMAN-SERVANT (*climbing with her hands*): So! So! So! My lord David! So! So! Swing him not against the wall, O spiteful rope. So! So! He kicks free! Yea! And God be praised, he is on the ground, looking an instant at his hands. So he looks up and departs! Lifts his hand and departs!

MICHAL: Is he gone? Draw in the rope, and hide it safe.

WOMAN-SERVANT: That I will!

> *Meanwhile* MICHAL *has flung back the curtain of the recess where the low earthen bank of the bed is seen, with skins and covers. She takes the wooden image of a god and lays it in the bed, puts a pillow at its head, and draws the bed-cover high over it.*

MICHAL (*to herself*): Yea, and my house's god which is in my house, shall lie in my husband's place, and the image of my family god, which came of old from my mother's house, shall deceive them. For my house has its own gods, yea, from of old (*enter* BOY), and shall they forsake me?

BOY: They demand to enter. The King asketh for David, that he go before the King's presence.

MICHAL: Go thou, say to them: My lord and my master, David, is sick in his bed.

BOY: I will say that.

> *Exit.*

WOMAN-SERVANT: Sit thou nigh the bed. And if they still will come up, thou shalt say he sleepeth.

MICHAL: Yea, will I. (*Sits by bed.*) O god of my household, O god of my mother's house, O god in the bed of David, save me now!

> *Enter* BOY.

BOY: They will e'en set eyes on my master.

MICHAL: Stay! Say to them, that their captains shall come up, two only: but softly, for my lord David hath been sick these three days, and at last sleepeth.

BOY: I will tell them.

> *Exit.*

WOMAN-SERVANT: And I too will go bid them hush.

> *Exit.* MICHAL *sits in silence.*
>
> *Enter two* CAPTAINS *with the* WOMAN-SERVANT.

WOMAN-SERVANT: There he sleepeth in the bed.

MICHAL: Sh-h-h!

1ST CAPTAIN: I will go even now and tell the King.

> *Exeunt the* CAPTAINS *after a pause.*
>
> *Curtain*

Curtain rises after a short time on same scene.

WOMAN-SERVANT (*rushing in*): They are coming again down the street, but boldly now.

MICHAL: Yea! Let them come! By this time is David beyond their reach, in the secret place.

WOMAN-SERVANT: Oh, and what shall befall thee! Oh!

MICHAL: I am the King's daughter. Even Saul shall not lift his hand against me. Go down thou to the door, and hold the men whilst thou mayst. Why should we admit them forthwith? Say that Michal is performing her ablutions.

WOMAN-SERVANT: Will I not!

Exit.

MICHAL: And shall I strip the bed? They will search the house and the fields. Nay, I will leave it, and they shall see how they were fools. O teraphim, O my god of my own house, hinder them and help me. O thou my teraphim, watch for me!

Sound of knocking below.

VOICE OF SERVANT: Ho, ye! Who knocks, in the Lord's name?

VOICE OF CAPTAIN: Open! Open ye! In the name of the King.

VOICE OF SERVANT: What would ye in this house of sickness?

VOICE OF CAPTAIN: Open, and thou shalt know.

VOICE OF SERVANT: I may not open, save Michal bid me.

VOICE OF CAPTAIN: Then bid Michal bid thee open forthwith.

VOICE OF SERVANT: O thou captain of the loud shout, surely thou wert here before! Know then, my master is sick, and my mistress performeth her ablutions in the sight of the Lord. At this moment may I not open.

VOICE OF CAPTAIN: An thou open not, it shall cost thee.

VOICE OF SERVANT: Nay, now, is not my mistress King's daughter, and is not her command laid on me? O Captain, wilt thou hold it against me, who tremble between two terrors?

VOICE OF CAPTAIN: Tremble shalt thou, when the terror nips thee. E'en open the door, lest we break it in.

VOICE OF SERVANT: Oh, what uncouth man is this, that will break down the door of the King's daughter, and she naked at her bath, before the Lord!

VOICE OF CAPTAIN: We do but the King's bidding.

VOICE OF SERVANT: How can that be? What, did the King indeed bid ye break down the door of his daughter's house, and she uncovered in the Lord's sight, at her ablutions?

VOICE OF CAPTAIN: Yea! The King bade us bring before him instantly the bed of David, and David upon the bed!

VOICE OF SERVANT: Oh, now, what unseemly thing is this! Hath not the King legs long enough? And can he not walk hither on his feet? Oh, send, fetch the King, I pray thee, thou Captain. Say, I pray thee, that Michal prays the King come hither.

VOICE OF CAPTAIN: Word shall be sent. Yet open now this door, that the bird escapes me not.

VOICE OF SERVANT: O Captain! And is my master then a bird? O would he were, even the young eagle, that he might spread wing! O man, hast thou no fear what may befall thee, that thou namest David a bird? O Israel, uncover now thine ear!

VOICE OF CAPTAIN: I name him not.

VOICE OF SERVANT: And what would ye, with this bird my master! Oh, the Lord forbid that any man should call him a bird!

VOICE OF CAPTAIN: We e'en must bring him upon his bed before the King.

VOICE OF SERVANT: Now what is this! Will the King heal him with mighty spells? Or is David on his sick-bed to be carried before the people, that they may know his plight? What new wonder is this?

VOICE OF CAPTAIN: I cannot say—— Yet I will wait no longer.

MICHAL: Open, Maiden! Let them come up.

VOICE OF SERVANT: Oh, my mistress crieth unto me, that

I open. Yea, O Michal, I will e'en open to these men. For who dare look aslant at the King's daughter?

CAPTAIN (*entering, followed by soldiers*): Is David still in the bed? An he cannot rise, will we carry him upon the bed, before the King.

MICHAL: Now what is this?

CAPTAIN: Sleeps he yet? Ho, David, sleepest thou?

2ND SOLDIER: We will take up the bed, and wake him.

3RD SOLDIER: He stirs not at all.

CAPTAIN (*to* MICHAL): Yea, rouse him and tell him the King's will.

MICHAL: I will not rouse him.

CAPTAIN (*going to the bed*): Ho, thou! Ho! David! (*He suddenly pulls back the bed-cover.*) What is this? (*Sudden loud shrilling laughter from the* WOMAN-SERVANT, *who flees when the men look round.*)

SOLDIERS (*crowding*): We are deceived. Ha-ha! It is a man of wood and a goats'-hair bolster! Ha-ha-ha! What husband is this of Michal's?

MICHAL: My teraphim, and the god of my house.

CAPTAIN: Where hast thou hidden David?

MICHAL: I have not hidden him.

> *Pause.*

VOICE OF SAUL (*on the stair*): Why tarry ye here? What! Must the King come on his own errands? (*Saul enters.*) And are ye here?

MICHAL: The Lord strengthen thee, my Father.

SAUL: Ha! Michal! And can then David not rise from his bed, when the King sendeth for him?

CAPTAIN: Lo! O King! Behold the sick man on the bed! We are deceived of Michal.

SAUL: What is this? (*Flings the image across the room.*)

MICHAL: Oh, my teraphim! Oh, god of my house! Oh, alas, alas, now will misfortune fall on my house! Oh, woe is! woe is me! (*Kneels before teraphim.*)

SAUL: Where is David? Why hast thou deceived me?

MICHAL: O god of my house, god of my mother's house, visit it not upon me!

SAUL: Answer me, or I will slay thee!

MICHAL: God of my house, I am slain! I am slain!

SAUL: Where is David?

MICHAL: O my lord, he is gone; he is gone ere the sun made day.

SAUL: Yea, thou hast helped him against me.

MICHAL (*weeping*): Oh! Oh! He said unto me: *Let me go; why shouldst thou make me slay thee, to trouble my face in the sight of men.* I could not hinder him, he would have slain me there!

SAUL: Why hast thou deceived me so, and sent away mine enemy, that he is escaped?

MICHAL (*weeping*): I could not prevent him.

SAUL: Even when did he go?

MICHAL: He rose up before the Lord, in the deep night. And then he would away, while no man saw.

SAUL: Whither is he gone?

MICHAL: Verily, and verily, I know not.

Pause.

SAUL: He hath escaped me! And my flesh and my blood hath helped mine enemy. Woe to you, Michal! Woe to you! Who have helped your father's enemy, who would pull down thy father to the ground. Lo! My flesh and my blood rebel against me, and my seed lies in wait for me, to make me fall!

MICHAL: Oh, why must David be slain?

SAUL: Woe to you, Michal! And David shall bring woe to you, and woe upon you. David shall pull down Saul, and David shall pull down Jonathan; thee, Michal, he will pull down, yea, and all thy house. Oh, thou mayst call on the teraphim of thy house. But if thy teraphim love thy house, then would he smite David speedily to the death, for if David liveth I shall not live, and thou shalt not live, and thy brother shall not live. For David will bring us all down in blood.

MICHAL (*weeping*): O my Father, prophesy not against him!

SAUL: It shall be so. What, have I no insight into the dark!

And thou art now a woman abandoned of her man, and thy father castest thee off, because thou hast deceived him, and brought about his hurt.

MICHAL: O my Father, forgive me! Hold it not against me!

SAUL: Nay, thou hast bent thy will against thy father, and called destruction upon thy father's house.

MICHAL: Ah, no! Ah, no!

Curtain

SCENE XV: *Naioth in Ramah. A round, pyramid-like hill, with a stair-like way to the top, where is a rude rock altar. Many* PROPHETS, *young and old, wild and dressed in blue ephods without mantle, on the summit of the hill and down the slope. Some have harps, psalteries, pipes and tabrets. There is wild music and rough, ragged chanting. They are expecting something. Below,* SAMUEL *and* DAVID, *talking. Not far off a* PROPHET *in attendance.*

PROPHETS (*on hill—irregularly crying and chanting*): This is the place of the Lord! Upon us shines the Unseen! Yea, here is very God! Who dare come into the glory! O thou, filled with the Lord, sing with me on this high place. For the egg of the world is filled with God.

SAMUEL (*speaking to* DAVID): It is time thou shouldst go. As a fox with the dogs upon him, hast thou much fleeing to do.

DAVID: Must I always flee, my Father? I am already weary of flight.

SAMUEL: Yea, to flee away is thy portion. Saul cometh hither to seek thee. But surely shall he fall before the Lord. When he gets him back to his own city, enquire thou what is his will towards thee. And if it still be evil, then flee from him diligently, while he lives.

DAVID: And shall there never be peace between Saul's house and mine?

SAMUEL: Who knows the Lord utterly! If there be not peace this time, then shall there never in life be peace between thee and him, nor thy house and his.

DAVID: Yet am I his son-in-law, in Michal my wife! And my flesh yearneth unto mine own.

SAMUEL: Is the house of Saul thine own?

DAVID: Yea, verily!

SAMUEL: Dost thou say, *Yea, verily?* Hark, now! If this time there be peace between thee and him, it should be peace. But if not, then think of naught but to flee, and save thyself, and keep on fleeing while Saul yet liveth. The Lord's choice is on thee, and thou shalt be King in thy day. As for me, I shall never see thy day.

DAVID: Would I could make my peace with Saul! Would I could return to mine own house, and to mine own wife, and to the men of my charge!

SAMUEL: My son, once the Lord chose Saul. Now hath He passed Saul over and chosen thee. Canst thou look guiltless into the face of Saul? Can he look guiltless into thy face? Can ye look into each other's faces, as men who are open and at peace with one another?

DAVID: Yet would I serve him faithfully.

SAMUEL: Yea, verily! And in thine heart, art thou King, and pullest the crown from his brow with thine eyes.

DAVID: O my Father, I would not!

SAMUEL: Wouldst thou not? Willst thou say to me here and now: *As the Lord liveth, I will not be King! But Saul and his house shall rule Israel for ever: and Jonathan my friend shall be King over me!* Wilt thou say that to me?

DAVID: Does Samuel bid me say this thing?

SAMUEL: He bids thee not. But for Saul's sake, and for Jonathan's, and for Michal's, and for peace, wilt thou say it? Answer me from thine own heart, for I know the smell of false words. Yea, I bid thee, speak!

DAVID: The Lord shall do unto me as He will.

SAMUEL: Yea, for the Lord hath anointed thee, and thou

shalt rule Israel when Saul is dead, and I am dead, and
the Judges of Israel are passed away. For my day is
nearly over, and thine is another day. Yea, Saul has lived
in my day, but thou livest in thine own day, that I know
not of.

DAVID: O my lord, is there naught but wrath and sorrow
between me and Saul henceforth?

SAMUEL: The Lord will show! Knowest thou not?

DAVID: I would it were peace!

SAMUEL: Wouldst thou verily? When the wind changes,
will it not push the clouds its own way? Will fire leap
lively in wet rain? The Lord is all things. And Saul hath
seen a tall and rushing flame and hath gone mad, for the
flame rushed over him. Thou seest thy God in thine own
likeness, afar off, or as a brother beyond thee, who ful-
fils thy desire. Saul yearneth for the flame: thou for thy
to-morrow's glory. The God of Saul hath no face. But
thou wilt bargain with thy God. So be it! I am old, and
would have done. Flee thou, flee, and flee again, and
once more, flee. So shalt thou at last have the kingdom
and the glory in the sight of men. I anointed thee, but I
would see thee no more, for my heart is weary of its end.

DAVID: Wilt thou not bless me?

SAMUEL: Yea, I will bless thee! Yea, I will bless thee, my
son. Yea, for now thy way is the way of might, yea, and
even for a long space of time it shall be so. But after
many days, men shall come again to the faceless flame
of my Strength, and of Saul's. Yea, I will bless thee!
Thou art brave, and alone, and by cunning must thou
live, and by cunning shall thy house live for ever. But
hath not the Lord created the fox, and the weasel that
boundeth and skippeth like a snake!

DAVID: O Samuel, I have but tried to be wise! What should
I do, and how should I walk in the sight of men? Tell me,
my Father, and I will do it.

SAMUEL: Thou wilt not. Thou walkest wisely, and thy
Lord is with thee. Yea, each man's Lord is his own,

though God be but one. I know not thy Lord. Yet walk
thou with Him. Yea, thou shalt bring a new day for
Israel. Yea, thou shalt be great, thou shalt fight as a
flower fighteth upwards, through the stones and alone
with God, to flower in the sun at last. For the yearning
of the Lord streameth as a sun, even upon the stones.
(*A tumult above among the* PROPHETS. SAMUEL *looks up
—continues abstractedly.*) Yea, and as a flower thou
shalt fade. But Saul was once a burning bush, afire with
God. Alas, that he saw his own image mirrored in the
faces of men! (*A blare of music above.*)

SAMUEL (*to* PROPHET): What see ye?

PROPHETS (*shouting*): The sun on the arms of the King.

SAMUEL (*to* DAVID): Now shalt thou go! For I, too, will not
set mine eyes upon Saul the King.

DAVID: Bless me then, O my Father!

SAMUEL: The Lord fill thy heart and thy soul! The Lord
quicken thee! The Lord kindle thy spirit, so thou fall
into no snare! And now get thee gone! And when Saul
is returned to his own place, enquire thou secretly his
will towards thee. And then act wisely, as thou knoweth.

DAVID: I go forth into the fields, as a hare when the hound
gives mouth! But if the Lord go with me . . .

    Exit.

SAMUEL (*to* PROPHET): Is Saul surely in sight?

PROPHET: Verily, he is not far off. He has passed the well
of Shecu.

SAMUEL: Has he company of men?

PROPHET: Ten armed men has he.

SAMUEL: Will he still bring armed men to the high place?
Lo! Say thou to him: Samuel hath gone before the Lord,
in the hidden places of the Hill.

PROPHET: I will e'en say it.

SAMUEL: Say also to him: David, the anointed, is gone, we
know not whither. And let the company of the prophets
come down towards the King.

PROPHET: It shall be so.

Exit SAMUEL.

PROPHET (*climbing hill and calling*): O ye Prophets of the Lord, put yourselves in array, to meet Saul the King.

2ND PROPHET (*on hill with flute—sounds flute loudly with a strong tune—shouts*): Oh, come, all ye that know our God! Oh, put yourselves in array, ye that know the Name. For that which is without name is lovelier than anything named! (*Sounds the tune strongly.*)

> PROPHETS *gather in array—musicians in front; they chant slowly. As* SAUL *approaches they slowly descend.*

CHORUS OF PROPHETS: Armies there are, for the Lord our God!

Armies there are against the Lord!

Wilt thou shake spears in the face of Almighty God?

Lo! in thy face shakes the lightning.   *Bis.*

Countest thou thyself a strong man, sayest thou Ha-ha!

Lo! We are strong in the Lord! Our arrow seest thou not!

Yet with the unseen arrows of high heaven

Pierce we the wicked man's feet, pierce we his feet in the fight.

Lo! the bow of our body is strung by God.

Lo! how He taketh aim with arrow-heads of our wrath!

Prophet of God is an arrow in full flight

And he shall pierce thy shield, thou, thou Lord's enemy.

Long is the fight, yet the unseen arrows fly

Keen to a wound in the soul of the great Lord's enemy.

Slowly he bleeds, yet the red drops run away

Unseen and inwardly, as bleeds the wicked man.

Bleeding of God! Secretly of God.

SAUL (*entering with* ARMED MEN—PROPHETS *continue to chant*): Peace be with you!

PROPHET: Peace be with the King!

SAUL: Lo! ye prophets of God! Is not Samuel set over you?

PROPHET: Yea! O King!

SAUL (*beginning to come under the influence of the chant and to take the rhythm in his voice*): Is Samuel not here?

PROPHET: He hath gone up before the Lord!

SAUL: Surely the Lord is in this place! Surely the great brightness (*looks round*)—and the son of Jesse, is he among the prophets?

PROPHET: Nay, he has gone hence.

SAUL: Gone! Gone! What, has he fled from the high place! Surely he feared the glory! Yea, the brightness! So he has fled before the flame! Thus shall he flee before the flame! But gone? Whither gone?

PROPHET: We know not whither.

SAUL: Even let him go! Even let him go whither he will! Yea, even let him go! Yea! Come we forth after such as he? Let him go! Is not the Lord here? Surely the brightness is upon the hill! Surely it gleams upon this high place!

LEADER OF MEN-AT-ARMS: Tarry we here, O King? Where shall we seek the son of Jesse?

SAUL: Even where ye will.

LEADER: Tarrieth the King here?

SAUL: Yea! I will know if the Lord is verily in this place.

PROPHET: Verily He is here.

> *Company of* PROPHETS *still chant.*

SAUL (*going slowly forward*): Art Thou here, O Lord? What? Is this Thy brightness upon the hill? What? Art Thou here in Thy glory?

COMPANY OF PROPHETS: Fire within fire is the presence of the Lord!

> Sun within the sun is our God! *Bis.*
> Rises the sun among the hills of thy heart
> Rising to shine in thy breast? *Bis.*

SAUL: Yea! O Prophets! Am I not King? Shall not the Sun of suns rise among the hills of my heart, and make dawn in my body? What! Shall these prophets know the glory of the Lord, and shall the son of Kish stay under a cloud? (*Sticks his spear into the ground, and unbuckles his sword-belt.*)

LEADER OF ARMED MEN: Wilt thou go up before the Lord, O King? Then camp we here, to await thy pleasure.

SAUL: I will go up. Camp an ye will.

LEADER: Even camp we here. (*They untackle.*)

SAUL: Ha! Ha! Is there a glory upon the prophets? Do their voices resound like rocks in the valley! Ha! Ha! Thou of the sudden fire! I am coming! Yea! I will come into the glory! (*Advancing, throws down his woollen mantle. The* 1ST PROPHET *takes it up.*)

CHORUS OF PROPHETS: Whiteness of wool helps thee not in the high place,

Colours on thy coat avail thee naught.   *Bis.*

Fire unto fire only speaks, and only flame

Beckons to flame of the Lord!   *Bis.*

> The PROPHETS *divide and make way as* SAUL *comes up.*

SAUL: Is my heart a cold hearth? Is my heart fireless unto Thee? Kindler! it shall not be so! My heart shall shine to Thee, yea, unshadow itself. Yea, the fire in me shall mount to the fire of Thee, Thou Wave of Brightness!

SOLDIER (*below—with loud and sudden shout*): The sun is in my heart. Lo! I shine forth!

SAUL (*with suddenness*): I will come up! Oh! I will come up! Dip me in the flame of brightness, Thou Bright One, call up the sun in my heart, out of the clouds of me. Lo! I have been darkened and deadened with ashes! Blow a fierce flame on me, from the middle of Thy glory, O Thou of the faceless flame. (*Goes slowly forward.*) Oh, dip me in the ceaseless flame!

> Throws down his coat, or wide-sleeved tunic, that came below the knee and was heavily embroidered at neck and sleeves in many colours: is seen in the sleeveless shirt that comes half way down the thigh.

SOLDIER (*below*): Kings come and pass away, but the flame is flame forever. The Lord is here, like a tree of white fire! Yea, and the white glory goes in my nostrils like a scent.

SAUL: Shall a soldier be more blessed than I? Lo! I am not dead, thou Almighty! My flesh is still flame, still steady flame. Flame to flame calleth, and that which is dead is cast away. (*Flings off his shirt: is seen, a dark-skinned man in leathern loin-girdle.*) Nay, I carry naught upon me, the long flame of my body leans to the flame of all glory! I am no king, save in the Glory of God. I have no kingdom, save my body and soul. I have no name. But as a slow and dark flame leaneth to a great glory of flame, and is sipped up, naked and nameless lean I to the glory of the Lord.

CHORUS OF PROPHETS: Standeth a man upon the stem of upright knees

Openeth the navel's closed bud, unfoldeth the flower of the breast!

Lo! Like the cup of a flower, with morning sun

Filled is thy breast with the Lord, filled is thy navel's wide flower!

SOLDIER: Oh, come! For a little while the glory of the Lord stands upon the high place! Oh, come! before they build Him houses, and enclose Him within a roof! Oh, it is good to live now, with the light of the first day's sun upon the breast. For when the seed of David have put the Lord inside a house, the glory will be gone, and men will walk with no transfiguration! Oh, come to this high place! Oh, come!

SAUL: Surely I feel my death upon me! Surely the sleep of sleeps descends. (*Casts himself down.*) I cast myself down, night and day; as in death, lie I naked before God. Ah, what is life to me! Alas that a man must live till death visit him!—that he cannot walk away into the cloud of Sun! Alas for my life! For my children and my children's children, alas! For the son of Jesse will wipe them out! Alas for Israel! For the fox will trap the lion of strength, and the weasel that is a virgin, and bringeth forth her young from her mouth, shall be at the throats of brave men! Yea, by cunning shall Israel prosper, in the days of the seed of David: and by cunning and lurking in holes of the earth shall the seed of Jesse fill the earth. Then the Lord of Glory will have drawn far off, and gods shall be pitiful, and men shall be as locusts. But I, I feel my death upon me, even in the glory of the

Lord. Yea, leave me in peace before my death, let me retreat into the flame!

    A pause.

ANOTHER SOLDIER: Saul hath abandoned his kingdom and
his men! Yea, he puts the Lord between him and his
work!

PROPHET: E'en let him be! For his loss is greater than another's triumph.

SOLDIER: Yea! But wherefore shall a man leave his men
leaderless—even for the Lord!

1ST SOLDIER (*prophesying*): When thou withdrawest Thy
glory, let me go with Thee, O Brightest, even into the
fire of Thee!

CHORUS OF PROPHETS: Cast thyself down, that the Lord
    may snatch thee up.

Fall before the Lord, and fall high.

All things come forth from the flame of Almighty God,

Some things shall never return!   *Bis.*

Some have their way and their will, and pass at last

To the worm's waiting mouth.   *Bis.*

But the high Lord He leans down upon the hill,

And wraps His own in His flame,

Wraps them as whirlwind from the world,

Leaves not one sigh for the grave. . . .

    Curtain

SCENE XVI: *Late afternoon. A rocky place outside Gilgal.*
DAVID *is hiding near the stone Ezel.*

DAVID (*alone*): Now, if Jonathan comes not, I am lost. This
is the fourth day, and evening is nigh. Lo! Saul seeketh
my life. O Lord, look upon me, and hinder mine enemies! Frustrate them, make them stumble, O my God!
So near am I to Gilgal, yet between me and mine own

house lies the whole gap of death. Yea, Michal, thou art not far from me. Yet art thou distant even as death. I hide and have hidden. Three days have I hidden, and eaten scant bread. Lo! Is this to be the Lord's anointed! Saul will kill me, and I shall die! There! Someone moves across the field! Ah, watch! watch! Is it Jonathan? It is two men; yea, it is two men. And one walks before the other. Surely it is Jonathan and his lad! Surely he has kept his word! O Lord, save me now from mine enemies, for they compass me round. O Lord my God, put a rope round the neck of my enemy, lest he rush forward and seize me in the secret place. Yea, it is Jonathan, in a striped coat. And a man behind him carryeth the bow. Yea, now must I listen, and uncover my ears, for this is life or death. O that he may say: *Behold, the arrows are on this side of thee, take them!* For then I can come forth and go to my house, and the King will look kindly on me.—But he comes slowly, and sadly. And he will say: *The arrows are beyond thee*—and I shall have to flee away like a hunted dog, into the desert.—It will be so! Yea! And I must hide lest that lad who follows Jonathan should see me, and set Saul's soldiery upon me. (*Exit after a pause.*)

    Enter JONATHAN *with bow, and* LAD *with quiver.*

JONATHAN (*stringing his bow*): Lo! this is the stone Ezel. Seest thou the dead bush, like a camel's head? That is a mark I have shot at, and now, before the light falls, will I put an arrow through his nose. (*Takes an arrow.*) Will this fly well? (*Balancing it.*)

LAD: It is well shafted, O Jonathan.

JONATHAN: Ay! Let us shoot. (*Takes aim—shoots.*) Yea, it touched the camel's ear, but not his nose! Give me another! (*Shoots.*) Ah! Hadst thou a throat, thou camel, thou wert dead. Yet is thy nose too cheerful! Let us try again! (*Takes another arrow—shoots.*) Surely there is a scratch upon thy nose-tip! Nay, I am not myself! Give me the quiver. And run thou, take up the arrows ere the shadows come.

LAD: I will find them.

> *He runs, as he goes* JONATHAN *shoots an arrow over his head. The* LAD *runs after it—stops.*

JONATHAN: Is not the arrow beyond thee?

LAD: One is here! Here, another!

JONATHAN: The arrow is beyond thee! Make speed! Haste! Stay not!

LAD: Three have I! But the fourth——

JONATHAN: The arrow is beyond thee! Run, make haste!

LAD: I see it not! I see it not! Yea, it is there within bush. I have it, and it is whole. O master, is this all?

JONATHAN: There is one more. Behold it is beyond thee.

LAD (*running*): I see it not! I see it not! Yea, it is here!

JONATHAN: It is all. Come, then! Come! Nay, the light is fading and I cannot see. Take thou the bow and the arrows, and go home. For I will rest here awhile by the stone Ezel.

LAD: Will my master come home alone?

JONATHAN: Yea will I, with the peace of day's-end upon me. Go now, and wait me in the house. I shall soon come.

> *Exit* LAD. JONATHAN *sits down on a stone till he is gone.*

JONATHAN (*calling softly*): David! David!

> DAVID *comes forth, weeping. Falls on his face to the ground and bows himself three times before* JONATHAN. JONATHAN *raises him. They kiss one another, and weep.*

DAVID: Ah, then it is death, it is death to me from Saul?

JONATHAN: Yea, he seeks thy life, and thou must flee far hence.

DAVID (*weeping*): Ah, Jonathan! Thy servant thanks thee from his heart. But ah, Jonathan, it is bitter to go, to flee like a dog, to be houseless and homeless and wifeless, without a friend or helpmate! Oh, what have I done, what have I done! Tell me, what have I done! And slay me if I be in fault.

JONATHAN (*in tears*): Thou art not in fault. Nay, thou art

not! But thou art anointed, and thou shalt be King. Hath not Samuel said it even now, in Naioth, when he would not look upon the face of Saul! Yea, thou must flee until thy day come, and the day of the death of Saul, and the day of the death of Jonathan.

DAVID (*weeping*): Oh, I have not chosen this. This have I not taken upon myself. This is put upon me, I have not chosen it! I do not want to go! Yea, let me come to Gilgal and die, so I see thy face, and the face of Michal, and the face of the King. Let me die! Let me come to Gilgal and die! (*Flings himself on the ground in a paroxysm of grief.*)

JONATHAN: Nay! Thou shalt not die. Thou shalt flee! And till Saul be dead, thou shalt flee. But when Saul has fallen, and I have fallen with my father—for even now my life follows my father—then thou shalt be King.

DAVID: I cannot go!

JONATHAN: Yea! Thou shalt go now. For they will send forth men to meet me, ere the dark. Rise now, and be comforted. (DAVID *rises.*)

DAVID: Why shouldst thou save me! Why dost thou withhold thy hand! Slay me now!

JONATHAN: I would not slay thee, nor now nor ever. But leave me now, and go. And go in peace, forasmuch as we have sworn both of us in the name of the Lord, saying: *The Lord be between me and thee, and between my seed and thy seed for ever.*

DAVID: Yea, the covenant is between us! And I will go, and keep it.

> *They embrace in silence, and in silence* DAVID *goes out.*

JONATHAN (*alone in the twilight*): Thou goest, David! And the hope of Israel with thee! I remain, with my father, and the star-stone falling to despair. Yet what is it to me! I would not see thy new day, David. For thy wisdom is the wisdom of the subtle, and behind thy passion lies prudence. And naked thou wilt not go into the fire. Yea, go thou forth, and let me die. For thy virtue is in thy wit, and thy shrewdness. But in Saul have I known the magnanimity of a man. Yea, thou art a smiter down of giants, with a smart stone! Great men and magnanimous, men of the faceless flame, shall fall from Strength, fall before thee, thou David, shrewd whelp of the lion of Judah! Yet my heart yearns hot over thee, as over a tender, quick child. And the heart of my father yearns, even amid its dark wrath. But thou goest forth, and knowest no depth of yearning, thou son of Jesse. Yet go! For my twilight is more to me than thy day, and my death is dearer to me than thy life! Take it! Take thou the kingdom, and the days to come. In the flames of death where Strength is, I will wait and watch till the day of David at last shall be finished, and wisdom no more be fox-faced, and the blood gets back its flame. Yea, the flame dies not, though the sun's red dies! And I must get me to the city.

Rises and departs hastily.

THE ZEAL OF THY HOUSE

A Play

DOROTHY SAYERS

The Zeal of Thy House was first presented, in a slightly shortened form, at the Canterbury Festival, 1937, by the Friends of the Cathedral; Producer: Harcourt Williams, in association with Frank Napier.

My best thanks are due to Miss Margaret Babington and the Friends of Canterbury Cathedral for inviting me to write the play and for much hospitable kindness; to Mr. Laurence Irving and Miss Elizabeth Haffenden, who designed the stage and the costumes respectively; to Mr. G. H. Knight, who arranged the music; to the large cast of professional and amateur actors who interpreted the play with so much skill and enthusiasm; and, last but not least, to Mr. Williams and Mr. Napier, who, in addition to playing the important parts of William of Sens and Theodatus, coped so patiently and generously with the problems of production presented to them by an inexperienced playwright.

DOROTHY L. SAYERS

DRAMATIS PERSONÆ

Angelic Persons:

MICHAEL ⎫
RAPHAEL ⎬ *Archangels*
GABRIEL ⎭

CASSIEL, *the Recording Angel*

A YOUNG CHERUB, *Thurifer to Raphael*

Religious:

THE PRIOR OF CHRISTCHURCH ⎫
STEPHEN, *the Treasurer*
THEODATUS, *the Sacristan*
MARTIN, *the Guest-Brother and Infirmarian*   *Choir*
AMBROSE, *the Choirmaster*   *Brothers*
WULFRAM, *the Director of the Farm*   *and*
ERNULPHUS, *the Director of the Kitchen and*   *members*
    Distillery   *of the*
PAUL, *the Gardener*   *Cathedral*
HILARY, *the Almoner*   *Chapter*
SILVESTER, *the Painter*
GERVASE, *the Historian and Clerk* ⎭

HUBERT, *an Oblate, Superintendent of the Rough Masons*

Laymen:

WILLIAM OF SENS, *Architect to the Cathedral*

JOHN OF KENT ⎫
HENRY OF YORK ⎬ *Rival Architects*

SIMON ⎫
WALTER ⎬ *Workmen*
HUGH
GEOFFREY ⎭

A YOUNG BOY

THE LADY URSULA DE WARBOIS

MONKS; LAY-BROTHERS; WORKMEN; PILGRIMS OF BOTH SEXES
    TWO CANTORS AND A CHOIR OF MIXED VOICES

The action takes place during the years 1175-1179.

NOTE.—The names Michaël, Raphaël, are to be pronounced
as trisyllables throughout.

I: *At the opening of the play, the scene is set as for a meeting of the Chapter, with seats about a long table. The* CHOIR *having entered and taken their places, they sing the hymn following:*

CHOIR:
> Disposer supreme, and judge of the earth,
> Thou choosest for Thine the weak and the poor;
> To frail earthen vessels and things of no worth
> Entrusting Thy riches which aye shall endure.
>
> Those vessels soon fail, though full of Thy light,
> And at Thy decree are broken and gone;
> Then brightly appeareth the arm of Thy might,
> As through the clouds breaking the lightnings have
> shone.
> > *During the singing of the second half of this verse,*
> > *there enter* MICHAEL, RAPHAEL *with his* THURIFER,
> > GABRIEL *and* CASSIEL *the Recorder. They pass slowly*
> > *to the steps while the next verse is sung.*
> Like clouds are they borne to do Thy great will,
> And swift as the wind about the world go;
> All full of Thy Godhead while earth lieth still,
> They thunder, they lighten, the waters o'erflow.

℣. He maketh His Angels spirits.
℟. And His ministers a flaming fire.

MICHAEL:
> I am God's servant Michael the Archangel;
> I walk in the world of men invisible,
> Bearing the sword that Christ bequeathed His Church
> To sunder and to save.

RAPHAEL:
> > > I am God's servant
> Raphael the Archangel; and I walk

271

In the world of men invisible; I receive
Prayer spoken or unspoken, word or deed
Or thought or whatsoever moves the heart,
Offering it up before the Throne.

GABRIEL:

I am
God's servant the Archangel Gabriel,
The heavenly runner between God and man,
Moving invisible.

CASSIEL:

God's Recorder, I,
That keep the Book and cast up all accounts,
Cassiel, chief scrivener to the Courts of Heaven.

℣. Their sound is gone out into all lands.
℞. And their words into the ends of the world.

> *During the singing of the following verse, the* ANGELIC PERSONS *depart severally,* MICHAEL *standing above* RAPHAEL *on the right side of the steps, and the* THURIFER *kneeling below them;* CASSIEL *with his book on the left side of the steps with* GABRIEL *above.*

CHOIR:

Oh, loud be Thy trump and stirring the sound,
To rouse us, O Lord, from sin's deadly sleep;
May lights which Thou kindlest in darkness around
The dull soul awaken her vigils to keep.

> *The Recorder,* CASSIEL, *sits at his desk;*
> RAPHAEL *hands his censer to the* THURIFER, *and sits.*

MICHAEL: What is our business here to-day in Canterbury?

CASSIEL (*slapping the Book rather sharply open and running his finger down the page*): A meeting of the Cathedral Chapter to choose an architect for the rebuilding of the Choir after the great fire of 1174.

RAPHAEL (*reminiscently*): Ah, yes—the choir. I was sorry to see the old one go. It was very beautiful, and a favourite haunt of mine. Prayer had soaked into the stones and sanctified them.

CASSIEL (*austerely*): Mankind are exceedingly careless of their possessions. I have an entry against one Tom Hogg, neatherd, who neglected to clean his chimney and so had his thatch set on fire. The sparks were blown across the road and lodged under the lead roof of the church. In a short time all was ablaze.

GABRIEL: A heavy consequence for a light offence. Was that your doing, Michael?

MICHAEL: It was. I bore the flame betwixt my hands and set it among the rafters. We fanned it with our wings, my angels and I, riding upon the wind from the south.

CASSIEL (*muttering to himself over the Book*): . . . and seven, twenty-six . . . and three, twenty-nine . . . and nine, thirty-eight. . . .

RAPHAEL: Was it done to avenge the murder of the Archbishop?

CASSIEL: . . . and six. Put down four and carry eight.

MICHAEL: I do not know. I am a soldier. I take my orders.

CASSIEL (*casting up a column and ruling a line beneath it*): We all do that, Michael. Your interference in the matter does not affect the debit against Tom Hogg. He stands charged with Sloth to a considerable amount. What use was made of his sin is neither here nor there. It is a question of economics.

MICHAEL: Quite so. I could have done the work perfectly well myself, with a thunderbolt. Hogg's sin was not in the least necessary.

GABRIEL (*in humorous resignation*): Nothing that men do is ever necessary. At least, that is my experience. I find them very amusing.

> *The sound of the* "VENI CREATOR" *is heard from the lower end of the Chapter-House as the* CHOIR-MONKS *enter in procession.*

RAPHAEL: I find them very pathetic.

GABRIEL: You see them at their best, Raphael; as Michael sees them at their worst.

MICHAEL: I find them very perverse. If God were not infinite, they would surely exhaust His patience.

CASSIEL: They make a great deal of work in the counting house. Happily, being an angel, and not a man, I like work. The hatred of work must be one of the most depressing consequences of the Fall.

GABRIEL: Some men work like angels—and whistle over their work. They are much the most cheerful kind.

In the meantime, RAPHAEL *has met the* MONKS *at the foot of the steps and now precedes them to the Chapter, swinging his censer before them. The last verse of the hymn is sung by the* MONKS *standing about the table. Then all sit.* RAPHAEL *comes down to sit beside* MICHAEL. CASSIEL *opens the Book at a fresh page and prepares to take minutes of the meeting.*

PRIOR: Brethren, the business before us is, as you know, the appointment of an architect for the new choir. Our earlier discussions have brought the number of suitable candidates down to three. To-day we have to make our final choice.

THEODATUS: Under God's guidance.

PRIOR: Under God's guidance, of course, Father Theodatus. The three men in question are John of Kent, William of Sens, and Henry of York.

STEPHEN: Have we got the estimates, Father Prior?

PRIOR (*handing papers to* STEPHEN): I have two of them here. Henry of York's is lower than John of Kent's. He thinks he can restore the existing fabric without pulling it all down and rebuilding.

WULFRAM: Will that be safe? Some of the masonry looks to me very insecure. John of Kent is a local man—he has had more opportunity to judge. Besides, it would look well to give the work to a local man.

ERNULPHUS: John is very young—young men are always full of extravagant ideas. No experience.

HILARY: One must encourage young men. The future is with the young.

STEPHEN: John's estimate is certainly rather high. I don't think we can countenance extravagance.

PRIOR: We must consider expense, of course, Father Treasurer. Perhaps we had better have the architects in and hear what they have to say. Father Gervase—if you will be so good——

GERVASE *goes out by door, right.*

AMBROSE: Speaking as Choirmaster, may I urge here and now that we should get a man who understands something about acoustics. The old choir——

PAUL: What we want is the old choir restored to what it was before. I dislike this trivial modern stuff they are putting up all over the place, with its pointed arcading and flourishy capitals. Give me something solid, like Ely.

HILARY: One must move with the times, Father Paul. Now William of Sens is a progressive man.

WULFRAM: He is a foreigner. Why should we have a foreigner? Isn't an Englishman good enough? Money should be kept in the country.

STEPHEN: We do not seem to have had an estimate from William of Sens.

Re-enter GERVASE *right with* JOHN OF KENT, WILLIAM OF SENS, *and* HENRY OF YORK.

PRIOR: Not yet. He writes to me here—— Ah, good morning sirs. Pray come to the table. We have received your letters and considered your qualifications. We are now minded to hear your further opinions, after inspection of the site. You, Master Henry, have submitted a very conservative estimate of the cost of reconstruction.

HENRY: My Lord Prior, I have kept the expense down to the lowest possible figure; and after examination of the standing masonry I have prepared a plan and elevation.

Producing it.

PRIOR: Let us have that.

HENRY *puts the plan before the* PRIOR *and moves across to left of table.*

HENRY: You will see that I have allowed for keeping the

greater part of the standing fabric. (THEODATUS *and*
ERNULPHUS *on* PRIOR's *left examine the plan.*) With the
exception of the more grievously damaged portions
which I have marked, I see no reason why the present
structure may not be restored——

He passes plan down to the MONKS, *on left.*

JOHN: My Lord Prior——

HENRY: ——and put into good order along the original lines.
The existing outer walls may be retained——

WULFRAM: You think they are not too much weakened by
the action of the fire?

JOHN: Weakened? They are calcined in places almost to
powder.

HENRY: They can be patched and grouted, Master John;
and by the addition of supporting buttresses and by
altering the pitch of the roof so as to lessen the
thrust——

SILVESTER (*who has been studying the plan with* MARTIN):
Will not the effect of the buttresses be somewhat
clumsy?

MARTIN: There is something a little mean in the propor-
tions of this roof.

AMBROSE (*who is a man of one idea*): I should think it
would be bad for sound. After all, the chief use of a
choir is to hold services in.

MARTIN: The sooner we get a choir the better. The singing
has been very bad lately. I am ashamed to hear sacred
words so howled.

Hands back plan to HENRY, *who takes it across
right, to* WULFRAM.

AMBROSE (*defensively*): The nave is very awkward to sin
in. What with the west end boarded up——

HILARY: Well, we can't be expected to hold our services in
full view, not to say smell, of the common people.

AMBROSE: And the east end boarded up——

ERNULPHUS *quietly falls asleep.*

WULFRAM (*taking plan*): The draughts are appalling. I
caught a shocking cold last Tuesday.

AMBROSE: We are singing in a wooden box. You can't sing properly in a box.

PRIOR: Time is certainly of some importance.

STEPHEN: The cost is still more important.

HENRY (*moving up again left of table*): To repair, according to my plan, will be very much cheaper and quicker than to pull down and rebuild. I could engage to be ready within two years——

JOHN: And in two years more you will have to rebuild again. My Lord Prior——

PRIOR: You, Master John, recommend a complete reconstruction?

JOHN: Recommend? It must be done. Do not be deceived. This botching is useless and dangerous. It is unworthy——

HENRY: Master John, I am older than you and more experienced——

JOHN: You never in your life built anything bigger than a parish church.

PRIOR: Master John, Master John!

JOHN: This is the Cathedral Church of Christ at Canterbury. It must be the wonder of the realm—nay, of the world! Will you insult God with patchwork? Give me the commission, Lord Prior, and I will build you a church worth looking at!

> *Producing plan and elevation, which he passes to* STEPHEN.

HENRY: To the greater glory of Master John of Kent!

JOHN: To the glory of God and of the blessed Saints Dunstan and Elphege.

STEPHEN (*aside to the* PRIOR): And the entire depletion of the Treasury. Will somebody please tell me where the money is to come from?

THEODATUS: The devotion of the common people is most touching. A poor widow yesterday brought us five farthings, all her little savings.

STEPHEN: Our Lord will reward her. But that will not go very far.

MARTIN: I think we ought to take the long view. Canterbury is the most important church in the Kingdom, and attracts a great many people to the town. What with the visitors and the great increase in the number of pilgrims since the lamented death of the late Archbishop——

ALL: Blessed St. Thomas, pray for us.

They cross themselves.

MARTIN: A little money spent now on building will repay itself handsomely in donations and bequests.

STEPHEN *passes the plan to* HILARY.

THEODATUS (*rather loudly*): If the fire was a Divine judgment for the Archbishop's murder——

ERNULPHUS (*waking with a start*): Eh? the Archbishop? Blessed St. Thomas, pray for us.

He crosses himself and falls asleep instantly.

THEODATUS: I say, if the fire was a judgment, then the new building is a reparation to God, and should be an offering worthy of its high destination and a sufficient sacrifice for the sins of this country.

SILVESTER: No artist can do his best work when he has to consider every halfpenny. Thou shalt not muzzle the ox——

THEODATUS: All this talk about money is sheer lack of faith. God will provide.

STEPHEN: No doubt. But, humanly speaking, the accounts will have to go through the Treasury, and I feel responsible.

HILARY (*passing design to* PAUL): There is a good deal of elaborate and expensive ornament here, Master John.

PAUL: Modern nonsense, modern nonsense. Let us have the old choir back. Here is a groined roof and a clerestory and a lot of fiddle-faddle. How long is all this going to take?

JOHN (*uncompromisingly*): Seven years—perhaps more.

MARTIN: Seven years! Have we to put up with half a cathedral for seven years? Why, God made the world in six days!

PRIOR: God, Father Martin, was not subject to limitations of funds or material.

JOHN (*angrily aside to* WILLIAM): Nor to the cheese-paring parsimony of a monastic chapter.

WILLIAM (*who has listened to all this with a quiet smile; with a touch of humour*): Possibly God is an abler architect than any of us.

PRIOR: We have not yet heard your opinion, Master William. Do you think it possible to restore the remaining fabric?

WILLIAM: Oh, I should think very likely. I should certainly hope to save some of it.

JOHN (*angrily to* WILLIAM): That is *not* what you said to us outside.

WILLIAM: But I really cannot say—I do not see how anybody can say—without prolonged and careful examination.

AMBROSE: That's very true. Very reasonable.

WILLIAM: That is why I have as yet prepared no estimate or plan. But I have brought some drawings of the work entrusted to me at Sens and elsewhere which will give you some idea of the kind of thing I should like to do here.

Hands papers to PRIOR.

PRIOR: Now, I like that. Extremely fine and dignified. And very modern in feeling.

STEPHEN: And not too ornate.

WILLIAM *hands them on down right.*

GERVASE: It is wonderful. It is like a poem in stone. I should dearly love to see it. How light—and yet how majestic!

He looks admiringly at WILLIAM.

WILLIAM: Time and cost would depend on the extent of the work. I suggest making a thorough survey before getting out a preliminary plan and estimate. Naturally, I should commit you to nothing without the advice and approval of yourself, Lord Prior and the Father Treasurer.

STEPHEN: Just so. We should object to nothing in reason.

WILLIAM (*he has now got the ear of the house*): I should be obliged (*firmly*) to stipulate for the best materials.

THEODATUS: God's service demands the best materials.

WILLIAM: But we can effect an economy by making good use of local talent, of which I am sure we must possess a great deal——

WULFRAM: I am all in favour of local talent.

WILLIAM: And we may reduce the cost of shipping and carriage by the use of certain mechanical devices of my own invention, which I need not say I shall be happy to place at the disposal of the authorities without extra fee.

PRIOR: Thank you—that is very proper, very generous. . . . H'm. Well, Brethren, I think we have now the facts before us. If these gentlemen would kindly retire for a few moments. . . .

General movement, GERVASE *goes up, right, to door.*

ERNULPHUS (*waking with a start*): Eh, what? what? Have we finished?

SILVESTER: No, Father Ernulphus. The architects are retiring while we deliberate.

ERNULPHUS: Oh, I see. Very good.

He falls asleep again.

HENRY: Two or three years only, Lord Prior—say four at most—and a strict regard for economy.

Exit HENRY.

JOHN: Consider, Lord Prior—a structure worthy of its dedication—and safety to life and limb, if you think that matters.

Exit JOHN.

WILLIAM: Sir, if I am chosen, I will do my best.

Exit WILLIAM. GERVASE *follows them off. The rest examine the plans and documents.*

GABRIEL: The motives of mankind are lamentably mixed.

RAPHAEL: They mean well, I assure you.

MICHAEL: Then it is a pity they do not say what they mean.

CASSIEL: It is most confusing. I have worn out my pen trying to keep up with them.

GABRIEL: That is easily remedied. Allow me.

He plucks a feather from his own wing and hands it to CASSIEL *as* GERVASE *re-enters and shuts the door.*

CASSIEL (*trimming the feather into a pen*): Thank you.

PRIOR: Well, Brethren?

SILVESTER: I must say, Master Henry's plan seems rather makeshift.

WULFRAM: He is a Yorkshire man. I would as soon have a foreigner as a Yorkshire man.

STEPHEN: He is too anxious to please. First he says two years—then three or four. I should not rely on his estimate.

PRIOR: Are we agreed, then, not to appoint Henry of York? (*The* MONKS *signify agreement.*) Then that leaves us the choice between John of Kent and William of Sens.

MICHAEL: What will they make of that?

CASSIEL: They will choose the man whom God has appointed.

GABRIEL: I shall see to it that they do.

WULFRAM: Let us have John. He is a local man.

As the MONKS *give their votes,* GERVASE *notes them down.*

MARTIN: Yes; his church will attract attention and bring people into the town.

PAUL: Too new-fangled and showy. I am for William. I distrust these go-ahead young men.

HILARY: I have said William all along.

GERVASE: Clearly William is a great craftsman—let us choose him.

THEODATUS: We know nothing about him personally. John is a young man of devout life.

STEPHEN: What has that to do with it? Besides, his manners are abominable. I give my voice for William.

SILVESTER: I like John's plan—we haven't seen William's.

AMBROSE: John's plan looks good from the musician's point of view.

PRIOR: I must not influence you—but I admit I am greatly impressed by William of Sens. . . . Father Gervase, how does the voting stand?

GERVASE: Five have spoken for John and five for William.

GABRIEL: This is where I interfere.

He goes up into the Chapter-House.

PRIOR: Somebody has not voted. Who is it?

Everybody stares round at ERNULPHUS.

MARTIN: It is Father Ernulphus.

THEODATUS: He has been asleep all the time.

GABRIEL *stands behind* ERNULPHUS.

PAUL: He is getting very shaky, poor old soul.

THEODATUS (*loudly in* ERNULPHUS' *ear*): Father Ernulphus!

ERNULPHUS (*starting into consciousness*): Eh? eh? what?

THEODATUS (*shouting in his ear*): Do you vote for John of Kent or William of Sens?

GABRIEL (*in his other ear*): William of Sens.

ERNULPHUS (*to* THEODATUS): Eh? Yes, of course. William of Sens. Certainly.

He closes his eyes again.

THEODATUS (*vexed*): He hasn't heard a word. (*Loudly*) Father Ernulphus!

ERNULPHUS (*suddenly alert*): You needn't shout. I'm not deaf. I have followed everything very carefully. I said William of Sens and I mean William of Sens.

He shuts his eyes tight with an air of finality.

THEODATUS: Really, Father Prior!

STEPHEN: You will never move him now.

A pause.

PRIOR: The vote of the Chapter, then, is for William of Sens. If there is no further business, the Chapter is dissolved.

ALL (*rising*): Glory be to the Father, and to the Son, and to the Holy Ghost. As it was in the beginning, is now and ever shall be, world without end. Amen.

GABRIEL *goes up and stands above.*

PRIOR (*as the* MONKS *begin to file down, left and right*):
Father Gervase, pray inform the architects of this decision. Thank those that are not chosen for their pains; they shall receive their journey-money from the Father Treasurer. Ask Master William to come and see me. No time must be lost in putting the work in hand, for the night cometh wherein no man can work.

> *Exit* GERVASE, *right, as the* PRIOR *follows the* MONKS *out.*

℣. Be strong, all ye people of the land, saith the Lord, and work; for I am with you, saith the Lord God of Hosts.

℟. No man, having put his hand to the plough, and looking back, is fit for the Kingdom of God.

℣. There is nothing better than that a man should rejoice in his own works, for that is his portion.

℟. Ascribe ye greatness unto our God; He is the Rock, His work is perfect.

> *Re-enter* GERVASE, *right, with* JOHN, HENRY *and* WILLIAM.

JOHN (*indignantly to* WILLIAM): Trickery, Master William, sheer trickery and cheating. You know well enough that you *cannot* restore a single stone of it.

HENRY (*with equal indignation*): You will tell any lie in order to get the job. You promise economy, and you will spend their money like water. It is treacherous—it is dishonest——

WILLIAM: *You* would not only promise, you would *do* them a dishonest piece of work. *That* is treachery, if you like, Master Henry.

> HENRY *bounces down the steps with an angry exclamation.*

JOHN: But why must you flatter and fawn on them? Why pander to all their ridiculous foibles? Cannot you tell them the truth as I do and let the best man win?

WILLIAM: The trouble with you, my lad, is want of tact. You can handle stone, but you can't handle man. You must learn to humour fools if you want to get anything done.

JOHN: You stinking fox!

> JOHN *joins* HENRY, *and they go off muttering to-gether, sinking their differences in their common grievance.*

GERVASE (*troubled*): Master William, is it true, what they say?

WILLIAM: Listen to me, young man. At my age one learns that sometimes one has to damn one's soul for the sake of the work. Trust me, God shall have a choir fit for His service. Does anything else really matter?

> *He and* GERVASE *follow the others out.*

> *During the singing of the following Interlude, the scene-shifters set the stage to represent the site of the choir. The other three* ANGELS *go up and stand above with* GABRIEL.

Every carpenter and workmaster that laboureth night and day, and they that give themselves to counterfeit imagery, and watch to finish a work;

The smith also sitting by the anvil, and considering the iron work, he setteth his mind to finish his work, and watcheth to polish it perfectly.

So doth the potter sitting at his work, and turning the wheel about with his feet, who is always carefully set at his work, and maketh all his work by number.

All these trust to their hands, and every one is wise in his work.

Without these cannot a city be inhabited, and they shall not dwell where they will nor go up and down;

They shall not be sought for in public council, nor sit high in the congregation;

But they will maintain the state of the world, and all their desire is in the work of their craft.

II: *About two years have passed since the previous scene.* WORKMEN *go in and out, fetching tools and barrows from door, left, which appears to lead to some kind of office or store-room, and carrying out, right, blocks of dressed stone on hand-barrows, etc. About half a dozen* LAY BROTHERS *and* WORKMEN *remain to work on the stage. A general impression of bustle and movement is accentuated by the entrance of a number of respectably dressed* PILGRIMS, *chattering like jackdaws,—right.*

PILGRIMS (*they enter by twos and threes, gape vaguely about and pass on and out by way of the steps*): Beautiful, beautiful; and everything in such good taste. . . . I wonder what it costs to keep the shrine going in candles. . . . Two years they've been building now— goodness knows how long it's going to take. . . . Dickon, you bad boy, leave that saw alone. . . . Who did you say the architect was? Wilfrid somebody? . . . My poor, dear husband—such a sad sufferer—I was determined to make the pilgrimage. . . . No doubt, it will be all very fine when it's finished, but I don't think it's a patch on Lincoln. . . . Shocking bad dinners they give you at the "Lamb"—you'd better come and have a bite with us. . . . I beg your pardon, madam, was that your foot? Ah, the poor, dear, martyred Archbishop! Such a charming man. I saw him when he came back from France—yes, really, he was as close to me as I am to you. . . . Have you heard the one about the three fat friars and the tinker's widow? Well, there were three begging friars. . . . So I said to her, "Very well, you may take your wages and go." . . . It came to me as I was kneeling there that God would most surely have pity upon my sister. . . . I must say it comes out more expensive than I'd reckoned for. And I was abominably cheated that night we lay at Rochester. . . . The King must be a very naughty man to have killed the poor Archbishop. . . . There! I told you it was only putting ideas into the child's head. . . . Bad business, that fire, and if you ask me, I don't believe the true story ever came out. . . . Yes, darling, ever so sorry—barefoot in a white sheet. . . . Indeed, I have a very great devotion to St. Thomas. . . . This Purbeck marble's all the rage, but I don't care about it myself . . . etc., etc.

They trail away, still chattering. During the confusion, GERVASE *and* WILLIAM *have made their entrances, right,* GERVASE *crossing the stage and vanishing into doorway, left, while* WILLIAM *sits at a trestle-table, centre, and waits resignedly for his workshop to get clear. As the stage empties, the* ANGELS *come down again and take up their former positions.*

CASSIEL:

Two years of toil are passed; what shall I write
About this architect?

MICHAEL:

       A schedule here,
Long as my sword, crammed full of deadly sins;
Jugglings with truth, and gross lusts of the body,
Drink, drabbing, swearing; slothfulness in prayer;
With a devouring, insolent ambition
That challenges disaster.

CASSIEL:

       These are debts;
What shall I set upon the credit side?

GABRIEL:

Six columns, and their aisles, with covering vaults
From wall to arcading, and from thence again
To the centre, with the keystones locking them,
All well and truly laid without a fault.

CASSIEL:

No sum of prayer to balance the account?

GABRIEL:

Ask Raphael, for prayers are in his charge.

CASSIEL:

Come, Raphael, speak; or is thy censer cold?
Canst thou indeed find any grace in William
The builder-up of Canterbury?

RAPHAEL: Yes.

He swings his censer, which gives out a cloud of incense.

Behold, he prayeth; not with the lips alone,
But with the hand and with the cunning brain
Men worship the Eternal Architect.
So, when the mouth is dumb, the work shall speak
And save the workman. True as mason's rule
And line can make them, the shafted columns rise
Singing like music; and by day and night
The unsleeping arches with perpetual voice
Proclaim in Heaven, to labour is to pray.

MICHAEL: Glory to God, that made the Firmament!

Enter GERVASE, *left.*

GERVASE: Here are the letters for you to sign, Master William. These to Caen, about the next shipment of stone; these to Dover, with instructions for the unloading and carriage. I have mentioned the matter of the damaged crane and told them it must be made good at their own expense.

Hands pen and inkhorn.

WILLIAM: Thanks, Father Gervase.

Signs letters.

GERVASE: This is the invoice for the oak roofing-beams. And there is an enclosure I can't quite understand. Something about the commission.

WILLIAM (*hastily*): That has no business to be there. Idiots! It refers to a private transaction. Give it to me. I will deal with it myself. Anything more?

Taking paper and pocketing it.

GERVASE: Do you mind looking at this consignment note? We seem to be fifty scaffold-poles short; but I will have them checked again.

WILLIAM: Good. I can trust you to get it put in order. I

don't know what we should have done these two years
without your vigilant eye and skilful pen.

GERVASE: I wish I could do more to help. But my hands
are no good for anything but writing. I should have
loved to take a more active part in the work. (*Smiling.*)
I must be content to be the man with only one talent,
and make it go as far as I can.

 Enter HUBERT, *right.*

WILLIAM: If every one would make good use of his own
talent and let others do the same, the world would move
faster. Well, Brother Hubert, what's the trouble?

HUBERT: Well, sir, if you'd kindly take a look at this here
last lot of lime (*presenting specimens of lime and mortar
on a shovel*). If lime you can call it. What they've done
to it I *don't* know, but it don't seem to have no body in
it as you might say. It don't bind right. You should hear
what my lads has to say about it.

WILLIAM: Yes. Poor slack stuff. Where did this come
from?

GERVASE: From Jocelyn's. You remember, the Father Treasurer wanted the order given to them. He said Thomas
Clay's price was excessive.

WILLIAM: I wish the Father Treasurer would allow me to
know my own job. Tell him—no, don't tell him anything. Order in a fresh lot from Thomas Clay's as before,
instructing him to charge it up at Jocelyn's price and
send me a private note of the difference. We can adjust
it on that timber account. Do you understand? If these
timber merchants are knaves enough to offer me a five
per cent commission for giving them the contract and
Father Stephen is fool enough to grudge a few pounds
extra for first-class material, all right. We play off the
knave against the fool, get what we want, and save argument.

HUBERT: Ay, that's so. What the Father Treasurer don't
see won't worry him.

GERVASE: But is it honest?

HUBERT: All I know is, this here lime ain't honest. Prior Wibert, him as built the Water-Tower, wouldn't never have asked his masons to put up with cheap rubbish like this here.

WILLIAM (*to* GERVASE): No, of course it's not honest. And it's not exactly safe. That is, it's liable to misconstruction, if proclaimed upon the housetops. But the Lord commended the unjust steward.

HUBERT: You can't make bricks without straw, nor yet mortar without lime. And if Prior Wibert, rest his soul, was alive, he'd say the same.

WILLIAM: Cheer up, little churchman. Take thy bill and sit down quickly and write fifty. Nobody's robbing the Church.

Exit GERVASE, *left, still a trifle unhappy about it.* H'm. Unfortunate. He'll lie awake all night wrestling with his conscience, and probably let the whole thing out to the Father Treasurer. Can't be helped. Sufficient for the day. . . . How about the new arch? D'you think she's settled in? I'd like to get those supports out to-day.

HUBERT: Been over every inch of her, sir, and I think she'll do. We're getting the tackle up now.

WILLIAM: Let me know when you're ready; I don't want anything started till I come. What do you think of the plan for the roof and clerestory?

HUBERT: Grand, sir, grand. I only wish Prior Wibert, good man, was alive to see it. Always a man for new ideas, was Prior Wibert. Ah! He'd have loved that tall shafting and the way the cross-ribbing is made to carry the span. "Mark my words, Hubert," he used to say to me, "the arch is the secret of building. We ain't half learned yet," he'd say, "what the arch can carry when it's put to it."

WILLIAM: He was right, there. But we're finding out. We're finding out every day. Greece never guessed it; Rome only half understood it; but our sons will know in the years to come. (*With rising excitement.*) We all have our dreams, Hubert. Churches we shall never live to see. Arch shouldering arch, shaft, vault and keystone, window and arcading, higher and wider and lighter, lifting roof, tower, spire, into the vault of heaven—columns slender as lily-stalks—walls only a framework for the traceries—living fountains of stone——

HUBERT: That's so, Master, that's so. That's the way to build. Each stone carrying his neighbour's burden, as you might say.

WILLIAM: A triumph of balance, eh, Hubert? A delicate adjustment of interlocking stresses. Look! there was an idea came into my head last night.

He sketches on a block of stone.

Enter STEPHEN *and* MARTIN, *right.*

STEPHEN: Well, I must say, it's rather inconsiderate. Still, we mustn't let the opportunity slip.

MARTIN: Certainly not; rich benefactors have to be humored. Nobody knows that better than he does. Will you tackle him?

STEPHEN: If you like. Er—Master William!

WILLIAM: What can I do for you, Father Treasurer?

STEPHEN: Forgive me for interrupting you—I know you're very busy, but the fact is, we have a visitor——

MARTIN: Rather an important visitor.

STEPHEN: The Lady Ursula de Warbois——

Enter THEODATUS, *right. He has his sleeves tucked up, and a coarse apron over his habit, and carries a trowel.*

MARTIN: We had been hoping she would come——

STEPHEN: She has just arrived and asked to see the Father Prior.

MARTIN: She is with him now. Father Theodatus, have you heard? The Lady Ursula is with the Father Prior!

THEODATUS: Indeed?

He goes across to speak to one of the WORKMEN.

WILLIAM: Come, sirs. All this excitement is scarcely be-

coming to your cloth. Is the lady young and beautiful?
And what is she doing with the Father Prior, or he with
her.

    WORKMEN *snigger*.

THEODATUS: Master William! Pray control your tongue.

WILLIAM: There! you see you have shocked Father Theodatus.

STEPHEN: The Lady Ursula is the widow of an exceedingly
wealthy knight.

MARTIN: She has come to reside in Canterbury; and has
several times expressed interest in the work. To-day
she has come and wants to see over the new choir——

STEPHEN: If she is pleased with what she sees, she will
probably be good for a handsome subscription.

WILLIAM: Oh, very well. Take her where you like. Better
stand clear of the new arch, though. We're going to get
the supports out, and it might come down. You never
know—eh, Hubert?

HUBERT: That's right. You never know.

STEPHEN: Yes—but the point is, she particularly wants to
meet the architect and be shown round personally.

MARTIN: She wants to see the plans, and have everything
explained to her.

WILLIAM: T'cha! women always want explanations. But
they never listen, and wouldn't understand a word if
they did. I've no use for women—not in working hours.

THEODATUS (*gloomily*): The curse came by a woman.

WILLIAM: Well—if it comes to that, so did *you*, Father
Theodatus.

HUBERT: That's right. Women are a curse—but we can't
get *into* the world, nor *on* in the world without 'em.

MARTIN: Well, Master William, I'm sure you will oblige
her. People always like to talk to the architect. The
human touch, you know. It's always good publicity.

WILLIAM: Oh, very well, I suppose one must make one's
self a martyr to publicity. Go and keep an eye on the
lads, Hubert; I'll come as soon as I'm free.

Going, STEPHEN *and* MARTIN *offer to accompany him.*

No, thanks. I can find my own way. Don't you run your heads into temptation. *Sed libera nos a malo*—deliver us from the apple and all its consequences.

Exit, right, with HUBERT.

STEPHEN: Dear me! I hope he will behave with discretion.

MARTIN: Never fear. He can bridle his tongue when he likes. He is a politic man. Remember how he persuaded us into the expense of re-building.

STEPHEN: Yes—we have had some experience of his policy. Well—he wheedled money out of us; let him now wheedle it out of the Lady Ursula.

MARTIN: At any rate, he is a first-class workman. He gives us good value for our money.

STEPHEN: Does he? I hope he does. Sometimes I have my doubts. From something one of the carriers let fall the other day, I am inclined to suspect him of—some irregularities.

MARTIN: Oh, surely not! The accounts all go through your hands and the correspondence through those of Father Gervase.

STEPHEN: Father Gervase? Do you think a crafty old fox like that hasn't the wit to hoodwink a young and innocent churchman like Father Gervase? Is he in the office, by the way? I am inclined to give him a caution. (*Calling left.*) Father Gervase!

GERVASE (*emerging, left, with letters*): Yes, Father Stephen?

STEPHEN: Tell me; since you have been handling Master William's letters, have you ever had any reason to suspect any financial irregularities?

GERVASE (*taken aback*): Financial irregularities?

STEPHEN: Tampering with the estimates? Fudging the accounts? Pocketing commissions and that sort of thing? Doing little deals on the side?

GERVASE (*recovering himself; with confidence*): I am quite positive, Father Stephen, that Master William has never cheated the Church of a single penny, and never would. He thinks of nothing, lives for nothing, but the integrity of his work. If you knew him as well as I do, working with him these two years, you would be sure of that.

STEPHEN: I am glad to hear it. But keep your eyes open. I have heard stories, and I am not altogether satisfied.

GERVASE: Would it not be better to speak openly to Master William himself?

THEODATUS: Of course it would; but they are afraid to. Why? Because the man has managed to get the ear of the Father Prior—and because they don't want him to throw up the job in the middle—and because, having once put their hands to dirty tools, they don't know how to draw back. (*To* STEPHEN *and* MARTIN) No man can serve God and mammon. God's House should be built with prayer. You are trying to build it with worldly wisdom and worldly lucre. Look at all those pilgrims! How many of them have clean hands and pure hearts?

MARTIN: We cannot see into their hearts.

THEODATUS: Have you listened to their talk? One in ten may be sincere. The rest are idle men and gadding women, making pilgrimage an excuse for a holiday trip —compounding for old sins by committing new ones. All they come for is to drink and gossip in alehouses, tell each other dirty stories, pick up loose companions, waste their own time and other people's, and gabble through a few perfunctory prayers at top speed, so as to have more time for sight-seeing.

GERVASE: Are you not a little uncharitable?

STEPHEN: Most of them are very worthy people. And after all, we can't do without their money.

THEODATUS: If you had faith, you could. You degrade the Church by these vulgar and dubious methods of publicity.

MARTIN: Really, Father Theodatus! This is monstrous. The Father Prior himself entrusted me with the publicity side of the appeal. I have taken great pains to get these pilgrimages properly advertised. And this is my reward!

GERVASE: Brethren! brethren! All the workmen are listening to you.

Enter WILLIAM, *right, with* URSULA.

MARTIN: Let them listen!

THEODATUS: I do not care who hears me!

WILLIAM: Pray, madam, mind your head—the doorway is rather low. One step down. Allow me. This is just a little corner of our workshop, where—— Walter! Hugh! Simon! Is nobody doing any work to-day? Do you take it for the Feast of St. Lazybones? (*The* WORKMEN *hurriedly return to their tasks.*) Walter—that corner is out of true. And here, you! Is that the way to treat your tools? . . . I beg your pardon, madam. The moment my back is turned, everything seems to come to a standstill.

URSULA: No wonder. Without the heart, how can the limbs do their office? You are the heart of the undertaking.

WILLIAM (*formally*): It is very good of you to say so. I think you know Father Stephen, the Treasurer? Father Martin, the Guest-Brother? Father Theodatus, the Sacristan? And Father Gervase, who is Clerk and Historian to the Chapter, and is good enough to deal with my correspondence in his spare time. (*To* GERVASE) Have those letters gone?

GERVASE: I am just taking them to the messenger.

Exit GERVASE, *right.*

MARTIN: And what, madam, do you think of our Cathedral?

URSULA: I think it must be the most beautiful in the world. And how glorious the new choir will be when it is finished! Master William has described it all to me and has promised to show me all his plans and drawings. That was a promise, was it not, Master William?

WILLIAM: Certainly—if you are really interested.

URSULA: Of course I am interested. I am glad I have come to live in Canterbury. It will be so exciting to watch the work going on from day to day. A widow needs an interest in life. And it will be a great comfort to live under the protection of blessed St. Thomas.

MARTIN: Thousands of the suffering and bereaved have already found healing and consolation by his benign intervention. Only a few weeks ago, out of a large congregation of worshippers who attended a special service——

Bell begins to ring. MONKS *enter, right, and file across the stage and down the steps.* WORKMEN *lay down their tools and go out, right, with dinner-baskets.*

THEODATUS: That is the bell for nones.

Exit down steps.

MARTIN: I will tell you presently about the special service.

Exeunt STEPHEN *and* MARTIN *down steps.*

WILLIAM: Do you propose to attend nones? The lower part of the nave is available for the laity.

URSULA: No; I propose to see those drawings of yours.

WILLIAM: I do not think you came here to see architectural drawings.

URSULA: I came—to see the architect. (*Pause.*) Did you realise this was not the first time we had met?

WILLIAM: I realised it perfectly. I had the honour to pick up your glove yesterday in the market-place.

URSULA: I was much indebted to you for the courtesy.

WILLIAM: I was much indebted to you for the opportunity. I am an opportunist. So, I fancy, are you. We have that much in common.

URSULA: Is that an impertinence, I wonder?

WILLIAM: Yes.

URSULA: I ought to be offended with you.

WILLIAM:
If you are wise, you will be. Let us be plain.
The first time our eyes met, we knew one another
As fire knows tinder. You have seen what havoc
Fire works. Let be.

URSULA:

              I do not fear the fire.

WILLIAM:

My fire should be a lamp to light the world,
Fed with my life, consuming only me;
Will you not learn that it is perilous
To play with fire? That it is death to come
Between the man and the work? In one man's life
Is room for one love and no more—one love;
I am in love with a dream.

URSULA:

                      Tell me your dreams
Sitting by the fire, seeing pictures in the fire,
Visions and dreams.

WILLIAM:

                    Your old men shall dream dreams
And your young men see visions—but not your women.
What use have women for the dreams of a man
Save to destroy them? What does a woman know
Of the love of knowledge, passing the love of women?
The passion of making, beside which love's little passion
Shows brittle as a bubble?—To raise up beauty from
    ashes
Like the splendour of resurrection; to see the stone
Knit unto stone and growing, as in the womb
Bone grows to bone; to build a world out of nothing—
That is my dream; that is the craftsman's dream,
The power and the glory, the kingdom of God and
    man—
Of man, never of woman. Women create
Passively, borne on a wind of lust, for a whim,
At the caprice of a man, in a smile, in a spasm
Of the flesh; we, with the will, with the blood, with the
    brain,
All the desire of the soul, the intent of the mind.

Now do you understand what my dreams are
And why they are not for you?

URSULA:

                        I understand.
Knowledge and work—knowledge is given to man
And not to woman; and the glory of work
To man and not to woman. But by whom
Came either work or knowledge into the world?
Not by the man. God said, "Ye shall not know;
Knowledge is death." And Adam was afraid.
But Eve, careless of peril, careless of death,
Hearing the promise, "Ye shall be as gods,"
Seized knowledge for herself, and for the man,
And all the sons of men; knowledge, like God;
Power to create, like God; and, unlike God,
Courage to die. And the reward for her
Was sorrow; but for Adam the reward
Was work—of which he now contrives to boast
As his peculiar glory, and in one breath
Denies it to the woman and blames her for it,
Winning the toss both ways. My simple Adam,
It is too late to scare woman with risks
And perils—woman, that for one splendid risk
Changed the security of Paradise,
Broke up the loom and pattern of creation,
Let in man's dream on the world, and snatched the
    torch
Of knowledge from the jealous hand of God
So that the fire runs in man's blood for ever.

WILLIAM (*carried away*):
So that she runs like fire in a man's blood
For ever! Take what thou wilt—the risk, the sorrow,
The fire, the dream—and in the dream's end, death.

GABRIEL:
Thus Eve cast down the gauntlet in God's face:
"My will for Thine; man's purpose against God's;

Slay me and slay the man, slay all my seed,
But let man's knowledge and man's work go on."

MICHAEL:

Thus God took up the gauntlet in Eve's face.
Having, like man, courage to look on death:
"My Son for thy sons, and God's blood for man's;
Crucify God, but let the work go on."

CASSIEL:

By man came sin.

RAPHAEL:

O felix culpa, quae
Talis et tanti meruit Redemptoris!

HUBERT (off): Master William! Master William!

WILLIAM: There! that means work. You see what happens
when one starts this kind of thing. Go now. They are
coming out of church. Quickly—or we shall have Father
Martin and the special service all over again. I will
come to your lodging after supper.

URSULA (on the steps): Bringing your dreams with you.
Exit down steps. Enter HUBERT, *right.*

HUBERT: Master! The arch is ready when you are.

WILLIAM: I am coming. Work, Hubert, work. Sometimes
one persuades one's self that it all means something to
somebody.

HUBERT: Do you think the gracious lady will be moved to
contribute to the building fund?

WILLIAM: H'm. I had forgotten that aspect of the matter.
Yes—I shouldn't be surprised if she did.

HUBERT: The blessed saints be praised for it.

WILLIAM: I wonder!
Exeunt WILLIAM *and* HUBERT, *right.*

THE YOUNG CHERUB (suddenly): Why did God create
mankind in two different sorts, if it makes so much
trouble?
The ANGELS *are inexpressibly shocked.*

RAPHAEL: Hush! you mustn't ask Why.

MICHAEL: Angels never ask Why.

GABRIEL: Only men ask Why.

CASSIEL: And you see what happened to them, just for asking Why.

MICHAEL: Do you want to eat of the Tree of Knowledge, like Adam and Eve?

GABRIEL: And find Michael there, with his big sword?

RAPHAEL: And put our Master to the trouble and pain of another crucifixion?

CASSIEL: Or start another war, like that lost brother whom we must not name?

ALL: Criticising God's creation! I never heard of such a thing!

CHOIR: Shall we that are but worms, but silk-worms, but glow-worms, chide God that He hath made slow-worms, and other venomous creeping things?

Shall we that are all discord, quarrel the harmony of His creation or His providence?

Can an apothecary make a sovereign treacle of vipers and other poisons, and cannot God admit offences and scandals into His physic?

As soon as he had made light (which was His first creature) He took pleasure in it; He said it was good; He was glad of it; glad of the sea, glad of the earth, glad of the sun, and moon, and stars, and He said of every one, It is good.

III: *The scene is as before; two more years have passed; WALTER, HUGH and GEOFFREY, lay workmen, are engaged in polishing marble rather up-stage.*

Enter SIMON, *right, and crosses to door, left.*

SIMON (*sings*):
  The animals went in two by two,
    Hey, ho, nonny!

Said the dog, Bow-wow! said the cat, Mew, mew!
   Spring is the time for love!
   Exit left.

WALTER: Spring, indeed! I wish the spring were here. It hasn't stopped raining for three months.

HUGH: More like four. We've had vile weather ever since the eclipse last September. What a climate!

WALTER: I knew that eclipse meant bad luck.

GEOFFREY: Well, it's not raining to-day.

HUGH: Bad luck? If we never get worse luck than a bit of bad weather, I don't care how many eclipses we have.

WALTER: We ain't heard the last of the eclipse yet, mark my words.

HUGH: You and your prophecies! What are you grumbling about? Job's going well enough, ain't it? Four years, and here we've finished the triforium and the clerestory, and the key of the great arch will be put in to-day. Not too bad, in four years.

   Re-enter SIMON, *left, trundling a coil of rope, wound on a drum.*

GEOFFREY: Ah! he's a good worker, is Master William. And a fast worker. Knows what he's about. He's the sort of master I can do with. Strict, and drives you like the devil, but I don't mind that.

HUGH: That's right. I respect a master that's a good worker. When Master William works, he works.

WALTER: And when he plays (*with a meaning grin*), he plays! Him and the Lady Ursula!

HUGH: Well, I don't mind that, either. That's their affair.

SIMON: Quite right, Hugh. The day for labour and the night for—sleep.

   (*Sings*) Two by two they went into the ark,
       Hey, ho, nonny!
     The doors were shut, they were all in the dark,
       Spring is the time for love!

GEOFFREY: She's somewhere about the place now.

WALTER: Who is? Lady Ursula?

GEOFFREY: Yes. Takes a lot of interest. Always putting up
a bit o' prayer, or coming to see how the job's getting
on, or calling on the Father Treasurer with a little dona-
tion to something.

SIMON (*sings*):
But when old Noah opened the door,
 Hey, ho, nonny!
They all came out by three and four,
 Spring is the time for love!

  Enter PRIOR *and* THEODATUS, *right.*

HUGH: It's a wonder the good fathers don't see through it.
GEOFFREY: Maybe they do. Maybe it pays them to wink
t'other eye. Lady Ursula's rich. It don't do to offend
rich folks.
THEODATUS: You hear that, Father Prior?
WALTER: All the same, mark my words, no good will come
of it. That eclipse wasn't sent for nothing.
HUGH: Ah, come off it. You and your eclipse!

SIMON (*sings*):
Who d'ye think had been playing tricks?
 Hey, ho, nonny!
They went in two and they came out six,
 Spring is the time for love!

THEODATUS: For shame, my son, for shame! We cannot
have these lewd songs here.
 He comes down past SIMON *to the steps, with the*
 PRIOR.
SIMON: Sorry, Father.
 He goes out, left.

THEODATUS:
So it goes on, Father, day after day—
Songs in the workshop, sniggering in the dortour,
Unbecoming gossip among the novices,
Heads wagged in the market-place, and tales going round

In the ale-house, fingers pointed everywhere
At William of Sens, the Cathedral architect—
A notorious evil liver, a seducer of women,
A taker of bribes——

PRIOR (*mildly*):

That was not proved, I fancy.

THEODATUS:

A cunning liar, that boasts of pulling the wool
Over the eyes of the fat, innocent monks;
A man without truth, without shame. It is not
    respectable;
It is not right.

PRIOR:

You must not say, without truth,
Lest you should hear the very stones cry out
Against you. Truth is glorious; but there is one
Glory of the sun, another of the moon,
And all the truth of the craftsman is in his craft.
Where there is truth, there is God; and where there is
    glory,
There is God's glory too.

THEODATUS (*sullenly*):

Craft is the word.
We could do better without William's craft
In more ways than in one. I would rather have
A worse-built church with a more virtuous builder.

PRIOR:

Make God the loser for your conscience' sake?
This is God's House, and if on any pretext
We give him less than the best, we shall cheat God
As William never cheated God, nor us.
He that bestowed the skill and the desire
To do great work is surely glad to see
That skill used in His service.

THEODATUS:

Skill is not all.
The kingdom of Heaven is won by righteousness,
Not skill. He cannot wish His work performed
Save with clean hands and a pure heart.

PRIOR:

My son,
Will you not let God manage His own business?
He was a carpenter, and knows His trade
Better, perhaps, than we do, having had
Some centuries of experience; nor will He,
Like a bad workman, blame the tools wherewith
He builds His City of Zion here on earth.
For God founded His Church, not upon John,
The loved disciple, that lay so close to His heart
And knew His mind—not upon John, but Peter;
Peter the liar, Peter the coward, Peter
The rock, the common man. John was all gold,
And gold is rare; the work might wait while God
Ransacked the corners of the earth to find
Another John; but Peter is the stone
Whereof the world is made. So stands the Church,
Stone upon stone, and Christ the corner-stone
Carved of the same stuff, common flesh and blood,
With you, and me, and Peter; and He can,
Being the alchemist's stone, the stone of Solomon,
Turn stone to gold, and purge the gold itself
From dross, till all is gold.

THEODATUS:

To purge—to burn!
He makes His ministers a flaming fire—
And are not we His Ministers? Shall not we
Lay axe to the rotten root, trunk, branch? destroy,
Make bonfire of this scandal in the Church
And burn God's honour clean?

PRIOR:

God is a man,
And can defend His honour, being full-grown
In wisdom and in stature. We need not
Play nursemaid to the Babe of Bethlehem
To shield Him from the harlot and the thief,
Or keep those tender, innocent hands from harm
That bear the sharp nails' imprint, and uphold
The axis of the spheres. He can touch dirt
Without defilement, for Himself hath said,
"What I have cleansed, that call not thou unclean."

THEODATUS:

But while His laws are broken in our sight
Must we stand by, and smile, and still do nothing?

PRIOR:

Do your own work, while yet the daylight lasts.
Look that it be well done; look not beyond it.
I charge you, on your holy obedience,
Set charity as a bridle on your tongue;
Talk not of William's nor another's faults,
Unless to God, Who hears but spreads no scandal.
Of this be sure: who will not have the Gospel
Shall have the Law; but in God's time, not ours.

> *Enter* SIMON *by door, left, carrying a small wind-lass.*

SIMON (*bursting irrepressibly into song*):
Every bird had found her mate,
  Hey, ho, nonny!
They all came out by seven and eight,
  Spring is the time for love!
    He sets the windlass down, centre. Enter WILLIAM,
    right.

WILLIAM: You are merry, Simon. Is that the rope to rig the travelling cradle?

SIMON: Yes, sir.

WILLIAM: See that every inch of it is well tested before I go up. I'm not as young or as light as I was. Good morning, Father Prior. Ah! Father Theodatus, you are just the man I was looking for. Pray will you help Simon to test that rope? It is to hoist me up to the top of the great arch, and I have a value for my neck.

THEODATUS: Oh, by all means.

> *Moving up, left.*

WILLIAM: Simon is a good lad enough, but I would rather trust your vigilance. Young men's minds are apt to run astray.

> *During the following dialogue,* THEODATUS *takes the free end of the rope and begins to wind it off on to the windlass.* SIMON *stands by the drum, so that, as the rope is slowly wound off, they can both examine it for flaws. They occupy the stage from centre to left.*

PRIOR: *Young* men are not alone in that, Master William. The talk of the town comes to our ears sometimes, dull-witted old churchmen though we be. It seems that even a master architect may find interests outside his work.

WILLIAM: Outside his working *hours*, Father Prior.

PRIOR: I quite appreciate that. My dear son, as your father in God I might find many things to say to you. . . .

WILLIAM: But as a man of the world you doubt whether I should listen. It is a rare virtue to refrain even from good words.

PRIOR: Then I will speak only as a man of the world and urge the value of discretion.

WILLIAM: Father Theodatus would say, of hypocrisy.

PRIOR: Father Theodatus is not your employer. The Church is your employer, and it is my duty to speak for the Church.

WILLIAM: Very well. As my *employer*, to use your own blunt term, what fault have you to find with my private amusements?

PRIOR: This; that instead of attending to their work, your workmen waste their time in gossip and backbiting about you. If you choose to be damned, you must; if you prefer to make a death-bed repentance, you may; but if an idle workman does an unsound job now, no repentance of yours will prevent it from bringing down the church some day or other.

WILLIAM (*after a pause*): You are quite right. I congratulate you. You have found the one argument to which I am bound to listen. Were you a diplomat before you were a churchman?

PRIOR: Perhaps.

Exit, right.

WILLIAM (*looking after him*): Or a soldier. The old man's a hard hitter and knows where to plant his blows. (*He goes up, back, to overlook the work of* WALTER *and* GEOFFREY, *speaking to* THEODATUS *and* SIMON *as he goes*): Test it with the eye and the hand—don't trust to either alone.

MICHAEL:

Are there no fires in Heaven, that every man
With his own hand, upon the anvil of sin
Forges the sword of judgment? Gabriel, Raphael,
There is a sword in the making; look you to it.

 RAPHAEL *goes up and stands near* THEODATUS, *centre, and* GABRIEL *near* SIMON, *left.*

℣. The eyes of the Lord are in every place, beholding the evil and the good.

℟. Shall we continue in sin that grace may abound? God forbid.

℣. He maketh His sun to rise on the evil and on the good;

℟. And sendeth rain upon the just and unjust.

 Enter URSULA, *right.*

URSULA: William!

WILLIAM (*turning quickly and coming to meet her*): Ah! You have come at a very good moment.

 He leads her forward to the steps.

SIMON (*watching them with interest*): Oho! look at that!

WILLIAM: We are just about to put in the key of the great arch.

THEODATUS: Turn away mine eyes from beholding vanity!

WILLIAM: If you will stand here presently and watch, you will see me fly up to the top of the scaffold in a machine of my own devising—and down again, like blessed St. Paul in a basket!

THEODATUS (*hastily with averted eyes*):
Sancta Maria, ora pro nobis;
Sancta Dei genetrix, ora pro nobis;
Sancta Virgo virginum, ora pro nobis.

RAPHAEL *sets his censer gently swinging.*

URSULA: How amusing! I hope it is safe.

SIMON (*over his shoulder to* GEOFFREY): More headaches for Father Martin! He don't like these goings-on. Says they look bad, and shock influential patrons.

WILLIAM: Never fear for that. But, hark'ee—we're in disgrace with the Prior.

THEODATUS:
Mater castissima, ora pro nobis;
Mater inviolata, ora pro nobis;
Mater intemerata, ora pro nobis.

URSULA: Oh! I ought not to have come.

WILLIAM: That was my fault. I asked you. I wanted you here.

GABRIEL: Take care, Simon! There is a flaw in the rope.
SIMON, *with his eyes on* WILLIAM *and* URSULA, *pays no attention.*

SIMON (*sings*):
The cat, the rat, the sow, the hen,
Hey, ho, nonny!
They all came out by nine and ten,
Spring is the time for love!

The rope runs through his heedless fingers. GABRIEL *makes a despairing gesture, and looks across at* RAPHAEL. *The scandalised* THEODATUS *continues to pray with his eyes tight shut.*

THEODATUS:

Virgo veneranda, ora pro nobis;
Virgo praedicanda, ora pro nobis;
Virgo potens, ora pro nobis.

URSULA: What does the Prior complain of? Scandal in the Cathedral?

WILLIAM: Something like that.

THEODATUS:

Vas honorabile, ora pro nobis;
Vas insigne devotionis, ora pro nobis;
Rosa mystica, ora pro nobis.

RAPHAEL: Take care, Theodatus! There is a flaw in the rope.

THEODATUS:

Turris Davidica, ora pro nobis;
Turris eburnea, ora pro nobis;
Domus aurea, ora pro nobis.

RAPHAEL *flings away the censer, which rolls clanging down the steps. The rope, flaw and all, is wound off.*

URSULA: At least he cannot say that you think more of me than of your work.

WILLIAM: No, he has not said that.

THEODATUS:

Agnus Dei, qui tollis peccata mundi, parce nobis Domine;
Agnus Dei, qui tollis peccata mundi, exaudi nos, Domine;
Agnus Dei, qui tollis peccata mundi, miserere nobis.

The rope is now all wound off.

URSULA: He will not take the work away from you?

WILLIAM: He is too shrewd for that. Besides, God would not let him; He has put me here and will keep me here, Prior or no Prior.

WORKMAN (*putting his head in at the door, below*): Master Hubert says, is that rope ready?

SIMON: Here you are, mate.

He picks up the windlass and takes it down to WORKMAN, *who carries it out.*

URSULA: Do we presume too much upon God's mercy?

WILLIAM:

We are the master-craftsmen, God and I—
We understand one another. None, as I can,
Can creep under the ribs of God, and feel
His heart beat through those Six Days of Creation;
Enormous days of slowly turning lights
Streaking the yet unseasoned firmament;
Giant days, Titan days, yet all too short
To hold the joy of making. God caught His breath
To see the poles of the world stand up through chaos;
And when He sent it forth, the great winds blew,
Carrying the clouds. And then He made the trees
For winds to rustle through—oak, poplar, cedar,
Hawthorn and elm, each with its separate motion—
And with His delicate fingers painted the flowers,
Numberless—numberless! why make so many
But that He loved the work, as I love mine,
And saw that it was good, as I see mine?—
The supple, swift mechanics of the serpent,
The beautiful, furred beasts, and curious fish
With golden eyes and quaintly-laced thin bones,
And whales like mountains loud with spurting springs
Dragons and monsters in strange shapes, to make
His angels laugh with Him; when He saw those
God sang for joy, and formed the birds to sing.

And lastly, since all Heaven was not enough
To share that triumph, He made His Masterpiece,
Man, that like God can call beauty from dust,
Order from chaos, and create new worlds
To praise their maker. Oh, but in making man
God over-reached Himself and gave away
His Godhead. He must now depend on man
For what man's brain, creative and divine
Can give Him. Man stands equal with Him now,
Partner and rival. Say God needs a church,
As here in Canterbury—and say He calls together
By miracle stone, wood and metal, builds
A church of sorts; *my* church He cannot make—
Another, but not that. This church is mine
And none but I, not even God, can build it.
Me hath He made vice-gerent of Himself,
And were I lost, something unique were lost
Irreparably; my heart, my blood, my brain
Are in the stone; God's crown of matchless works
Is not complete without my stone, my jewel,
Creation's nonpareil.

URSULA:

        Hush! God will hear you—
The priests say He is jealous. Tempt Him not
Lest He should smite and slay.

WILLIAM:

           He will not dare;
He knows that I am indispensable
To His work here; and for the work's sake, He,
Cherishing, as good masons do, His tools,
Will keep me safe. When the last stone is laid
Then may He use me as He will; I care not;
The work is all; when that is done, good night—
My life till then is paramount with God.

URSULA:

You make me shake to hear you. Blasphemy! blasphemy!

WILLIAM:
    Sound sense. Fear nothing. I must leave you now;
    The work waits for me, and that must not be;
    Idleness is the only sin. Like God
    I must be doing in my little world,
    Lest, lacking me, the moon and stars should fail.
        He goes out down the steps.

URSULA (*watching him go*): I am afraid; have mercy on
    him, Christ!
CASSIEL: Draw thy sword, Michael; the hour is come.
        MICHAEL *follows* WILLIAM *out, with his sword
        drawn in his hand.*
℣. Except the Lord build the house, their labour is but
    lost that build it.
℟. Except the Lord keep the city, the watchman waketh
    but in vain.
℣. The zeal of thine house hath eaten me up; and rebukes
    are fallen upon me.
℟. For Thou art great and doest wondrous things; Thou
    art God alone.
        *During the singing of these versicles, the three re-
        maining* ANGELS *stand side by side at the top of the
        steps, with* URSULA *below them. Now they go up
        and stand on the plinth at the back of the stage,*
        RAPHAEL *and* GABRIEL *to right and left, with* CAS-
        SIEL *centre.*
CHOIR: The Lord is known to execute judgment; the un-
    godly is trapped in the work of his own hands.
    For he hath said in his heart, Tush, I shall never be cast
    down; there shall no harm happen unto me.
    The snares of death compassed me round about, and the
    pains of hell gat hold upon me.
    I shall find trouble and heaviness, and I will call upon
    the name of the Lord: O Lord, I beseech Thee, deliver
    my soul.
        The stage gradually fills with MONKS *and* WORKMEN;
        among them is a YOUNG BOY.

MONKS AND WORKMEN: This is a brave day . . . the great arch finished . . . See, they are making ready to drop in the keystone . . . It is wonderful how well Master William's machines work—they have halved the labour of building . . . there's old Hubert—he'll be a proud man to-day . . . Laus Deo! our new choir will be ready for us within the year . . . There it goes! No, they're waiting for something . . . They're waiting for the architect . . . There he is, slung half-way up in the travelling cradle . . . Can't you see? Come on, lad, up on my shoulder . . . There's the keystone slung aloft on the crane . . . Hurray! Master William's up now—just getting to the top of the scaffolding . . . Get ready to cheer, boys. . . .

THE YOUNG BOY (*from his perch on the workman's shoulder, shrilly*): Oh, look! look at the angel—the terrible angel!

ALL: What's that? An angel? What? Where? Nonsense!

THE YOUNG BOY: High on the scaffold, with the drawn sword in his hand!

URSULA: Mother of God!

She falls upon the steps.

A shout from the stage is succeeded by a heavy crash without from the far end of the building. Men run in, right.

ALL: He's fallen . . . Master William's down . . . He's killed . . . fifty feet at least . . . His foot slipped . . . No, the rope broke . . . What's happened? . . . God have mercy on us! . . . Run for help! . . . Blessed Mary, pray for us! . . . Send for the Prior . . . Fetch a chirurgeon . . . The devil is abroad . . . No, it was an angel . . . Where's that boy who saw the angel? . . . Here, the lady's fainted—give us a hand here to carry her in . . . Come along, let's see what's happened . . .

There is a general rush down the steps.

URSULA (*to the men who are supporting her*): Take me

with you. (*But she is unable to stand.*) No—leave me!
Run and bring me word.

> *They leave her crouched on the steps and run out.*
> *The three* ANGELS *come down and follow the crowd*
> *out. Nobody is left but* THEODATUS, SIMON *and* UR-
> SULA.

SIMON: The rope! God forgive me—I was talking and
laughing. Father Theodatus, what have we done?

THEODATUS: The rope! God is avenged. But I did not mean
—I did not think—if it had not been for your lewd songs
and his own behaviour with this woman——

URSULA: Could You not break me and not him, O God?

SIMON: We have killed him among us.

CHOIR: Out of the deep have I called unto Thee. O Lord,
hear my voice.

O let Thine ears consider well the voice of my com-
plaint.

If Thou, Lord, wilt be extreme to mark what is done
amiss, O Lord, who may abide it?

For there is mercy with Thee, therefore shalt thou be
feared.

I look for the Lord, my soul doth wait for Him, in His
word is my trust.

My soul fleeth unto the Lord; before the morning watch,
I say, before the morning watch.

O Israel, trust in the Lord, for with the Lord there is
mercy, and with Him is plenteous redemption;

And He shall redeem Israel from all his sins.

> *During the singing of the psalm, the* PRIOR *has re-*
> *entered from the lower end, with* HUBERT, GERVASE
> *and the* YOUNG BOY. *They mount the steps.*

URSULA: Father! Father! In pity, tell me—is he dead?

PRIOR: No, my poor child. But sorely maimed.

HUBERT: He will never be the same man again.

URSULA: Let me go to him.

PRIOR: Presently. The leech is with him now, seeing to his
hurts. Trust me, you shall see him presently. (*He goes*

on up steps and sits, right.) Now, Hubert, I must know how all this came to pass.

HUBERT: My Lord Prior, there is no doubt at all. There was a flaw in the rope. Just as the cradle came up to the level of the scaffolding, bearing Master William, I saw with my eyes the strands spring asunder. I stretched out my hands to catch him, but I could not reach. If I could have done anything—anything! I would gladly have given my life.

GERVASE: So would I, Hubert.

PRIOR: I am sure you would.

HUBERT: Such a craftsman! such a craftsman! So kind a master! Just, zealous, generous—no fault in him at all.

GERVASE: So faithful a servant of the Church! Who will finish his work now? . . . He was my friend, too.

HUBERT: What I should like to know is—who had the testing o' that there rope?

SIMON (*flinging himself at the* PRIOR's *feet*): It was I—it was my neglect. I have no excuse. I shall never forgive myself.

URSULA: It was my fault. I was talking to William—distracting the attention of them all. This is a judgment for our sin—his and mine.

THEODATUS: True; it was a judgment. Ask this boy here. Did he not see the angel thrust him down?

PRIOR: Yes, child. What is this about an angel?

THE YOUNG BOY: It is true. I saw a great angel stand between heaven and earth—all in gold and scarlet, with a drawn sword. Oh, and he had great wings, too. He cut the rope and the cradle fell.

THEODATUS: There, you see! it was a divine judgment.

HUBERT: Divine judgment! The boy's dreaming. It was rank carelessness. Simon—who was at the other end of the rope when you tested it? (SIMON *looks round at* THEODATUS, *waiting for him to speak.*) Speak up, man! Who was it?

PRIOR: I was there, Theodatus.

THEODATUS: Well, it was I. But I had nothing to do with it. You heard what the child said. It was a miracle.

PRIOR: I think we sometimes make disasters, and then call them miraculous judgments. Did you at any moment take hand or eye from the rope while you were testing it?

THEODATUS: I cannot remember. (*Under the* PRIOR's *eye, he abandons this line of defence.*) *She* was there with William. For my soul's sake I could not look at them. I was saying my prayers . . .

HUBERT: Sayin' your prayers! With the master's safety depending on you!

THEODATUS: God himself laid the seal upon my eyes. I was His appointed instrument to overthrow the wicked man.

PRIOR:

Think what you say, my son. It is not for us
To ordain ourselves the ministers of vengeance;
For it must needs be that offences come,
But woe unto that man by whom the offence
Cometh; 'twere better he had not been born.
This is thy sin: thou hast betrayed the work;
Thou hast betrayed the Church; thou hast betrayed
Christ, in the person of His fellow-man.
What was the prayer wherein thou offer'dst up
Thy brother's life?

THEODATUS:

The Litany of the Virgin.

PRIOR:

Go to the church; repeat it once again,
Saying at every line: "This was the spear
With which I pierced the body of the Lord,"
Then come to me and ask for absolution.

THEODATUS: I will obey.

Exit THEODATUS, *right.*

PRIOR:
> For you, my son and daughter,
> You see how sin brings its own suffering;
> Do not despair; God's mercy is very great. (*He rises.*)
> Thou that hast visions of angels, come with me.
> I am an old man. Let me have thy shoulder.
> So. Thou shalt tell me more about the angel.
>> *Exeunt* PRIOR *and* YOUNG BOY, *right.*

GERVASE (*helping* URSULA *to her feet*):
> Madam, pray do not weep so. He would be sorry to see it.
> I loved him, too. Let us go together to visit him.

URSULA: And supposing he can never work again? What comfort in this world for him? And what forgiveness for any of us?
> *Exeunt* GERVASE *and* URSULA, *right.*

HUBERT: Well, Simon, you've made a nice mess of it. There, there, lad, I can see you're sorry. Don't 'ee lose heart, now. It's a bad business, but we must make the best of it.

SIMON: Oh, Hubert!
> *Exeunt* HUBERT *and* SIMON, *right.*
> *During the singing of the following hymn, the* AN-
> GELS *return and take up their places as at the be-*
> *ginning of the play.*

CHOIR:
> Plebs angelica
> phalanx et archangelica
> principans turma, virtus
> Uranica,
> ac potestas
> almiphona.
>
> Dominantia
> numina divinaque

subsellia, Cherubim
aetherea
ac Seraphim
ignicoma,

Vos, O Michael
caeli satrapa,
Gabrielque vera
dans verba nuntia,

Atque Raphael,
vitae vernula,
transferte nos inter
Paradisicolas.

IV: *Six months have passed since the preceding scene. During the singing of the interlude,* GERVASE, *assisted by a* LAY-BROTHER, *is making up a couch in the centre of the stage. Enter, right,* MARTIN, *carrying a couple of large sheepskins.*

MARTIN: They told me you wanted some extra coverings for Master William's bed.

GERVASE: Thank you, brother. Why, this is very kind! Surely these are the best fleeces.

MARTIN: They are usually kept for distinguished visitors. But Father Wulfram specially asked that you should have them. They will make Master William warm and comfortable—since he has taken this fancy for lying here.

GERVASE: We are in hopes he may sleep better close to his work. He is so restless. Day and night he thinks of nothing but the building, and frets to lie helpless and so far away. From here he can see the sun shine on the arches he has raised; and when he lies wakeful in the early dawn it will comfort him to hear the clink of the mason's trowel and the carver's hammer heralding in the day.

The LAY-BROTHER *sets a stool near the head of the couch, down-stage, and goes out, right.*

MARTIN: Poor soul! Well, let us praise God for this warm and seasonable weather. Now that the summer is come, he will take no hurt from his change of lodging.

The LAY-BROTHER *returns with a jug of water, a horn drinking-vessel, and a candlestick, which he places on the stool.*

GERVASE: May it refresh him, soul and body! But I fear he undertakes more than his strength will bear. He has insisted to-day on being carried to view the progress of the roof over the Choir and Crosses. It is impossible to move him without causing severe pain—and then he gives orders and excites himself. Indeed, it is too much for him.

MARTIN (*with some hesitation*): I suppose nothing would induce him to resign the appointment?

GERVASE: Part him from his work? Oh, no! It would be more bitter to him than death. And where should we get another like him?

Exit LAY-BROTHER, *right.*

MARTIN: Well, I don't know. It is true he has done magnificent work. But frankly, dear brother, a sick man with a crippled spine cannot have his eyes here, there and everywhere, and during this half-year since his accident things have not gone quite so well.

GERVASE: You know why that is. Some of the brethren do not work so loyally for Brother Hubert as they did for him.

MARTIN: Isn't that natural? Hubert is an excellent craftsman, but, after all, he is only an oblate, and a man of no education. Now if Master William had appointed, let us say, Father Hilary——

GERVASE: Father Hilary does fine carving very prettily, but he's quite out of his depth when it comes to the practical side of building. Now, Brother Hubert understands his job inside out.

MARTIN: Of course, but—— Well, there you are! You can't deny that there has been a certain amount of ill-feeling.

GERVASE (*bitterly*): Jealousy, vanity, hatred, malice and all uncharitableness! And these are churchmen, vowed to holy obedience and humility.

MARTIN: Beati pauperes spiritu. Beati mites.

GERVASE: Amen! (*He examines the couch critically and gives a punch to the pillows. Re-enter* LAY-BROTHER, *right, with a crucifix in his hand and a large bundle of papers under his arm.*) Ah, thanks, Brother Robert. (*He sets the crucifix on the stool with the other things.*) Better put the papers on that other stool for the moment. (LAY-BROTHER *puts them on stool, right.*) There! I think that is the best we can do.

Voices and footsteps off, right.

MARTIN: I think they are bringing our patient in now.

GERVASE: I hope he is not too much exhausted.

Enter, right, WILLIAM, *carried by* THEODATUS *and* SIMON.

WILLIAM: Ugh! ugh! Gently, you fools, gently. Do you want to kill me? You've had one good shot at it. Jolt, jolt, like a couple of pack-asses. Clumsy idiots.

They lay him on the couch, to a running accompaniment of groans and curses.

THEODATUS: I am sorry. Did I hurt you?

WILLIAM: Oh, no! Only jarred me to pieces, that's all.

GERVASE (*arranging pillows*): Is that a little easier? I'm afraid you have over-tired yourself. Are you in great pain?

WILLIAM: Oh, I daresay it'll be worse in Purgatory.

MARTIN (*pouring out water*): You have been out too long in the hot sun.

WILLIAM (*drinking*): Thanks. Sorry, Simon. Don't mind me, Father Theodatus. It's only bad temper. The Prior set you a hard penance when he appointed you beast of burden to a sick man.

Exit LAY-BROTHER.

THEODATUS: No, indeed. There is nothing I would more
gladly do. I deserve far more than that for the evil I did
you.

WILLIAM: Oh, stop blaming yourself. What's done can't be
helped. Blame God, or the devil, or whoever looks after
these things. Where's Hubert? I want him here. Go and
fetch Brother Hubert, for God's sake, somebody. (*Exeunt* SIMON *and* THEODATUS, *right.*) Why haven't my
papers been brought down?

GERVASE (*bringing stool with papers and setting it by the
couch up-stage*): They are all here. I will put them
handy for you.

MARTIN: Will you not rest a little first?

WILLIAM: No, I will not. Leave me alone, can't you? Gervase, find me the measurements for those corbels.
They've got them all wrong, as I knew they would.
(*Enter* HUBERT, *right.*) Just because I'm not there to
stand over them all the time—— Oh, Hubert, come and
look at this. What did I tell you? I knew it was not my
measurements that were wrong. Can't you remember
anything you're told?

HUBERT: I am sure, sir, I gave Father Hilary the measurements exactly as you gave them to me. But he would
have it as his own way was the right one, and he told
the men under him——

WILLIAM: Father Hilary! Why should they pay any attention to Father Hilary? If I had the use of my limbs I'd
give them something to remind them who's in charge
here. But I have to lie helpless as a log while you make
a mess of it among you. Never mind. Not your fault.
Gervase, give me pen and ink—I'll show you how you
can put it right. (GERVASE *fetches pen and ink from
bench, left.*) Lift me up, somebody. (MARTIN *lifts him
up.*) Ugh! Now, see here . . . I've got an idea about
this. . . .

*He begins to draw on the plan, but is overcome by
faintness.*

HUBERT: Dear master, leave it until to-morrow.

WILLIAM: It looks as though I shall have to. All right, Hubert. Don't worry. We'll put it straight in the morning. (GERVASE *and* MARTIN *take away the drawing materials and settle him back on his pillows.*) Oh, God! Shall I never be able to do anything again?

> *Enter* LAY-BROTHER, *right, with a bowl of soup and a trencher of bread.*

MARTIN (*soothingly*): You work too hard. You have overtired yourself. You will feel better when you have eaten. (GERVASE *takes the bowl and hands it to* WILLIAM, *and the* LAY-BROTHER *goes out.*) Come away now, Brother Hubert. He must be persuaded to rest. (*He bustles* HUBERT *away, right, then turns at the door as* ERNULPHUS *and* PAUL *pop their heads round it.*) Here are some visitors for you.

> *Enter* PAUL, *carrying a bunch of roses and something done up in a cabbage-leaf, and* ERNULPHUS, *obviously concealing some offering under his habit. Exeunt* MARTIN *and* HUBERT.

ERNULPHUS: May we come in? Pax tecum, my son, pax tecum.

WILLIAM (*in a dispirited growl*): Et cum spiritu tuo.

ERNULPHUS: And how do you feel this evening?

WILLIAM (*with a wry face, but not unkindly*): Horrible!

ERNULPHUS: T—t—t—t—t!

PAUL: It's this dreadful hot weather. Very trying. I don't know when I remember such a trying June. I'm sure we never had such unwholesome heat when I was a boy. I was nearly melted away, working in the garden. And the greenfly gets worse every year. There never was such a year for greenfly. Everything smothered. Still, I've managed to find a few roses (*presenting them*), and see! A dozen or so of the early strawberries. I thought you might like them for your supper.

WILLIAM (*genuinely touched*): That's very good of you, Father Paul. Are they the first?

PAUL: The very first. Nobody else has had any—not even

the Father Prior. I hope you will find them sweet. Though I must say, fruit doesn't seem to have the flavour it had in my young days. Still, such as they are, there they are.

He puts them on the stool, down-stage.

WILLIAM: I shall enjoy them immensely. I don't know anything more refreshing than early strawberries.

ERNULPHUS: Oho! don't you? I do. (*He produces a stout little flask from under his habit.*) Just you try this. A reviving cordial water from our own distillery. Not too fiery, and full of healthful properties. Made from herbs, according to our special recipe.

Puts it on the stool.

WILLIAM: Thank you; thank you very much. I will drink it to the healths of both of you.

PAUL: Oh, but it is your own health we must all wish and pray for. We do pray for you, of course. Night and morning. And remember you at Mass. Eh, Father Ernulphus?

ERNULPHUS: Always. All of us. So you mustn't lose heart. Oh, dear, no. Now we had better run away, or we shall tire you out. Good night, my son. May God watch over and restore you!

PAUL: Our Lady and all the blessed saints have you in their keeping.

PAUL *and* ERNULPHUS *trundel amiably off, right.*

WILLIAM: Good old souls! This is what I have come to, Gervase—to be nursed and coddled, and comforted like a child with strawberries. Ah, well. You can tuck me up for the night and leave me to my own hobgoblins.

GERVASE (*taking the supper things away and helping him to lie down*): To the holy Angels, rather. There! is that comfortable?

WILLIAM: Yes, thank you, my boy.

GERVASE (*with a little assumption of authority*): Do not forget your prayers.

WILLIAM: Very well, Father.

GERVASE: Benedicat te omnipotens Deus, Pater, et Filius et Spiritus Sanctus. Amen.

WILLIAM: Amen.

GERVASE (*going out, right*): Sleep in peace. Hubert and I will be at hand if you should need anything.

Exit, left.

WILLIAM *pulls out a rosary, mechanically counts the first decade, then tosses it away impatiently.*

CHOIR:

O lux beata trinitas,
Et principalis unitas,
Jam sol recedit igneus;
Infunde lumen cordibus.

RAPHAEL: Michael.

GABRIEL: Michael.

CASSIEL: Michael, thou watchman of the Lord! What of the night? Watchman, what of the night?

MICHAEL: The morning cometh, and also the night; if ye will enquire, enquire ye: return, come.

CHOIR:

Te mane laudum carmine,
Te deprecamur vesperi,
Te nostra supplex gloria
Per cuncta laudet saecula.

Enter THEODATUS, *right.*

THEODATUS: Master William, there is one without would speak with you.

WILLIAM: Who?

THEODATUS: The Lady Ursula.

WILLIAM: What is the use of this? I will not see her. It is always the same story. She asks to be my wife, my nurse, my servant—Heaven knows what; to devote her life, make reparation and all the rest of it. She shall not do it. I will not have people sacrificing themselves for me. It is monstrous. It is impossible. Tell her so.

THEODATUS: She says she is here for the last time. She is very unhappy. I think you ought—I beseech you to let her come.

WILLIAM: That is a new tune for you to sing, Father Theodatus.

THEODATUS: I have learnt a little charity of late. Let me beg of you.

WILLIAM: Oh, very well.

THEODATUS *beckons in* URSULA *and goes out, right.*

URSULA: William, I have come to say good-bye. I will not trouble you any more. Since I am nothing to you now, and the world without you is nothing to me, I can but take refuge at the Throne of Grace and pray for both of us.

WILLIAM: That is folly, my dear. You, in a convent of nuns! Go and be happy, and forget me.

URSULA: That is the one thing I cannot do. No other man shall have me, if not you.

WILLIAM: I am not a man, Ursula. I am a cripple with a broken back—a stock, a stone—I am nothing. A marriage-bond with me would be a bond indeed. Let the dead past bury its dead. Our dream is over.

URSULA: "Sitting by the fire, seeing pictures in the fire, visions and dreams"—do you remember?

WILLIAM: I have no dreams now—only nightmares. Nobody can bring back my dreams. Some of them even grudge me my work here—all that is left to me.

URSULA: I have broken what I cannot mend. William, tell me—had I at any time, even for a moment, any part in your dream?

WILLIAM: I hardly know. But once, high in a corner of the clerestory, where none but God will look for it, I carved an angel with your face.

URSULA: Ah, my dear! . . . And you will still have me go?

WILLIAM: Yes; go. I am sorry. Go.

URSULA *goes without protest.*

Father Theodatus! (THEODATUS *looks in*) Pray conduct the Lady Ursula to the convent gate and ask the Father Prior if he can come and see me.

THEODATUS: I will, my son.

> *Exit* THEODATUS *with* URSULA, *right*.

CHOIR: My days are consumed away like smoke, and my bones are burnt up as it were a fire-brand.

My heart is smitten down and withered like grass, so that I forget to eat my bread.

For the voice of my groaning, my bones will scarce cleave to my flesh.

And that because of Thine indignation and wrath; for Thou hast taken me up and cast me down.

> *Enter* PRIOR, *right*.

PRIOR: You sent for me, my son?

WILLIAM: Yes. I scarcely know why, save that I am in hell and can see no way out.

PRIOR: Is there some sin troubling your conscience?

WILLIAM: All the sins there are—or most of them, any way. Not that they ever troubled me till I was punished for them. But now—they rise up round me in the night and stifle me.

PRIOR: My son, will you not confess them and receive absolution?

WILLIAM: Confess? if I were to confess them all, you would be here till to-morrow. I cannot remember when I last made a confession.

PRIOR (*removing the papers from the stool up-stage and sitting down*): In general, then, my son, and as well as you can remember them, tell me your sins.

WILLIAM:

I do confess to God
The Father and the Son and Holy Ghost,
To Mary Mother of God the ever-virgin,
To the most holy Apostles Peter and Paul,

To blessed Michael and all his angels
And the whole company of Heaven, and thee,
Father, that I have sinned exceedingly,
In thought, in word, in action, by my fault,
By my own fault, my own most grievous fault.
I have lusted as men lust; I have eaten and drunk
With the drunken; I have given way to wrath,
Taking God's name in vain, cursing and smiting;
I have been too much eager after gold
And the brave things of the world, that take the eye
And charm the flesh. Now, smitten in my flesh
My sins have left me, and I see perforce
How worthless they all were. I am sorry for them.
Though yet I think I was not the worse craftsman
Because in me the lusty flesh rejoiced,
Lending its joy to all I did. Some men,
Fettering the body, fetter the soul, too,
So that the iron eats inward; thereof come
Cruelties, deceits, perversities of malice,
Strange twistings of the mind, defeats of spirit,
Whereof I cannot with sincerity
Accuse myself. But if it be a sin
To make the flesh the pander to the mind,
I have sinned deep. Of the means, not of the end,
I heartily repent.

PRIOR:

                Son, they mistake
Who think God hates those bodies which He made.
Freedom, not licence, must be given the body,
For licence preys upon itself and others,
Devouring freedom's gifts. Have others suffered
Through lust, wrath, greed of yours?

WILLIAM:

                        I do confess it,
And ask their pardon and God's pardon for it
Most humbly.

PRIOR:

In this world as in God's heaven
There is no power to match humility:
It breaks the horns of the unicorns, and makes
The wand of justice flower like Aaron's rod.
Stoop to repent, and God will stoop to pardon.

WILLIAM:
I do repent.

PRIOR:

Indeed I hope thou dost.
For all these injuries, see thou make amends
So far as may be done; the irreparable
God's grace shall turn to good, since only He
Can lead out triumph from the gates of hell,
As He hath done by thee, using thy faults
To further His great ends, by His sole power,
Not Thine.

WILLIAM:

I understand. A year ago
An idle mason let the chisel slip
Spoiling the saint he carved. I chid him for it,
Then took the tool and in that careless stroke
Saw a new vision, and so wrought it out
Into a hippogriff. But yet the mason
Was not the less to blame. So works with us
The cunning craftsman, God.

PRIOR:

Thou hast a mind
Apt to receive His meaning. But take heed:
The mind hath its own snares. What sins of the mind
Trouble thee now?

WILLIAM:

I do not know of any.

PRIOR:

I cannot read the heart; but I am old
And know how little one need fear the flesh
In comparison of the mind. Think, I beseech thee,
If any sin lie yet upon thy conscience.

WILLIAM:

Father, I know of none.

PRIOR:

The Tree of Life
Grew by the Tree of Knowledge; and when Adam
Ate of the one, this doom was laid upon him
Never, but by self-knowledge, to taste life.
Pray now for grace, that thou may'st know and live.

WILLIAM:

Wilt thou not give me present absolution?

PRIOR:

Of all thy fleshly faults, humbly confessed,
Truly repented, I do absolve thee now
In the name of the Father and of the Son and of
The Holy Ghost. Amen.

WILLIAM:

Amen.

PRIOR:

Good night;
Peace be with thee.

WILLIAM:

And with thy spirit. Good night.
Exit PRIOR. WILLIAM *tosses restlessly.*

℣. The ministers of God are sons of thunder, they are falls
of water, trampling of horses, and running of chariots;
and if the voices of these ministers cannot overcome

thy music, thy security, yet the Angels' trumpets will.
> *Distant trumpet.*

CHOIR:

> Quantus tremor est futurus
> Quando judex est venturus
> Cuncta stricte discussurus.
>> GABRIEL *goes up and stands behind* WILLIAM.
> Tuba mirum spargens sonum
> Per sepulchra regionum
> Coget omnes ante thronum.
>> MICHAEL *goes up and stands with drawn sword before* WILLIAM.
> Liber scriptus proferetur
> Inquo totum continetur
> Unde mundus judicetur
>> CASSIEL *goes up and stands at the foot of* WILLIAM'S *bed, with the Book open before him.*
> Quid sum miser tunc dicturus,
> Quem patronem rogaturus,
> Cum vix justus sit securus?
>> RAPHAEL *goes up and stands with his censer at the head of* WILLIAM'S *bed.*

WILLIAM:

> Sleep! while these voices wail through aisle and cloister
> Howling on judgment? Cannot Father Ambrose
> Keep his monks quiet—let a sick man rest?
> I am confessed, absolved. Why think of judgment?
> My soul is heavy even unto death,
> And something not myself moves in the dusk
> Fearfully. Lights! lights! lights!

GABRIEL (*laying his hand on* WILLIAM's *eyes*):
>> Let there be light!
>> WILLIAM *becomes aware of the presence of the* ANGELS.

℣. Behold, the angel of the Lord, standing in the way, and his sword drawn in his hand.

℞. And he was afraid, because of the sword of the angel of the Lord.

℣. My flesh trembleth for fear of Thee, and I am afraid of Thy judgments.

℞. God is a righteous judge, strong and patient, and God is provoked every day.

WILLIAM:

So—it is come; first death and then the judgment.
Thou standest there and holdest up the Book
Wherein my sins show black. But I am shriven.
Christ's blood hath washed me white. What then art thou,
Threats in thy hand, and in thy face a threat
Sterner than steel and colder?

MICHAEL:

                I am Michael,
The sword of God. The edge is turned toward thee:
Not for those sins whereof thou dost repent,
Lust, greed, wrath, avarice, the faults of flesh
Sloughed off with the flesh, but that which feeds the soul,
The sin that is so much a part of thee
Thou know'st it not for sin.

WILLIAM:

                What sin is that?
Angel, what sins remain? I have envied no man,
Sought to rob no man of renown or merits,
Yea, praised all better workmen than myself
From an ungrudging heart. I have not been slothful—
Thou canst not say I was. Lust, greed, wrath, avarice,
None ever came between my work and me;
That I put first; never by nights of lust
Too spent to labour in the dawning day;
Never so drunken that I could not set
Level to stone or hold the plumb-line true;

Never so wroth as to confound my judgment
Between the man and the work, or call the one
Ill-done because I wished the other ill;
Never so grasping as to take reward
For what I did not, or despised to do.
If I neglected lip-service to God,
My hands served for me, and I wrought His praise
Not in light words puffed from a slumberous mind
Like wind, but in enduring monuments,
Symbol and fruit of that which works, not sleeps.
Answer me, Angel, what have I ever done
Or left undone, that I may not repent
Nor God forgive?

MICHAEL:

There where thy treasure is
Thy heart is also. Sin is of the heart.

WILLIAM:
But all my heart was in my work.

MICHAEL:

Even so.

WILLIAM:
What, in my work? The sin was in my work?
Thou liest. Though thou speak with God's own voice
Thou liest. In my work? That cannot be.
I grant the work not perfect; no man's work
Is perfect; but what hand and brain could do,
Such as God made them, that I did. Doth God
Demand the impossible? Then blame God, not me,
That I am man, not God. He hath broken me,
Hath sought to snatch the work out of my hand——
Wherefore? . . . O now, now I begin to see.
This was well said, He is a jealous God;
The work was not ill done—'twas done too well;
He will not have men creep so near His throne

To steal applause from Him. Is *this* my fault?
Why, this needs no repentance, and shall have none.
Let Him destroy me, since He has the power
To slay the thing He envies—but while I have breath
My work is mine; He shall not take it from me.

MICHAEL:

No; thou shalt lay it down of thine own will.

WILLIAM:

Never. Let Him heap on more torments yet——

MICHAEL:

He can heap none on thee, He hath not borne——

WILLIAM:

Let Him strike helpless hands as well as feet——

MICHAEL:

Whose Feet and Hands were helpless stricken
   through——

WILLIAM:

Scourge me and smite me and make blind mine eyes——

MICHAEL:

As He was blindfolded and scourged and smitten——

WILLIAM:

Dry up my voice in my throat and make me dumb——

MICHAEL:

As He was dumb and opened not His mouth——

WILLIAM:

Cramp me with pains——

MICHAEL:

                    As He was cramped with pains,
Racked limb from limb upon the stubborn Cross——

WILLIAM:
Parch me with fever——

MICHAEL:
He that cried, "I thirst"——

WILLIAM:
Wring out my blood and sweat——

MICHAEL:
Whose sweat, like blood,
Watered the garden in Gethsemane——

WILLIAM:
For all that He can do I will not yield,
Nor leave to other men that which is mine,
To botch—to alter—turn to something else,
Not mine.

MICHAEL:
Thou wilt not? Yet God bore this too,
The last, the bitterest, worst humiliation,
Bowing His neck under the galling yoke
Frustrate, defeated, half His life unlived,
Nothing achieved.

WILLIAM:
Could God, being God, do this?

MICHAEL:
Christ, being man, did this; but still, through faith
Knew what He did. As gold and diamond,
Weighed in the chemist's balance, are but earth
Like tin or iron, albeit within them still
The purchase of the world lie implicit:
So, when God came to test of mortal time
In nature of a man whom time supplants,
He made no reservation of Himself

Nor of the godlike stamp that franked His gold,
But in good time let time supplant Him too.
The earth was rent, the sun's face turned to blood,
But He, unshaken, with exultant voice
Cried, "It is finished!" and gave up the ghost.
"Finished"—when men had thought it scarce begun.
Then His disciples with blind faces mourned,
Weeping: "We trusted that He should redeem
Israel; but now we know not." What said He
Behind the shut doors in Jerusalem,
At Emmaus, and in the bitter dawn
By Galilee? "I go; but feed My sheep;
For Me the Sabbath at the long week's close—
For you the task, for you the tongues of fire."
Thus shalt thou know the Master Architect,
Who plans so well, He may depart and leave
The work to others. Art thou more than God?
Not God Himself was indispensable,
For lo! God died—and still His work goes on.

℣. Thou that destroyest the temple and buildest it in three
days, save thyself. If thou be the Son of God, come
down from the cross.

℟. Thinkest thou that I cannot now pray to My Father,
and He shall presently give Me more than twelve
legions of angels? But how then shall the scriptures be
fulfilled, that thus it must be?

RAPHAEL:

Lord, I believe; help Thou mine unbelief.

WILLIAM:

Lord, I believe; help Thou mine unbelief.

CHOIR:

Faithful Cross, above all other
    One and only noble Tree,
None in foliage, none in blossom,

None in fruit thy peer may be;
Sweetest wood and sweetest iron,
    Sweetest weight is hung on thee.

WILLIAM:

O, I have sinned. The eldest sin of all,
Pride, that struck down the morning star from Heaven
Hath struck down me from where I sat and shone
Smiling on my new world. All other sins
God will forgive but that. I am damned, damned,
Justly. Yet, O most just and merciful God,
Hear me but once, Thou that didst make the world
And wilt not let one thing that Thou hast made,
No, not one sparrow, perish without Thy Will
(Since what we make, we love)—for that love's sake
Smite only me and spare my handiwork.
Jesu, the carpenter's Son, the Master-Builder,
Architect, poet, maker—by those hands
That Thine own nails have wounded—by the wood
Whence Thou didst carve Thy Cross—let not the Church
Be lost through me. Let me lie deep in hell,
Death gnaw upon me, purge my bones with fire,
But let my work, all that was good in me,
All that was God, stand up and live and grow.
The work is sound, Lord God, no rottenness there—
Only in me. Wipe out my name from men
But not my work; to other men the glory
And to Thy Name alone. But if to the damned
Be any mercy at all, O send Thy spirit
To blow apart the sundering flames, that I
After a thousand years of hell, may catch
One glimpse, one only, of the Church of Christ,
The perfect work, finished, though not by me.

℣. Save me from the lion's mouth; Thou hast heard me
    also from among the horns of the unicorns.

℞. For why? Thou shalt not leave my soul in hell, neither
    shalt Thou suffer Thine holy one to see corruption.
        Trumpet.

CASSIEL:

Sheathe thy sword, Michael; the fight is won.

RAPHAEL:

Close the book, Cassiel; the score is paid.

GABRIEL:

Give glory, Raphael; the race is run.

MICHAEL:

Lead homeward, Gabriel, the sheep that strayed.

ALL:

Eloi, Eloi, Eloi,
Glory to God in the highest; holy is He!

MICHAEL:

How hardly shall the rich man enter in
To the Kingdom of Heaven! By what sharp, thorny ways,
By what strait gate at last! But when he is come,
The angelic trumpets split their golden throats
Triumphant, to the stars singing together
And all the sons of God shouting for joy.
Be comforted, thou that wast rich in gifts;
For thou are broken on the self-same rack
That broke the richest Prince of all the world,
The Master-man. Thou shalt not surely die,
Save as He died; nor suffer, save with Him;
Nor lie in hell, for He hath conquered hell
And flung the gates wide open. They that bear
The cross with Him, with Him shall wear a crown
Such as the angels know not. Then be still,
And know that He is God, and God alone.

℣. Who suffered for our salvation; descended into hell,
rose again the third day from the dead.

℟. He ascended into Heaven, He sitteth on the right hand
of the Father, God Almighty; from whence He shall
come to judge the quick and the dead.

CHOIR:

Eloi, Eloi, Eloi,

Glory to God in the highest; holy is He!

While this is sung, the ANGELS *go up and stand side
by side across the stage behind the couch.*

WILLIAM:

I shall not die but live, and declare the works of the
Lord. Who is there? I was dreaming. Gervase! Hubert!

GERVASE *and* HUBERT *run in, left and right.*

GERVASE:

William?

HUBERT:

Dear master?

WILLIAM:

God hath changed my mind.

I must submit. I must go back to France.

I do but hinder the work, lingering here,

Kicking against the pricks.

GERVASE:

Do not say so!

HUBERT:

What should we do without you?

WILLIAM:

I am not

The only architect in the world—there are others

Will do the work as well, better perhaps.

Stay not to chide me—listen, there is one,

William the Englishman, a little man,

But with a mounting spirit and great vision;

Send now for him. I think we quarrelled once,

Not seeing eye to eye—but that is nothing;

He will respect my work as I do his,
And build a harmony of his and mine
To a nobler close than mine. I'll not dictate
Conditions to the Chapter; but, should they choose
William the Englishman to follow me,
He'll do such work for them as honours God
And them and all good craftsmen. As for me,
My place is here no more. I am in God's hand.
Take me and bear me hence.

HUBERT:

Dear master, whither?

WILLIAM:

To the Lady Ursula's lodging. If unto her
I can make any amends, then I will make it.
To all of you, I owe a debt of love
Which I will pay with love. Only to God,
That royal creditor, no debt remains.
He from the treasure of His great heart hath paid
The whole sum due, and cancelled out the bond.

GERVASE:

Laus Deo!

> GERVASE *and* HUBERT *carry* WILLIAM *out, right.*

CHOIR:

O quanta qualia sunt illa sabbata,
Quae semper celebrat superna curia,
Quae fessis requies, quae merces fortibus,
Cum erit omnia Deus in omnibus.

Vere Jerusalem illic est civitas,
Cujus pax jugis est summa jucunditas,
Ubi non praevenit rem desiderium,
Nec desiderio minus est praemium.

Illic ex sabbato succedit sabbatum,
Perpes laetitia sabbatizantium,

Nec ineffabiles cessabunt jubili,
Quos decantabimus et nos et angeli.

> MICHAEL *comes down to the foot of the steps and addresses the congregation; the other three* ANGELS *standing above him.*

MICHAEL: Children of men, lift up your hearts. Laud and magnify God, the everlasting Wisdom, the holy, undivided and adorable Trinity.

Praise Him that He hath made man in His own image, a maker and craftsman like Himself, a little mirror of His triune majesty.

For every work of creation is threefold, an earthly trinity to match the heavenly.

First: there is the Creative Idea; passionless, timeless, beholding the whole work complete at once, the end in the beginning; and this is the image of the Father.

Second: there is the Creative Energy, begotten of that Idea, working in time from the beginning to the end, with sweat and passion, being incarnate in the bonds of matter; and this is the image of the Word.

Third: there is the Creative Power, the meaning of the work and its response in the lively soul; and this is the image of the indwelling Spirit.

And these three are one, each equally in itself the whole work, whereof none can exist without other; and this is the image of the Trinity.

Look then upon this Cathedral Church of Christ: imagined by men's minds, built by the labour of men's hands, working with power upon the souls of men; symbol of the everlasting Trinity, the visible temple of God.

As you would honour Christ, so honour His Church; nor suffer this temple of His Body to know decay.

THE BLOODY TENET

A Play

JAMES SCHEVILL

". . . *liberavi animam meam: I have not
hid within my breast my soul's belief."*
ROGER WILLIAMS *in his* The Bloody Tenet
of Persecution for Cause of Conscience

To Marvin Halverson and the
National Council of Churches,
and to Lawrence Durgin and the
members of the Central Congregational
Church in Providence, Rhode Island,
where this play was first performed.

CHARACTERS

IN THE PROLOGUE AND THE EPILOGUE:

THE EVANGELIST, *Mrs. Simpsen, a prominent American evangelist.*

THE JOURNALIST, *Edward Miller, a writer of books and articles on the history of religion.*

IN THE REMAINING SCENES:

GOVERNOR HAYNES, *Governor of Massachusetts Bay and Presiding Officer of the General Court.*

THOMAS DUDLEY, *Governor of the Bay before and after Haynes. At the time of Williams's trial, a leading magistrate.*

JOHN WINTHROP, *Ex-Governor of the Colony. Reduced to magistrate at the time of Williams's trial because of his "leniency to disaffected souls."*

JOHN COTTON, *Renowned theologian among the Puritans in England and the Calvinists on the continent. Who assured the world that the congregational system needed a vigorous magistracy. An implacable foe of Williams, Cotton dreamt of a theocracy modeled on the Biblical image of Israel.*

THOMAS HOOKER, *With Cotton a renowned minister, but a minister with a special reputation as a great preacher.*

ROGER WILLIAMS, *The defendant at the trial held in Hooker's Church, Newtown, October 8, 1635.*

MARY WILLIAMS, *His wife.*

CANONICUS, *The Chief of the Narragansett Indians.*

SIR EDWARD COKE, *Chief Justice of the Star Chamber under Queen Elizabeth. The great English lawyer and mentor of Williams.*

Note: Since Canonicus does not speak, this part can be doubled. The cast for performance, then, consists of eight men and two women.

PROLOGUE

SCENE I: *The church is dark. The light comes up to reveal the* JOURNALIST *waiting for the* EVANGELIST. *A banner, reading* THE TEMPLE OF RADIANT REDEMPTION, *hangs on the wall. The* JOURNALIST *is a middle-aged intellectual, shrewd, aggressive and cynical. Nervously, he looks around the Temple before he speaks.*

JOURNALIST:
   She's late . . . I'll bet she keeps everyone waiting . . .
   All these statues . . . (*He gestures with disgust around the Temple*) I thought Protestants had gotten rid of idols.
   But she seems to have added a few of her own . . . (*He looks at the banner*)
   The Gospel of Radiant Redemption . . . There's a Simple-minded American evangelist for you.
   The latest tricks of Public Relations . . . (*Then bitterly*):
   I used to think of myself as a religious historian.
   Now I'm just a reporter who runs after evangelists
   For interviews . . . Sh . . . here she comes . . .
       He is startled as the EVANGELIST *makes an impressive entrance. She is dressed in a dazzling, long white gown, with a red sash across the front. There is no doubt of the magnetism of her personality.*

EVANGELIST (*extending her hand regally*):
   Mr. Miller? I'm sorry to keep you waiting.

JOURNALIST:

Thank you for seeing me, Mrs. Simpsen. (*Then ironically*):
Don't worry about keeping me waiting.
A journalist only kills time.

EVANGELIST:

Is this your first visit to
My Temple of Radiant Redemption?

JOURNALIST:

Yes, I'm afraid it is . . .

EVANGELIST:

Then stop a moment and listen . . . (*She stops him imperiously*)
Listen to the spirit of our ancestors
Who sing the Gospel of Radiant Redemption.

JOURNALIST (*puzzled*):

The ancestors of your Gospel?

EVANGELIST (*sweeping her arm around the church*):

There they are, in the air of eternity.
Sweet in the sunlight of His grace,
The heroes who have bled for Jesus.
Do you hear that voice in the corner?

JOURNALIST:

I don't hear anything.

EVANGELIST:

That is the soul of Saint Peter, crucified downwards,
Who knew the secret irony of a crucifixion
Forces the traitors still to look up at you.
(*She is about to lead him to another corner, but he stops her.*)

JOURNALIST:

But Saint Peter was a Catholic martyr . . .

EVANGELIST (*brushing this off firmly*):

Religious heroes, Mr. Miller, belong to Jesus
And not to any one religious order. (*She points to another corner*)
In this blessed corner of my Temple
Prays the martyr, John Huss, as the cruel flames
Burnt the flesh of earth from his body.
Jesus has always demanded sacrifice
To escape the hot temptation of Hell.

JOURNALIST:

Perhaps there is a danger of conformity in religion
And heretics are created as scapegoats, but
The saints and martyrs of God need no earthly recognition.
Why do you make them into a personal gallery of heroes?

EVANGELIST:

We forget their sacrifices too easily.
Religion has need of heroes today.

JOURNALIST:

You don't understand what I mean.
By praising martyrs and heretics
As heroes of religious revolt,
Aren't you destroying the unity
Of organized churches and setting up
New symbols of separation . . . ?

EVANGELIST:

There's nothing wrong with symbols.
I don't think God is a realistic geographer
Of Heaven and Hell, Mr. Miller.
Each soul is a fire escape and a fire trap
At the same time, you must know that.

JOURNALIST (*pointedly*):
  The danger of religious rebels is that
  They interpret scripture for their own ends.
  That's why the early Christian fathers
  Moved back from the cloudy symbols of the word
  To the traditions of the acts of Jesus.

EVANGELIST:
  Religion has no meaning
  Unless the symbol and the act are one.
  Don't try to deceive me, Mr. Miller.
  The danger of the scholar is that
  He wastes all his time poring over words
  And finally divides the act and the symbol
  Into two false worlds.

JOURNALIST (*nettled*):
  Perhaps you're right. That may be the scholar's danger,
  But what is the danger of the evangelist
  Who creates a world of romantic isolation
  Split apart from all other Christian churches?

EVANGELIST:
  I don't split myself away from other churches.
  Wherever I preach throughout the country,
  I try to cooperate with all churches
  On the March for Christ through an extensive follow-up
    system.

JOURNALIST:
  Isn't there a risk of turning religion into Public Relations
  With your March for Christ and your follow-up systems?

EVANGELIST (*scornfully*):
  Religion is not a guest home for Sunday visits
  As you conformist intellectuals would make it.
  You've lost your spirit working for a magazine
  That treats religion like a mummy in a museum.

Come to the services in my Temple, Mr. Miller,
And throw away your crutches of cynicism!

JOURNALIST (*stiffly*):

I think religion is a private matter between man and
    God.
Preaching to crowds in a Temple or on a street corner
    may
Hypnotize them, but it doesn't bring them closer to God.
This idea of mass religion is why
We've never had a real American heretic.

EVANGELIST:

A street corner for the soul is as good as a study
If the brain will descend to the smell of the street.
And you're wrong about an American martyr. There
    has been one.
You've even written about him. This is his heroic corner
In my Temple of Radiant Redemption. (*She points*)

JOURNALIST:

Who do you mean?

EVANGELIST (*fervently*):

Roger Williams, the founder of religious freedom,
The gentle soul who separated the church
Once and for all from the tyranny of state control.

JOURNALIST (*protesting*):

That's what I mean about your gallery of heroes.
You're not talking about the real Williams,
But a fantasy of your own creation.
Williams was hardly a gentle soul
And he certainly wasn't a martyr.
His opponents, Governor Haynes, Thomas Dudley,
John Winthrop, and the great ministers,
Thomas Hooker and John Cotton—
They were deeply religious men.

EVANGELIST:

Many false religious fires
Shine from the walls of Hell.

JOURNALIST:

I'm surprised to hear *you* say that.
The Puritans weren't insincere about Williams.
They thought he was a kind of stubborn crank.

EVANGELIST:

Sometimes God loves the stubborn shepherd
More than the meek sheep, Mr. Miller.

JOURNALIST:

What do you really know about Williams?
Do you remember his interpretation of the parable in
   Matthew 13?

EVANGELIST:

You mean the parable when God commands men to let
   alone
The weeds to grow up with the wheat until the harvest.

JOURNALIST:

Yes. Williams said the church lives wildly
In the wilderness of the world, and
Cannot ever find absolute truth. The weeds
In the parable, to Williams, were false Christians . . .

EVANGELIST (*emphatically*):

Mr. Miller, there are false *everythings* today.

JOURNALIST (*pointedly*):

Williams called these false Christians
Strange professors of the name of Jesus,
Sowers of ignorance and error in the night . . .

EVANGELIST (*indignantly*):

You imply that he would call me a strange professor of
Jesus?

JOURNALIST (*shrugging*):

I'm only a journalist. I'm asking you
If your Temple of Radiant Redemption
Is another one of the isolated groups
That grow wildly in our country today?

EVANGELIST (*calmly and with great confidence*):

Religion, I think, is not a bed of roses.
Your Williams chained in the false light of history
Is not as real as my view of his message of spiritual
freedom.
You have no right to judge the heroes inside the Lord's
garden.

JOURNALIST:

I don't judge anything. This is your Temple.

EVANGELIST:

The Lord knows I prefer the quiet of a chapel,
But the radiation of His eternal will
Drives my spirit to help men towards His grace.

JOURNALIST:

Is that why you play the role of Christ
When you stage the crucifixion every year?
Isn't that a heresy of pride
That cuts away the grace of God?

EVANGELIST:

No one can proclaim himself a heretic.
Only the Lord has that sacred power:
If there was no one to challenge conformity
The prosecutors of heresy would survive
In their cold masks of security.

JOURNALIST:

Without prosecution, there would be no society of law.

EVANGELIST:

No prosecutor can represent the love of God.
How can you know the torment of a Roger Williams
When he stands alone against a power of men?

JOURNALIST:

I don't know and I admit it, but I know
What Williams has come to mean in history.
You aren't the only one to distort his life.
In Geneva his statue stands as one of the leaders
Of the Protestant Revolution, the hero
Who separated the church from the state.
His knotty mind has been simplified to this one point,
And from that point flower all of the weird sects—
The strange professors of Jesus—
Who grow wildly in our country today.

EVANGELIST:

The strange professor of Jesus may be a danger
But God did not create every man to be ordinary.
It would cost the loss of many souls
If I turned from the Lord's power of radiant redemption.
I have often thought about the trial of Roger Williams
And I am sure there was only one central issue,
The true love of God . . .

JOURNALIST (*protesting*):

But the trial of Williams was a complicated one. There
were many issues involved . . .

EVANGELIST (*ignoring this*):

God has willed us to remember only the simple issue
Of freedom to love God in our own way.

JOURNALIST (*angrily*):

How could Williams, with his complicated mind,
Ever think of simplifying God?

EVANGELIST (*triumphantly*):

Didn't he teach the savage Indians?
In the same way Christ taught an almost illiterate people
and today we must call back that simplicity
And teach the power of God's love and fire!

> (*She is close to him, scorning him with the fire of her voice as the scene blacks out and the choir is heard singing:*
> *"The land is fair, the air is soft, etc."*)

SCENE II: *Hooker's Church. Newtown, now Cambridge, Massachusetts. 1635.*

HOOKER (*enters with* COTTON, DUDLEY, WINTHROP *and* HAYNES): It is a humble church, Governor Haynes. We have no comforts here.

HAYNES:

But a strong fortress for God's spirit, Mr. Hooker.
Every man in Massachusetts Bay honors your preaching
And I am told your voice haunts all the pulpits in the colony.

HOOKER:

If I am honored with a voice, Sir,
It is to speak God's word in this new state.

WINTHROP (*to* HAYNES):

Why did you ask us here?

HAYNES:

It is the case of Roger Williams of which an end must be made.

WINTHROP:

I cannot judge this case
For I have been his friend
Despite his nature of dissent.

HAYNES:

You were honored, Mr. Winthrop,
As first governor of all this Bay . . .

DUDLEY:

But then reduced to magistrate
For leniency to disaffected souls . . .

HAYNES:

Please, Mr. Dudley. (*then, to* WINTHROP)
This a case, Sir, in which we must request your aid
For we know your love of God and value all your judg-
    ments.

WINTHROP:

Mr. Williams is a man well-liked
Though his views seem wild and crankish.

DUDLEY:

Especially well-liked in old England.

HAYNES:

That is where our problem rests.
Mr. Williams demands the right of complete separation
For any church within this colony.
He demands this rigorous separation
Not only from the English church, which we might
    tolerate,
But also from our theocratic Bay authority.
He has many influential English friends
Who listen when he writes against our magistrates.

WINTHROP:

Has he taken action to support these views?

HAYNES:

> In order to foster this separation
> He has sent letters to all our churches in the Bay
> Accusing our magistrates of tyrannical interference
> With the free powers of his Salem congregation.

DUDLEY:

> This is a rage of rebellion, Sir. You cannot deny that.

WINTHROP:

> It is a wrong, but more I think
> A case of temper than ill will and plotting.

DUDLEY:

> Plotting or temper makes no difference
> To the welfare of the state. Both must be punished.
> We cannot let this rebel split apart
> Our unity of magistrates and ministers.

WINTHROP:

> What is it you mean to do, Mr. Dudley?

DUDLEY:

> Mr. Williams must be tried before the General Court.

WINTHROP:

> I ask to be excused.

HAYNES:

> You must assist us else the colony is split.
> The danger we face is absolute and clear.
> We are only a small settlement
> Surrounded by savage and heathen enemies.
> If we lose our central authority
> Our state cannot long survive.

DUDLEY (to WINTHROP):

> Would you have our land dissolve

And all your reputation gone
Because a man of overweening pride
Thrusts down our Bay his knife of separation?

WINTHROP:

He never seemed to my friendship
A man possessed by devil's pride. (*Turning to* HOOKER
and COTTON *for support*)
Has he been argued with by our honored ministers?

HAYNES:

I asked Mr. Cotton to contest with him
Because I thought no one could deny
The sacred scholarship of our leading theologian.

HOOKER (*to* WINTHROP):

Mr. Cotton has just returned from long and bitter days
In Salem and will tell you of his futile argument.

COTTON:

Sirs, I do not seek your praise of scholarship.
This is an unpleasant task where the word of the Lord
Is conflicted with in practice.
When I visited Mr. Williams I found him sick in bed
Where he did read with feverish haste
To find support within the Bible.

DUDLEY:

He cannot find a heresy in every town
Within the sacred fury of the Bible.

WINTHROP:

Is it a serious illness?

COTTON:

Mainly a sickness of the mind I think
That failed to keep his words from running riot.

WINTHROP:

You do not judge him by his independent tongue?

COTTON:

I have no doubt of his sincerity,
But he has a head that runs around
And begs all constant reason
With its shifting roundabout.
He is a lion for separation, so strong for it,
There seems nothing left but God from which to sepa-
rate;
And when I did strap him down on separation
He wriggled out on oaths of loyalty,
And when I questioned him on loyalty
He shifted to attack the magistrates
For threatening his Salem church.

HAYNES:

It is a grave accusation that threatens all our government.

WINTHROP:

Let us not forget we are fled from an England
Where the laws of men warped the peaceful ways of God
Into a force that shattered peace.
We must beware of civil law.

COTTON:

That was his question of me, asking, in Christ's words,
Should we not render unto Caesar the things that are
Caesar's,
And unto God the things that are God's?
But in our New England we have no forcing hand of
Caesar;
We have no civil government but stems from God's holy
word.
I asked Mr. Williams, would he have a Caesar here in
the Lord's state?
And he answered, there is only one Lord's state,

The Bible's Israel, and it was doomed by God.
He is a man who reads his Bible like a dreamer
And cannot see the factual hand of the Lord.

WINTHROP:

We must take care in judging dreamers.
A state that sharpens laws to pointed spears
Tears all dissent and dream on cruel steel
And sinks into oblivion like a stain of blood.
Was it not Joseph's brethren who said scornfully,
"Behold, this dreamer cometh"?

HAYNES:

Sir, I think no one takes this trial lightly.
If Mr. Williams is a dreamer, it is the act of his dream
We will judge and not the fantasy of his vision. (*To* COT-
TON)
What did he say to his letters attacking our magistrates?

COTTON:

He justified them as the freedom of his conscience.
Conscience moves in his every word like a devious worm
In underground soil until no man knows its way or goal.

WINTHROP:

Is it not true then, Mr. Cotton,
If we fail to uphold the freedom of conscience
We make a mockery of our new state?

COTTON:

It is a sacred duty, Mr. Winthrop,
Yet what is conscience but the soul of every man?
And while we must not punish the freedom of this soul
before God,
We must punish any soul if it sins against itself,
For the Lord commanded Moses, "Thou shalt have no
other God before me."
How then can a soul find salvation if it be permitted

To worship false idols under the disguise of conscience-
freedom?

HAYNES:

What did Mr. Williams answer to this thought?

COTTON:

He did evade it by answering, the Lord also commanded
"Thou shalt not bear false witness against thy neighbor."
But who has cried false witness against his neighbor?
I tell you it is a head that runs around.

DUDLEY:

But though confused a danger to our unity.
He must be stopped from sins against his conscience.

WINTHROP:

And we, Sir, must be careful of sins to ours. (*To* COTTON)
Did you question him further on the magistrates
In addition to the Salem incident?

COTTON:

He has a general principle, a storm of clouds in his words,
That magistrates may not punish any breach of the First
Table of the Decalogue.

HAYNES:

If this should ever occur our civil officers
Could not even enforce the Sabbath.

COTTON:

Then I quoted him the declaration of the First Helvetic
Conference that:
"The chief office of the magistrate is to defend religion
And to take care that the word of God is purely
preached."

WINTHROP:

He did deny that?

COTTON:

    No, but he stressed the words *defend* and *take care*
    And called them words of peace and not attack,
    And hinted darkly of invented devotions to the God of
        heaven.

HAYNES:

    What meant he by "invented devotions"?

COTTON:

    It is hard to find the force of clarity
    On the surface of a muddy stream,
    But it seemed he meant the magistrates.
    He thinks it wrong that clergymen have vested interests
    Together with the magistrates upon our state.
    But what these vested interests are,
    And where the ministers that sin, he cannot say.

HAYNES:

    What do you think of this, Mr. Hooker?

HOOKER:

    I have known Mr. Williams and liked him,
    But he is a danger wrapped in the cloak of simplicity.
    It is the seeming innocents who carry
    Tight beneath their friendly love the flame of a despotic
        will
    That burns the union of the church and state.

HAYNES (*to* WINTHROP):

    Are you convinced, Mr. Winthrop,
    Of the need for this reluctant trial?

WINTHROP:

    Must it be a session of the General Court?
    With time, can we not persuade him
    By a delegation of more ministers?

COTTON:

It is too late for that, but there is merit in your thought.
What if beside the magistrates and deputies upon the
    General Court,
We summon our ministers within the Bay?
Such a trial, with all our eminence of leadership,
Held here in this honored church of Mr. Hooker,
Must persuade him of his errors
And bring his soul back to aid our colony.

WINTHROP:

When would you hold the trial?

DUDLEY:

It must be soon for many churches threaten separation.

HAYNES:

Let us set the morning of October 8.

WINTHROP:

But he is sick upon his bed.
Is it just to force him to attend so soon?

DUDLEY:

Mr. Cotton thinks it but a sickness of the mind.

COTTON:

It seemed a sickness that can stand a trial's debate,
And sometimes in a mind's dark fever,
The light of grace strikes suddenly.

HAYNES:

Our magistrates and deputies must be notified.

DUDLEY:

I will arrange for them.

HAYNES (to COTTON and HOOKER):

And you, Sirs, I ask you to approach our ministers.

HOOKER:

We will do so.

HAYNES (*to* WINTHROP):

You will attend, Mr. Winthrop, and lend us your aid?

WINTHROP (*hesitating*):

I will hear the evidence.

> As the scene ends, the choir is heard singing
> "DAVID'S LAMENTATION" by WILLIAM BILLINGS:

> "*David the King was grieved and moved,*
> *He went to his chamber, his chamber and wept.*
> *And as he wept, he wept and said:*
> *'O my son, O my son,*
> *Would to God I had died,*
> *Would to God I had died.'*"

SCENE III: *The home of* ROGER WILLIAMS. *Only a rough cot is needed to indicate the change of setting.*

WILLIAMS (*enters, tired and dusty*):

Mary! I am home. (*He slumps down on the edge of the cot.*)

MARY (*enters*):

You were gone so long I was worried. Are you ill again?

WILLIAMS:

No, only tired and weak. Give me some water.
I have been riding many hours.

MARY (*She gives him some water and feels his forehead*):

You are feverish. Why did you ride?

WILLIAMS:

I had to ride today. And would not ride against your
wishes.

If you had known you would have begged me stay at
home.

MARY:

You were not busy with your trading duties?

WILLIAMS:

No, I rode this morning to keep a secret meeting with
Canonicus.

MARY:

Canonicus?

WILLIAMS:

Yes, the chief of the Narragansett Indians.

MARY:

But our people all distrust him.
They fear him for planning
Savage crimes against our settlers.

WILLIAMS:

The summons I expected came yesterday.
I must stand trial in three days
Before the General Court in Newtown.

MARY:

The General Court!

WILLIAMS:

They have charged me with heresy
And called me a danger to the state.
They have even asked their ministers to attend
And placed the trial in Hooker's Church
To sharpen my guilt under God's law.

MARY:

Why then did Mr. Cotton visit you?
You were companions in the flight from England.

WILLIAMS:

He sought to persuade me of my errors, but failed.
Mary, I know they will be strict at this General Court . . .

MARY:

They cannot take your life?

WILLIAMS:

Some might have the wish, but I do not think
They dare so far although I have bitter enemies.

MARY:

What will happen to you?

WILLIAMS:

I think they will plot to send me back to England,
Convicted of disloyalty, in a winter passage of shame
Before my friends. But I will not go.

MARY:

They are many and hold the power.

WILLIAMS:

I have bought land in Narragansett
From their chief, Canonicus,
And mean to found a colony there if I am exiled.

MARY:

Another colony? How can you trust this heathen savage?

WILLIAMS:

Mary, we have been guilty of great wrong to the Indians.
We have seized their land by force,
But I have made peace with Canonicus.

MARY:

What peace is there in another colony?
I remember Mr. Cotton preaching once from *Samuel:*
Moreover, I will appoint a place for my people Israel,
And I will plant them that they may dwell
In a place of their own and move no more.
They are words I have never forgotten.

WILLIAMS:

Would you have me compromise
And tell the Court all my acts were lies?

MARY:

How can I judge you? I am your wife.
Oh, I would help you but I have nothing of your learn-
ing.
I will always follow you and do as you ask me,
But do not ask my understanding.

WILLIAMS:

Do you think I understand myself?
What dreamer understands the wilderness of his dream?
Riding by the ocean this dawn
Where the boats rocked at their anchors,
I saw the sentinel gulls perched on their high posts
In patient time, and the leaves drifted deathwards
Back to matter on the still water, and I thought,
It is always God's time in the sun.
He moves towards birth and death in His mysterious
moment
And no man stands the luxury of His light.
How then can I understand the shadows of my dream?
But I think if that dream ever were extinguished
My little source of God's light is gone.

MARY:

Although I cannot share your dream
I would not fight against it.

WILLIAMS:

> We have a child, Mary, and you expect
> Another one within two months.
> No one will harm you here. They would not dare that,
> And when I have a free settlement in the land
> I shall, with God's love, call by the name of Providence,
> I will send for you and the children.
> Is it selfish of me to hold my views?

MARY:

> You were never a selfish man. Last month,
> When you separated from our Salem church as teacher,
> You let me go on praying there
> Despite the whisperings of many tongues.

WILLIAMS:

> It is your own conscience, Mary,
> And I have no right to interfere with that.

MARY:

> You always speak of conscience as mine or yours.
> Has not our family a conscience too?

WILLIAMS:

> Mary!

MARY:

> I cannot help my tongue.
> When we fled by ship from England
> Our company was Christian men.
> Now you deal with heathen Indians.

WILLIAMS:

> Your words are unjust. Here in the Bay
> The Indian is our torment and we persecute him
> With a bloody tenet because his religion is not ours.
> But I have bought this soil from Canonicus.
> His tribe will not disturb our settlement.

MARY:

And what will happen to our children? It is a risk for
them.

WILLIAMS:

The children will be safe. I will not send for you
Until I prove my faith with the Indians.

MARY:

I pray that your pride of conscience
Does not forsake the word of God.

WILLIAMS:

You must not judge me, Mary.
Conscience is only a persuasion
Fixed in the mind and heart of man
That forces him to choose his way to God.
I have seen the Gates of Hell and through them
Enter preachers as well as lawyers, artisans, farmers,
Men who had no conscience in their choice.

MARY:

Why must your conscience lead to my bitter isolation?
Why must I endure this loneliness?
An exile from my husband, and then another exile
In the wilderness from our holy church. (*She is crying
and fighting to control herself.*)

WILLIAMS:

This will not be an exile, Mary.
Do you remember what the Lord said to Rebekah?
"Two nations are in thy womb, and the one people
Shall be stronger than the other people
And the elder shall serve the younger."
Here in the Bay I think we are the elder nation
And have failed to find the true peace of God's will,
But there in Narragansett we of the Bay
Shall found and serve the younger nation,

That men may live and worship in peace
And the land be open before us. (*He pauses.*)
Mary, if all this is my vanity
Tell me and I will act against it.

MARY (*controlling herself*):
I think no woman can judge a man's pride
Before the Lord, least of all a wife her husband.
It is my duty to go with you where you will go.

WILLIAMS:
I would not have it a mere duty.

MARY (*after a slight pause*):
You must rest. I will get you food. (*She goes out.*)
WILLIAMS (*he picks up the Bible and begins to read*):
"And Isaac intreated the Lord for his wife, because she
was barren: and the Lord was intreated of him, and
Rebekah his wife conceived. And the children struggled
together within her; and she said, 'If it be so, why am I
thus?' And she went to enquire of the Lord. And the
Lord said unto her, 'Two nations are in thy womb . . .'"
> *Worn out, he falls asleep. The choir is heard sing-
> ing very softly, "*DAVID THE KING.*" The lights dim
> suddenly and the bloody, shadowy outline of the
> Indian chief,* CANONICUS, *is seen.* WILLIAMS *starts
> up.*

WILLIAMS:
Canonicus! Fever burns my brain.
This is a vision of blood. What have we done in New
  England?
Under the cross of the living God, with a prayer of
  Thanksgiving,
We have possessed the dead stones from the Indians,
With a greed for great portions of land
And a depraved appetite for the vanity of power.
Oh, Canonicus, can I ever make peace with you?
In the bloody thoughts you bring me

What are all the wars of this world about
But for greater dishes and bowls of gain?
We will drive your people from your land
And burn your crude huts and kill your warriors
And you will murder our Christian settlers.
But if you will let me build my Providence
Perhaps a small memory of gentle peace
Between the Indian and white man will live on,
A grain of conscience for the lies of vanity.
Having bought truth dear we must not sell it cheap,
Not the least grain of it for the whole world,
Least of all for the bitter sweetening
Of a little vanishing pleasure, for a little
Puff of reputation from the changeable breath of men,
For the broken bags of riches that fall from eagles' wings,
For a dream of those which on our deathbed
Vanish and leave tormenting flames behind them.
What are the leaves and flowers and smoke of earthly
    things
About which we poor fools disquiet ourselves in vain?
Eternity, eternity, is our business.

> *The figure of* CANONICUS *disappears. Agitated,* WIL-
> LIAMS *begins to read from the Bible again.*

"And he dreamed, and, behold, a ladder set up on the
earth, and the top of it reached to heaven: and, behold,
the angels of the Lord ascending and descending on it.
And, behold, the Lord stood above it, and said, 'I am the
Lord God of Abraham thy father, and the God of Isaac:
the land whereon thou liest, to thee will I give it, and
to thy seed; and thy seed shall be as the dust of the
earth, and thou shalt spread abroad to the west, and to
the east, and to the north, and to the south . . .'"

> *The figure of* SIR EDWARD COKE *appears. He is
> richly clothed in Elizabethan formal dress in con-
> trast to the severe Puritan clothing of* WILLIAMS.

COKE:

Sir, you speak too soon of eternity . . .

WILLIAMS:

Who are you?

COKE:

The dust of the earth of which you read.

WILLIAMS:

Sir Edward Coke!

COKE:

I thought your conscience had shadowed out a thought
of me.

WILLIAMS:

I have never forgotten you.

COKE:

You remember my power then?

WILLIAMS:

I could never forget the Chief Justice of England.

COKE:

After the death of Queen Elizabeth,
When I continued as Chief Justice
Of the Star Chamber under King James,
I made you my chief stenographer.

WILLIAMS:

Yes . . . there in the Star Chamber which I came to
think of
As a web of spiders weaving testimony of the
King's intrigues, I learned to dream of God.

COKE:

Was it of God you dreamt, or of the noblemen
Whose deaths I caused, beheaded Essex and Southamp-
ton?

WILLIAMS:

 I felt their shadows in that courtroom always—
 Trials in which I knew you took the throne's part,
 But knew not your exact role.

COKE:

 You knew the role I played, but shut your eyes
 For conscience-ease. You were a man who wrote short-
   hand
 As well as any clerk in England and enjoyed
 The pleasure of your trust, the glitter of
 London's dancing fairs, the full-dress executions on
   Tower Hill.

WILLIAMS:

 Do not mock me! I was born into the Age of Puritans
 And never knew the rule of Queen Elizabeth.

COKE:

 True, she died the year that you were born,
 But under King James's rule, you saw me preside
 Over the trial of the poisoners of Sir Thomas Overbury.

WILLIAMS:

 I hated all the nobles' cheating pomp and scorn of God!

COKE:

 You hated me when the wardrobe mistress, Mrs. Turner,
 A conspirator in the Overbury poisoning,
 The inventor of a yellow starch for cuffs, took the stand
 And I called her, "Whore, bawd, papist!" And had her
   hanged.
 You remember the executioner wore yellow starched
   cuffs.

WILLIAMS:

 I did hate the rule of James which brought a
 Bloody autumn of persecution for cause of conscience.

COKE:

What a peacock your conscience is
Preening itself with illusion.
Despite your revulsion from the Star Chamber
You sucked willingly on my power,
Attended college on my recommending word,
Nourished yourself on my patronage.

WILLIAMS:

I did ever admire your belief in the Common Law
And your fight for parliamentary rights against the King
Until I came to know the truer law of God's will.

COKE:

Hypocrite! You became a puritan as a boy,
A step your tailor father hated and so you hated your
    parents too!

WILLIAMS:

The tailor and the cruel court were bound together.
Without the tailor who could be a fop
And preen and ape indecent ways?

COKE:

This is your curse of conscience then, to hate your
    parents,
And all your youth to act the pure and godly rebel
While serving me inside the Star Chamber.

WILLIAMS (*agonizingly*):

I did ever dream of God, even in the Star Chamber!

COKE:

Even when you became a minister and chaplain
In the household of Sir William Masham at Otes
And fell in love with Lady Masham's daughter, Jug?
This lust was your dream of God?

WILLIAMS:

It is not true!

COKE:

But Lady Masham would not have you
As a low-born husband for her daughter
And so your conscience sank again.
In springtime of your sex and bitterness
You married your wife, Mary—
Who was nothing but Jug's maid.

WILLIAMS:

Devil, devil! Why do you torture me
When I did always love you?

COKE:

Devil of conscience perhaps,
Curse of pride. Is it not true?

WILLIAMS:

No, it is . . . half true. My pride caused me bitter
words
Against the Lady Masham, and my need turned me to
her maid,
My wife, Mary, whom I learned to love.

COKE:

But married from lust.

WILLIAMS:

Married from need of love perhaps, but not from lust.
It is true I feared God for my hate against Lady Masham
Who thought me low-born for her daughter;
This was my sin of pride.

COKE (scornfully):

What is the reward you seek then?

WILLIAMS:

I live only for the fear and grace of God.

COKE:

How can you hope for the grace of God
When you say you live in fear of His name?
Did not John preach: "Perfect love casts out fear"?

WILLIAMS:

You are the tempter conscience dreads,
And yet I think no human love is perfect.
The true love of God never casts out
The true fear of God but only that which is
False and counterfeit, the fear of beasts and slaves.
Men must learn to live with fear before they come to
love
And so it was the spirit of the fear of God
Poured down upon the Lord Jesus himself.

COKE:

Go to your trial of man's law then,
Go with your fear and seek your hope;
Go with your lust and seek deliverance;
Go with your pride and seek humility;
But remember your English past in the Star Chamber,
The parents whom you hated, and the passion of your
springtime love.
He vanishes.

WILLIAMS:

Mary! Mary!

MARY (*enters*):

Did you call? Is it pain again?

WILLIAMS:

Pain of conscience, Mary.

I dreamt I saw Sir Edward Coke
Who called me back to the Star Chamber.

MARY:

You must not go to court so soon.
It is cruel in your sickness to make you attend.

WILLIAMS:

I must go if God wills it.

MARY:

How can you judge God's will?
Can you not convince them of your innocence?

WILLIAMS:

Mary, I cannot convince even you
That I do not act from pride only.

MARY:

A proud man is like a tower in the sun.
Who can tell if the tower points to God
Or the vanity of man's dream?
You are my husband. I cannot judge your pride.

WILLIAMS:

Mary, I have done you wrong. I would not lose your
love.

MARY:

Love is not the daring of a dream
But of a daily harmony. When men and women marry
I think they know little of love
Which comes only with living together.

WILLIAMS:

We have been married six years, Mary.
Can you love my stubborn soul?

MARY:

> I pray against your pride
> And do not understand your actions
> But I know you seek in them the grace of God.
> I have not your words, but you have my love.

WILLIAMS:

> Mary, I am sick in mind. From my pride
> Humility can only flow with your love.
>> *He turns away from her, deeply moved.*
> I must study now. (*He picks up the Bible.*)

MARY (*going to him*):

> You must rest, not study.

WILLIAMS:

> I cannot rest until God's will is done at this trial.
> The Father of Spirits is my witness of the search
> My spirit has made after Him in all passages from the
>> Bible.
> The fruits I have suffered and gained from this sickness
> I hope I shall never forget. Mary, let me read to you.
>> *She sits beside him on the cot and he begins to*
>> *read to her from the Bible, from the Twenty-Fourth*
>> *Psalm:*

> *The earth is the Lord's, and the fulness thereof;*
> *The world, and they that dwell therein.*
> *For he hath founded it upon the seas,*
> *And established it upon the floods.*

> *Who shall ascend into the hill of the Lord?*
> *Or who shall stand in His holy place?*
> *He that hath clean hands and a pure heart;*
> *Who hath not lifted up his soul into vanity, nor*
>> *sworn deceitfully.*

> *He shall receive the blessing from the Lord,*
> *And righteousness from the God of his salvation.*

This is the generation of them that seek him,
That seek thy face, O Jacob.
Lift up your heads, O ye gates;
And be ye lift up, ye everlasting doors;
And the King of glory shall come in . . .

> *As he reads, the lights dim slowly as the scene ends*
> *and the choir is heard once more singing, "The*
> *Land is fair, the air is soft, etc."*

SCENE IV: *Hooker's Church in Newtown, now Cambridge,*
Massachusetts. October 8, 1635. At the left are seen
HAYNES, DUDLEY *and* WINTHROP. COTTON *and* HOOKER *are*
seated at the right in the first row of pews.

HAYNES (*turning and looking back, as if viewing the magis-*
trates):
Mr. Dudley, are all our magistrates assembled?

DUDLEY:
They are here, already seated, Governor Haynes.
We are fifty magistrates and deputies, many weary
From their day-long travels to attend this General Court.

HAYNES (*to* WINTHROP):
And the ministers we asked by special invitation?

WINTHROP (*pointing in the direction of* COTTON *and*
HOOKER):
They have arrived and are accounted in their seats.

HAYNES:
It is well. The added presence of
So many men of God must persuade Mr. Williams.
In these devout and honored souls he cannot help

But read his errors. Before we start the trial
I will talk with Mr. Hooker and Mr. Cotton.
> *He walks down toward the congregation and* HOOKER
> *and* COTTON *rise to greet him.*

DUDLEY (*to* WINTHROP):

It is a cold day for October.
God grant we do not freeze before this trial ends.

WINTHROP:

Mr. Dudley, it is the cold of the soul
Crawling on the dirt floor of this church
That is on trial this day. If we freeze, Sir,
It is not our flesh from the frost of winter weather
But our souls for unjust persecution.

DUDLEY (*angered*):

Do you call this solemn trial
Unjust before it has a start?

WINTHROP:

I speak only of our need to follow God's laws.
Much civil hatred has been raised against Mr. Williams
But he still has a strength of friends.

DUDLEY:

This is the General Court and he shall speak
Even if it be his toleration folly.
I hope you do not judge this rebel minister
Against the Bay because he was your friend.

WINTHROP:

I will hear the arguments . . . (*He turns away from*
DUDLEY)

HAYNES (*to* HOOKER):

Mr. Hooker, we are many officers

And bulge the walls of your small church,
But we are grateful for your hospitality.

HOOKER:

I am honored, Sir, to have my church
As host to all the General Court,
But shamed that Mr. Williams should be here on trial.

HAYNES:

As are we all and trust that he will change
When he does see the sacred weight and purpose
Of our magistrates and men of God. (*turning to* COTTON)
Mr. Cotton, it pleases me that
You and all our ministers are present.
It is a true and solemn meeting of God's will
And I thank you for this plan
To bring together ministers and magistrates.

COTTON:

This unity of minds must sway his stubborn views,
For he is a real danger, Sir. All people
Speak for him on sight and do not see beneath his mask
    of love
The Devil's swamp to which this toleration leads.

HAYNES:

After I question him on the letters he did write
Blocking our magistrates' authority and urging
His Salem church to separate completely from our
    churches
Of the Bay, I will ask Mr. Hooker to debate with him
And as arranged you will also press the Charges.

COTTON:

As God calls us to fight all heresy
That His original Nation may revive again,
It is an onerous duty I cannot avoid.

> HAYNES *returns to his seat.* COTTON *and* HOOKER
> *take their seats.*

HAYNES:

> Let Mr. Williams know the Court is ready.
>
>> *The choir is heard singing softly* "DAVID THE KING."
>> WILLIAMS *enters.* HAYNES *motions him to the defendant's chair.*

HAYNES:

> Before we begin the interrogation, Mr. Williams,
> The members of the General Court have been disturbed
> By your unwillingness to approve the authority
> Of the Bay government. I would like first to ask
> If you accept the responsibility and judgment of this
>> Court.

WILLIAMS:

> I do respect the members of this Court,
> But it is by God's word only that I desire
> To stand or fall in trial and judgment; for all flesh is
>> grass
> And the beauty of flesh is but the beauty of grass,
> Only the word of God stands fast forever.

HAYNES:

> You imply that members of the Court
> Do not speak God's word on earth?

WILLIAMS:

> I think, Sir, that man's wish is not always God's will.

DUDLEY:

> By that indirection, do you mean
> Your toleration of any cranks of God?

WINTHROP (*to* DUDLEY):

> It was a fair answer. Let Governor Haynes proceed with
>> the questions.

HAYNES:

> Mr. Williams, do you deny writing this seditious letter

To all our churches in the Bay, (*Showing the letter*)
Complaining of the magistrates
For their injustice to the Salem church?

WILLIAMS:

I do deny the letter was seditious.

HAYNES:

But you admit the letter.

WILLIAMS:

The letter I have written protested the magistrates' rights
To refuse the petition of our Salem church
For land in Marblehead Neck only for the reason
That Salem refused to cast me out as teacher.
Is it just to punish Salem because of me?

HAYNES:

Did not the Salem congregation elect you as teacher
And were they not aware of the letter?

WILLIAMS:

They did join with me in the letter.

HAYNES:

Do you admit the letter accused
The lawful magistrates and deputies, in your own words,
Of a "heinous sin and a breach of the rule of justice"?

WILLIAMS:

Is it justice to bring about an action
By an inaction and by threats?

DUDLEY:

Look how he avoids commenting
On the hot-blooded words, "heinous sin."

WILLIAMS:

My language was perhaps too prideful but I do think
There was a sin of error against the Salem church.

DUDLEY:

So you begin your admission but retreat from it.

WINTHROP:

I do not believe we are here
To judge Mr. Williams's intemperate language.
It is the danger of his actions we must test.

DUDLEY:

Is not the letter an action, Mr. Winthrop?

HAYNES:

Let me proceed with the questioning.

WILLIAMS:

Before we turn from this point, Sir,
May I ask why the magistrates and elders
Refused to read our Salem letter
To their congregations? Were they afraid?

DUDLEY (*beside himself*):

Is he to be permitted such insolence?

WINTHROP:

This is the General Court, Mr. Dudley.
We are not the Inquisition. Let Governor Haynes reply.

HAYNES:

We live in a young world of our Lord, Mr. Williams,
Surrounded by wilderness and heathen enemies of His
word,
And so must enforce a central government in God's
name
Lest petty camps of selfish gain destroy our faith.
Is your trust in the Salem congregation yet full?

WILLIAMS:

I think they are still my friends in God.

HAYNES:

> But we have heard you are no longer
> A teacher in the Salem church. Is this true?

WILLIAMS:

> You know it is true. I have separated.

HAYNES:

> Will you give us cause for this break?

WILLIAMS:

> When the Salem church was threatened
> The members decided to hold communion
> With the churches of the Bay
> And to accept the Marblehead Neck Land
> That was in dispute. So I withdrew.

DUDLEY:

> Threatened, you say, Mr. Williams, threatened!
> This is abstract and general, Sir. Who did this threatening?

WILLIAMS:

> I believe it was the magistrates of the Bay. (*General murmurs*)

DUDLEY:

> You would accuse us directly? Has your pride no bounds?

WINTHROP:

> Mr. Williams, it is a general and serious accusation.

HAYNES (*to* WILLIAMS):

> By your own admission you have left your Salem church
> And stand alone before this Court, accused
> Even by your Salem friends . . . I wish to show you a
> second letter.
> (*He produces the letter*) Do you deny this writing?

WILLIAMS:

No, it is my hand.

HAYNES:

This is a letter to your Salem church?

WILLIAMS:

It is.

HAYNES:

In which you seek to persuade your congregation
To renounce communion with all the churches in the
Bay
As . . . "full of anti-Christian pollution"?
Are those your words, Sir?

WILLIAMS (*after a pause*):

They are my words, if my merit is not gentle writing.
I do not deny them. I have always believed in
The separation of the church from any national or popish
organization.

DUDLEY (*enraged*):

You dare to call the Bay churches a popish organization?

WINTHROP:

Gentlemen, we are not here to argue
The organization of the Bay churches against the Salem
church.
Let us present the specific charges against Mr. Williams.

HAYNES:

Since the letters have been acknowledged I should like
First to give Mr. Williams a final chance to recant them.

WINTHROP:

Mr. Williams, will you reconsider the spirit of your
letters?
Revenge is not our purpose in this Court.

WILLIAMS:

    I do not deny a sinful pride
    That I work against in my person,
    But I cannot recant the spirit of my letters.

DUDLEY:

    What shall we do with a pride that condemns
    And prompts itself all in a locked unison?

WINTHROP:

    I can accept it, Mr. Dudley. Have you never felt it?

HAYNES:

    Please, Sirs, I ask Mr. Winthrop to read the specific
        Charges.
    Then I will appoint the arguer of the Charges.

WINTHROP (*reading*):"On this eighth day of October, in
    the year of our Lord, 1635, the General Court of Massa-
    chusetts, meeting in solemn session, does present the
    following Charges against Mr. Roger Williams of Salem:
    First, that Mr. Williams has constantly rebuked the
    churches of Massachusetts Bay for not abjuring all con-
    nection with the Church of England.
    Second, that Mr. Williams has disputed, refused to
    sign, and contended against the Resident's Oath of Fi-
    delity which the magistrates had ordered for safeguard
    of the colony.
    Third, that Mr. Williams has contested the validity of
    the charter of Massachusetts, granted to the colony by
    the King's hand.
    Fourth, that Mr. Williams has declared that the civil
    magistrates of the Bay have not the power to punish
    breaches of the First Table of the Decalogue.

HAYNES:

    You have heard the Charges, Mr. Williams,
    Drawn up by the fifty members of this Court

And attested by our ministers whom we have invited
here.
You will be given your chance to answer.
The Court has asked our honored minister,
Mr. Thomas Hooker, to debate with you.
The Court has also requested our learned Man of God,
Mr. John Cotton, to speak. I do think you will listen to
them
Since you have known them to speak the Lord's word.

WILLIAMS:

I respect them and desire that my rejoinders
Shall be as full of love as truth.

DUDLEY:

A mixed figure again, pricked with pride.

WINTHROP:

Let Mr. Hooker and Mr. Cotton debate with him, and
he must change
By the force of their gift. They are distinguished
speakers.

HAYNES:

Mr. Hooker will begin with the First Charge.

HOOKER (*rises*):

In the First Charge, the issue is one of separation,
Whether our Bay churches shall be secure and centrally
organized
Or split off completely from the Church of England.
I do not think Mr. Williams will now accuse me
Of a friendship with the English church under King
Charles.
He remembers well how Archbishop Laud suppressed
my lectureship
And drove me from the land on pain of death. It was the
gilded

English hierarchy, kin to the tyrannical structure of
  Rome,
Where no man could speak himself to God and
The voices of the congregation sank into a whisper,
That Mr. Williams, Mr. Cotton and myself did suffer
  from.
I ask Mr. Williams if he recalls the day of exile
When we three ministers rode together from our homes
Fleeing the Courts of Injustice for this new world?

WILLIAMS:

I do remember and honor that day of our friendship
And persuasion against the national church when it was
Bitter as death to me that Bishop Laud pursued us out
  of the land.

WINTHROP (*to* HAYNES):

It is well. He will be persuaded.

HOOKER:

Here in this green harbor of the Bay we began anew
The eternal task of salvation, surrounded by all perils
Of the wilderness and of the hidden, heathen savages;
And we considered gratefully God's words:
    "This is the token of the covenant which I make
    between me and you and every living creature
    that is with you, for perpetual generations: I do
    set my bow in the cloud, and when the bow shall
    be seen in that cloud, I will remember my cove-
    nant, and the waters shall no more become a
    flood to destroy all flesh."
It is God's bow we have seen in this clouded land
Commanding us to remember this eternal covenant,
And to unite forever the church and state.
In our congregations we have exercised a new freedom
And given them the privilege of election which belongs
To the people according to the blessed will and
Lasting law of God. But if we separate from our

English mother church and stifle the growth of
Our theocratic state, we cast aside all hope
Of law and unity, of peaceful growth in God's new land.
　　　Turning directly to WILLIAMS.
I pray with you, good friend, let not
This colony of Massachusetts be like that sheet
Let down from heaven, clung to by beasts and
Creeping things, but let it be a Garden of the Lord. (*He
sits down.*)

DUDLEY:

He cannot refute this gift of tongue!

WINTHROP:

It is well-spoken.

HAYNES:

Mr. Williams, what is your consideration of these words?

WILLIAMS:

Mr. Hooker has spoken well of God's covenant to Noah,
But I remind him of the Tower of Babel where God said:
　　"Behold, the people is one, and they have all one
　　language; and this they begin to do; and now
　　nothing will be restrained from them, which they
　　have imagined to do. Go to, let us go down, and
　　there confound their language, that they may not
　　understand one another's speech."
And therefore was the language of all men confounded
As a warning to man's soul from the Lord. I do not
　　believe
The Old Testament can be read in a complete and
　　solemn literalness.
It is figures, stories of God's will, and if you seek
To build from it again a nation modeled after ancient
　　Israel
Such a thing can never come to pass. The Lord did

Scatter men upon the face of earth that in their lonely
lives

They would seek God's grace and never build again a
unity of church and state.

DUDLEY:

It is heresy to take the Bible as mere figures!

HAYNES:

What does Mr. Cotton say to this?

COTTON:

For myself I find it sinful to take God's words

As anything but sense. Does not Mr. Williams remember

The honored Calvin's saying on those who speak of
stories in the Bible:

"It is better to confess ignorance than to play with
frivolous guesses"?

WILLIAMS:

I have read the learned Calvin's words,

But I do think that in the heart of man

We live by figures of good and evil;

And that when the witnesses of Jesus Christ

Have opened a gap in the wall of separation

Between the garden of the church and the wilderness of
the world,

God has ever broken down the wall and made His garden a wilderness again.

The word of God cannot be shown clearly by the stric-
tures of

A national church lest every conscience be forced into
a soul-rape.

DUDLEY:

Soul-rape indeed!

HAYNES:

You have spoken on the First Charge, Mr. Williams,

And we hear your words of passion with regret.
I ask Mr. Cotton to speak on the Second Charge.

COTTON (*he stands*):

    The Second Charge concerns the Resident's Oath of
        Fidelity
    Requested by the magistrates to insure due loyalty to
        God
    And to all lawful functions of the Bay authorities.
    This oath did arise upon hearing of some episcopal
    And malignant practices against the colony, when the
        magistrates
    And others of the General Court thought meet to take
        a trial
    Of the people's faith. In case any should refuse to sign
        the oath
    They would not be elected to public command.
    None can say that oaths are novel to this colony;
    In early times men swore by sacred rivers,
    The Jew swore with his sacred scrolls in his hand,
    Doctors have always taken oaths to cure
    And clergymen have read their solemn oaths of ordina-
        tion.
    In our mother England the practice of
    Kissing the Good Book and swearing arose in the Middle
        Ages.
    An oath is but a sign of man's allegiance to the Lord.

WILLIAMS (*rising*):

    I am not as versed in history of oaths
    As is the honored scholar, Mr. Cotton,
    But I do agree that oaths are not a universal evil.
    It is often just that men should swear to do God's will.

COTTON:

    Why then is it unjust that the Bay in time of growing
        need,

As security from savages and disloyal men,
Should demand allegiance to the ways of God?

WILLIAMS:

Because it is an oath of force and not of choice.
You would have every boy of sixteen years
And every man above that age within the Bay
Speak and sign that tight and lengthy oath.
Is this an act of freedom?

COTTON:

I fear, Sir, you will not face the facts.
We are few men within this narrow Bay
And ringed around by many heathen Indians.
If we do not command obedience to our church
How will this colony survive?

WILLIAMS:

If it is God's will, it will survive,
As rule by man's will alone will perish.
Since that first fall from the immortal Garden,
Religion is no longer the clear waters of God in which
Man swims toward the light, but a muddy surface
Armed with a fin which razors towards the soul.

COTTON:

Sir, this oath I think is not a razor. I bid you
Not become a haberdasher of small questions.

WILLIAMS:

Many questions, Mr. Cotton, for the Lord
Suit better than a lack of change into His mercy.

COTTON:

This is splinters, Mr. Williams, splinters.
Can you not give us clearer cause against the oath?

WILLIAMS:

An oath is but an act of worship and prayer,
An image of trust wrung freely from a loyal soul.

It does profane both acts of worship and of prayer
To force an oath on one whose lips it sounds
False and sinful. In *Matthew* and in *James*
Christ counsels, "Swear not at all."
If we consider this wise injunction,
Then we must fear the nature of false oaths.
An oath, being an invocation of God's truth, is
An action of deep spirit and religious nature.
Christian men ought not to take an oath
Merely to maintain mortal men in offices of power.

WINTHROP:

I think he speaks as many men agree.

DUDLEY:

He is contesting at us magistrates.

HAYNES:

Mr. Williams, you will not change upon this oath?

WILLIAMS:

I have not been persuaded.

HAYNES:

I beg you consider, Sir, the time is late.
We have honored your reputation and long tolerated
your dissent.
I beg you think if the honored names here gathered
In this Newtown church speak nothing more than air to
you.

WILLIAMS:

Sir, I listen to your charges with respect,
When you are many voices to my one.

HAYNES:

Let Mr. Hooker speak upon the Third Charge.

HOOKER (*he stands*):

In the Third Charge, it is the claim of Mr. Williams
That the Charter of our Bay, granted by the King,
Gives us no legal right to own the land.
For this puzzle I have no statement but a question.
We are a people of God in what was once the Devil's
territory.
Would Mr. Williams have us depart
And leave God's new land to the savages?

DUDLEY:

He is a haberdasher and cannot wriggle from that point.

WILLIAMS:

How can we leave the land to the Indians
When they were here before our ships arrived?
I have heard the men of this court speak of
The danger of savages and the security of this colony of
God.
I know what it is to study, to preach, to be an elder,
To be applauded—and yet also what it is to tug at the
oar
And dig with the spade in rocky soil, to plow and labor
And travel by day and night amongst English and those
you call Devils.
I have earned my family's food by barter with the
Indians
And have seen the same sun shine on the wilderness as
does
Shine upon the order of a garden. In that wilderness
How sweetly did I hear the several sorts of heaven's birds
Sing unto men the soaring praise of their maker's wis-
dom and goodness;
And to me the wilderness was a clear resemblance of
the world
Where greedy and furious men persecute and devour the
hinds and roes.

DUDLEY:

  There bloom his figures again.

WINTHROP:

  Mr. Hooker will answer him.

HOOKER:

  We have heard you have forsaken your minister's career
  For trade with the Indians. Do you consider it
  Just and truthful that those called by God
  Should learn and follow the ways of savages?

WILLIAMS:

  Your inference is that my time is lost
  Because not in the function of ministry.
  I admit the offices of Christ are the sacred
  And best callings, but generally they are the worst trades
  As they are practiced only for a maintenance,
  A place, a living, a benefice.

WINTHROP:

  That is twist for turn.

HOOKER:

  You confess, then, that you trade with savages
  And make no effort to bring them to God's word?

WILLIAMS:

  I spoke no confession. A great will can convert
  Many men, but the convert through will power
  Belongs to the will and not to God.

HOOKER:

  Sir, if it is right you trade with Indians,
  Why can we not minister to our Charter?

WILLIAMS:

  Because as God's children we know the world lies in
    wickedness,

A sea of wild beasts, and God is over this wild, foaming
  world,
Over the heathen Indians as well as Christians.
Where have you gained this Charter? From the Indians
Who had the land before a ship sailed into port,
Or from the King who never did set foot on it?

HOOKER:

Do I understand, Sir, you believe a Christian King
Cannot give title to a savage land
In God's name and for God's sacred word?

WILLIAMS:

I do contend the land was seized and sanctioned
By the King. There was no purchase from the Indians.

HOOKER:

Mr. Williams, you have spoken against oaths,
Saying unregenerate men cannot swear.
How then can a savage swear away a land by purchase?
Would not such acts blaspheme against the Lord?

WILLIAMS:

I have lived much with these Indians.
My soul's desire was to do them good
And God was pleased to give me a powerful, patient
  spirit
To lodge with them in their filthy, smoky holes
To gain their tongue. They have no clothes, books nor
  letters
And therefore are easily persuaded
That the God who made Englishmen is a greater God
Because He has endowed the English greater than
  themselves.
And yet amongst their government and justice
I could never discern that scandalous excess of sins
With which old Europe does abound. Is it just then to
Strike them with the civil sword and seize their lands?

HOOKER:

    You have slipped my question, Sir.
    How can a savage swear to a purchase?

WILLIAMS:

    It is not the savage who must swear
    But the Christian bound to God's word. I wish to say
    That what you are trying in me here is a desire,
    A desire more perfect than human actions,
    More beautiful than human aims,
    A desire for the clarity of God's grace.

WINTHROP:

    It is too perfect.

WILLIAMS:

    I do not think that search for Christian grace can come
    From smiting and killing savages, but only from
    The patient aim to bear and carry the cross and gallows
    Of our Lord and patiently to suffer with Him.

HOOKER:

    Mr. Williams, we live in a new wilderness
    And the Lord descends on this land as He descended
    In fire on Moses atop Mount Sinai. Then you remember
    There were thunder and lightnings and a thick cloud
    Upon the mount and the voice of the trumpet exceeding
        loud
    So that all the people in the camp trembled.
    This is the state of this colony in the Bay, Sir,
    And the Lord calls us as He called to Moses:
        "Thou shalt have no other Gods before me. Thou
        shalt not make unto thee any graven image . . .
        for I the Lord am a jealous God, visiting the in-
        iquity of the fathers upon the children . . ."
    This is a strict God for heathens, Mr. Williams.
    He commands our absolute faith and devotion
    And will punish ourselves if we deal with savages.

DUDLEY:

This word cannot be denied.

HAYNES (*to* WILLIAMS):

Sir, you have a last chance to refute this sense.

WILLIAMS:

I do speak against the bloody tenet of persecution for cause of conscience,

That forces men to use the sword in cause of Christ,

A tenet of high blasphemy against the Lord of peace who said,

"Blessed are the peacemakers for they shall be called the children of God,"

A tenet fighting the sweet end of Christ's coming which was

Not to destroy men's lives for their religions, but to save them;

A tenet against which the blessed souls under the altar

Cry aloud for vengeance, this tenet having cut their throats,

Torn out their hearts, and poured forth their blood in all ages;

A tenet which no uncleanness, no adultery, no incest,

Sodomy, or bestiality can equal—this ravishment and

Forcing of souls and conscience throughout the world.

I say to this Court this bloody tenet kindles the devouring flames of war

And is mingled with the murders and poisonings of kings and states.

If we do force the nature of the Prince of Peace against these heathens

We are that stiff-necked people whom the Lord accused to Moses.

The Christian church does not prosecute, no more than a lily

Does scratch the thorns, or a lamb pursue and tear the wolves.

HAYNES:

> Sir, we have permitted you to counter our General Court
> With lengthy passion, but this I must ask Mr. Cotton to
> refute.

COTTON:

> I will not exercise a vanity of pride.
> It is enough to speak the conscience of this Court,
> Our fifty magistrates and many ministers
> Who speak this colony's God-humbled will.
> Like Moses, we live in a new world of God,
> A new land of Israel, to war against idolaters,
> And in this war we speak the prayer of peace
> But carry a sword to defend ourselves and homes.
> It is the will of God, His truth,
> Never to kill or banish any for conscience,
> But this Court speaking in God's name
> Has the right and duty to punish those
> Who sin against their own true conscience
> Whether from pride, or other commandments of the
> Lord.

HAYNES:

> Mr. Williams has been refuted. If any officer
> Will add his thoughts I ask him now to speak. (*There is
> a tense silence.*)
> Mr. Cotton will present the final Charge.

COTTON:

> In the Fourth Charge, Mr. Williams declares steadfastly
> That the Civil Magistrate may not punish
> Breaches of the First Table of the Decalogue
> And declares us in danger of setting up a national church
> For that we punish breaches of this Table.
> It is his view that commandments in the First Table
> Pertain to man's duties to the Lord
> And therefore cannot be punished by civil officers.
> But it is my view that our congregational system,

Wherein each member of the church can freely voice
 God's word,
Requires for its maintenance a vigorous magistracy.
These magistrates are elders of the church and
Therefore strong-willed men of God. Does Mr. Williams
 think
Such men likely to rule against the Lord?

WILLIAMS:

Within this church and Court we speak upon the Bible's
 word,
But all of you, I think, do know and praise the words of
 Luther
When he said: "The laws of the civil magistrate's
 government extend no further than over the body
 and goods and that which is external; for over the
 Soul God will not suffer any man to rule."

COTTON:

It is a special situation, Sir.
Many of the civil magistrates whom Luther fought were
Bound to Rome. In a wild and savage country like this
 Bay
The foundation of the civil power must lie
In magistrates who do God's will, else must the heathen
 dancers
Prance once more around their Calf of Gold.

WILLIAMS:

You always harken back to ancient Israel,
A blessed nation dead in time. That wrath
And glory of God cannot ever be revived.

COTTON:

Must all states then be secular?
How would you guide this youthful land,
Open it wide to enemies of the church?

WILLIAMS:

I think the wilderness of every land is like the sea.
Out on this sullen sea goes many a ship
Crammed with hundreds of hungry souls,
Each with his own crude, common woes
And so this ship is like a commonwealth;
Upon it, sometimes, live both Turk and Jew,
Papist and Protestant, in common perils
And no one forces them together for ship's prayers.
Each prays according to his worth and need.

COTTON:

A soul-saving ship? You are a most
Prodigious minter of exorbitant novelties.
And who may rule this ship?

WILLIAMS:

I have never denied the ship's commander
Should command the ship's true course
And rule that peace and justice shall be kept.
If any seaman dare refuse his duty,
Or any passenger conceive a lawless deed,
The laws and orders of the ship should punish him.
But for the hungry souls that pray to God,
Within the private chambers of their hearts
This ship sails true to each man's prayer.

COTTON:

It is a sinking ship where each man drowns at a false
altar.

WINTHROP:

I think it is a separation we once did believe ourselves.

DUDLEY:

All he does is contend against the magistrates.
Question him on this finally.

COTTON:

    Mr. Williams, I have pleaded with you many times,
    For days before the meeting of this Court
    And now within this solemn session
    To persuade you from your pride's delusion.
    If the magistrates fail to rule for God
    Pagan anarchy will rule and then, Sir,
    We shall see new tables of stone
    Engraved with the terrible fiery finger of the Lord.

WILLIAMS:

    The name of Christian must deserve the name.
    Constantine and all the noted emperors are confessed to
      have done
    More hurt to the crown of Christ than did the bloody
      Neros.
    I say again the forcing of conscience is a rape of soul!
    The civil sword may make a nation of hypocrites
    And anti-Christians, but not one Christian.

DUDLEY:

    He calls us hypocrites!

WINTHROP:

    Ask him to recall.

HAYNES:

    Question him on this.

COTTON (to WILLIAMS):

    Sir, do you name our magistrates hypocrites?

WILLIAMS:

    I call that man a hypocrite who thinks the civil sword,
    Bloodied in God's name, will make a Christian world.
    And I desire Mr. Cotton and every soul in this Court
    Seriously to consider if the Lord Jesus were himself in
      person,

In old or in this New England, what church, what
    ministry.
What government, He would set up, and what prosecu-
    tion
He would practice toward them that would not receive
    Him?

HAYNES:

We have spoken patiently with you for long hours, Mr.
    Williams,
And have not silenced the pride of your tongue
Although you speak as one dissent against the word of
Many Godly men. We give you a last chance to recant
    these Charges.

WILLIAMS:

I will not recant these Charges. Whatever fate I suffer
It is but a shadow vanished. Eternity will pay for all.

WINTHROP:

He has spoken his fate.

HAYNES:

The hearing is concluded for today.
Mr. Williams, you will return tomorrow morning
For the judgment of this General Court. (WILLIAMS *goes
    out.*)

DUDLEY (*vehemently, as the members of the Court begin
    their deliberation*):
I say let men of God in court and churches watch
O'er such as do a toleration hatch!
    *The lights fade out as the scene ends and the choir
    is heard singing,* WONDROUS LOVE.

EPILOGUE

SCENE V: *As the lights go up, Governor Haynes is about to deliver the verdict to Williams.*

HAYNES: On this morning of our Lord, October 9, 1635, the General Court of Massachusetts, meeting in solemn session, does find you, Roger Williams of Salem, unpersuaded after many hours of the Lord's arguments as humbly submitted by magistrates and ministers of His Bay Colony. Therefore, the General Court does find you guilty as charged of the following points: First, persisting and preaching the false doctrine that the Churches of the Bay should profess separation. Second, denying that a magistrate can tender an oath of Civil Obedience to all men of the Bay. Third, falsely declaring that the Royal Charter fails to give the Colony a valid title to the land of New England. Fourth, asserting that the magistrates in whom resides the civil authority should not punish breaches of the first four Commandments. It is the judgment of this General Court that . . .

MAN'S VOICE: Wait!

> *The figures of the Court suddenly become stylized and stiff as if frozen in time. They hold these poses until Haynes completes the sentence at the end of the Epilogue. The lights dim around them and two figures in modern clothes become apparent, the* JOURNALIST *and the* EVANGELIST, *who are dressed as they were in the Prologue.*

WILLIAMS:

Who are you? What do you want? Why has the trial stopped?

JOURNALIST:

  The trial hasn't stopped. It will conclude presently.

EVANGELIST:

  We've come to show you the glorious past of Roger
    Williams!

WILLIAMS:

  Why should I listen to you?

JOURNALIST:

  But I'm not a devil, only a journalist,
  A historian of religion. I've studied the past of Roger
    Williams.

WILLIAMS:

  The pursuit of the past is a passion of death.

JOURNALIST:

  My study of the past is your future.

WILLIAMS:

  I care only for the future salvation of man's soul.

JOURNALIST:

  My dear Sir, I can't give you any kind of view
  Of *the* future. No man sees that sort of thing.

EVANGELIST (*to* WILLIAMS *while she scorns the* JOUR-
    NALIST):

  Don't listen to his cynical mind.
  You've liberated the church from the state's tyranny.
  I can show you the glory of your own radiant prog-
    ress . . .

JOURNALIST:

  She's only an evangelist. Let me begin . . .

WILLIAMS (*troubled, he speaks finally to the* JOURNALIST):

  My love is for the truth of God, and peace of conscience.
  If you can bring me that peace, begin . . .

JOURNALIST (*waving aside the* EVANGELIST *triumphantly*):
  I bring you the peace of History. This is 1958,
  More than 350 years after your birth. You were born
  At the end of the Elizabethan age when a great culture
    was dying.

WILLIAMS:
  I do not know what you mean by culture.
  I believed only in the search for God.

JOURNALIST:
  That's the irony of it, Mr. Williams.
  After all these years you've been
  Taken over by this Evangelist and other fanatics.
  Your heresy has become heroic
  Under the ironic name of religious freedom.

EVANGELIST:
  Don't listen to him!

WILLIAMS (*slowly*):
  I always dreamt of religious freedom
  For all churches in the wilderness of the world.

JOURNALIST:
  Men have twisted your ideal of religious freedom
  And spoken of you as the precursor of Jeffersonian de-
    mocracy,
  A founder of liberalism and rationalism,
  One of the makers of political freedom.

WILLIAMS:
  I never was a politician. I hated politics.
  My only belief was in the heaven of God
  And the search for God in man's soul.

EVANGELIST (*crying out*):
  That is my belief too!

JOURNALIST (*mocking her*):
   In History the Devil's question is not
   "Where is God?" but "What is the human church?"

WILLIAMS:
   Some men think the church an altar
   To expose the sacred mystery of our Lord,
   Where forever the longing of the heart
   May be stilled in the blessing of its need;
   While other men think of the church as God's word
   Sounding through a humble minister's voice
   Until the word of love lights up the sacred hall.

JOURNALIST:
   But you never thought of the church in these ways.
   In History men call you a Seeker.

WILLIAMS:
   That is true. To me the human church is but
   A house of error and of search and all men in it,
   Catholic, Protestant, or Jew, kneel there as eternal
      Seekers;
   For it is written: "Seek and ye shall find,"
   And what man finds is in the seeking,
   In the peril and pilgrimage of search
   Lies his only reward and salvation,
   Never to know on earth the light of paradise,
   But only a knowledge of suffering,
   Of the inseparable knots of hate and love.

EVANGELIST (*radiantly*):
   That is the meaning of faith.

JOURNALIST (*ironically*):
   That is the peace of History
   In which you have found your high place.

WILLIAMS (*to the* JOURNALIST):

Your history is only proof of the world's wilderness.
The peace of the true Seeker of God does not come
From knocking at the door of time,
But from knocking at the soul's timeless door . . .

JOURNALIST:

You have knocked at the door of time.
(*As* WILLIAMS *stares at him, the* EVANGELIST *moves
impatiently in front of the* JOURNALIST)

EVANGELIST:

Do not despair, Roger Williams, at men of little faith.
Christ must return in blazing light
And the Seeker nears the end of his search.
His history only sweats in the record of fleshly lust (*She
is scorning the* JOURNALIST)
But I can tell you of the soul's progress
And of man's longing steps toward God.

JOURNALIST:

She'll tell you sentimental lies.

WILLIAMS (*after a moment of hesitation, to the* EVANGEL-
IST):

Perhaps you are my truth. I will listen to you.

EVANGELIST (*from this point on, the fire of her voice increases*):

I bring you good tidings of a joyous God, from a time
When churches blaze over His green land and the sky is
Brilliant white with neon-lighted crosses to His name.

WILLIAMS (*uncertain*):

The joy of God is not the joy of man.

EVANGELIST:

Now God builds the innocent church and scorches
The guilty preacher with the power of His radiation.

JOURNALIST:

Her radiation means death today.

WILLIAMS (*to the* EVANGELIST):

How did you find His power of salvation?

EVANGELIST:

One night in the darkness of my room,
Poor and sick in a factory city, a dazzling light
Scarred the wall and the burning voice of His radiation
Spoke from the scorched plaster: "Wherefore seek ye
  not redemption?"

WILLIAMS:

What did you learn from this voice?

EVANGELIST:

The Lord healed me with His mercy, and I went into
  the world
To preach God's glory which
I call the Gospel of Radiant Redemption.

WILLIAMS:

Which you call or which God calls?
Are you my truth or my false pride?

JOURNALIST (*scornfully*):

This is the History which your pride has created.

EVANGELIST (*ecstatically*):

I feel His light every Sunday at my Sacred Radiation
  Service,
When I walk down the silver staircase and the spotlight
Flashes on the golden altar underneath the voice of the
  choir—
Then I feel His radiance burning through me,
Commanding me to preach His Gospel!

WILLIAMS:

A silver staircase and a golden altar as His Truth?
God commands no one to preach in vanity.
What proof have you of His will?

EVANGELIST:

Here, I give you charts of all our American churches,
(*She does so*)
Old and new, who have separated from the state
To create fresh hymns of glory as you willed.

WILLIAMS (*looking doubtfully at the charts*):

So many churches . . . These may be splinters of the
Devil's will. (*He pushes them away*)

JOURNALIST (*to* WILLIAMS):

You have created them yourself.

EVANGELIST:

In your name new religions of Jesus spread their
Warming currents and the air is charged with miracles
of hope.
God is a power like radiation to consume the body with
joy
And devour the evil mind into an ash of burning terror!

WILLIAMS (*tormented*):

I am that evil mind.

EVANGELIST:

Blessings on you, Roger Williams,
You have shown us the radiance of Jesus.

WILLIAMS:

I have shown you nothing.

JOURNALIST:

You have shown us the fate of History.

WILLIAMS:

My faith is not in the time of your History.

EVANGELIST:

You have shown us the simplicity of God
And the freedom of His eternal love.

WILLIAMS:

The danger of simplicity is always tyranny,
Of reducing the mystery of God's love
To the greed of man's love for power.

EVANGELIST (*in a last, ecstatic outburst, she pushes in
front of the* JOURNALIST):

His radiation and simplicity! Blessings on you, Roger
Williams.

Praise the Lord! Praise His name, His peace, His everlasting love,

His Love! . . .

The lights go up abruptly and the figures of the
JOURNALIST *and the* EVANGELIST *disappear. Just
after the echo of the* EVANGELIST's *last fervent cry of
"Love!", the frozen pose of Governor Haynes re-
laxes and he completes the verdict.*

HAYNES: . . . the hateful errors of pride must be driven
from this new land of God. Therefore, the General Court
of Massachusetts Bay, respecting and humbly praising
His divine mercy, sentences you to immediate and
eternal banishment. On pain of death you will never
again be permitted to live within the boundaries of this
colony. Is there anything final you wish to say?

WILLIAMS (*turning away from the members of the Court*):

I will not answer you for my own pride.
This Court has found in me false images,
But no more than I have found in myself.
In my need I have heard the word of God

That men distort in their bloody tenet
Of persecution for cause of conscience.
I have seen the acts of murder and war
Men commit in the name of the Prince of Peace.
I have felt the dangerous heresy of a future
When the cure of love is cried in false simplicity
And the material stones of life are called divine.
I know the common trinity of the world is
Profit, preferment, and pleasure—but still I believe
That the human weeds in the Lord's garden must be left
To His judgment; the music of God sings above man's
  bloody laws,

> *The choir begins to sing softly the last stanza of*
> "WONDROUS LOVE"

A music of the regal senses
Rising above a tyrant's rules of order.
Sometimes, this music seems disorder,
A luring echo of magical sounds,
And then we damn it with the name of Devil,
The fallen angel from the brilliant air.
Our danger then is that we damn all music
Until the rigid rules harden to hate.
In one moment God may reach us,
A moment of utter timelessness,
Yet we may reach God only through
An agony of separation from His love.
And so I pray against my pride and yours—
Oh Lord, let Thy music sing in the winter of man's exile!

> *After Williams finishes speaking, the choir repeats,*
> *full-voice this time, the last stanza of* "WONDROUS
> LOVE":

> > *And when from death I'm free*
> > *I'll sing and joyful be*
> > *And through eternity,*
> > *I'll sing on, I'll sing on,*
> > *And through eternity*
> > *I'll sing on.*